T0295658

Continuous and Embedded Learning for Organizations

Continuous and Embedded Learning for Organizations

Jon M. Quigley
Shawn P. Quigley

CRC Press
Taylor & Francis Group
Boca Raton London New York

CRC Press is an imprint of the
Taylor & Francis Group, an **informa** business

CRC Press
Taylor & Francis Group
6000 Broken Sound Parkway NW, Suite 300
Boca Raton, FL 33487-2742

© 2020 by Taylor & Francis Group, LLC
CRC Press is an imprint of Taylor & Francis Group, an Informa business

No claim to original U.S. Government works

Printed on acid-free paper

International Standard Book Number-13: 978-0-367-18387-5 (Hardback)

Visit the Taylor & Francis Web site at
http://www.taylorandfrancis.com

and the CRC Press Web site at
http://www.crcpress.com

Contents

List of Figures

Preface

Modern business is an entanglement of social and technical systems. Optimizing one at the expense of another is not the way to creating an high performing organization. An organization cannot rely upon the leadership solely to create a sustainable and growing company. For many years (the late 1800 to early 1900's) there has been a focus on the technical systems, measurements and analysis, or scientific management also referred to as Taylorism after the founder Frederick Taylor. Modern management and more importantly, leadership, recognizes the limits of an approach nearly entirely dedicated to measurements and the technical attributes. What started in the days of Deming from his 14 points, most notably number 8—drive out fear, could arguably be analogous to the modern psychological safety that is frequently discussed. Driving out fear, or psychological safety, no matter the name, is the sort of environment that encourages exploration, experimentation and learning.

Learning has a variety of approaches and produce a wide range of results. Some of our learning will be planned, some opportunistic, some to a specific application, some general principles or heuristics. Some will be directed at some improvement target or solving some known problem often referred to as corrective action. Corrective actions are especially interesting, as these are opportunities to remedy some failure, which may be due to some insufficient understanding or learning. Corrective actions have a target of understanding the reason(s) for the defect in either the product, project or process, and then determine a subsequent solution (learning) that will eliminate the problem from recurring. This requires elimination of a defensive posture by the individual. This defensive posture linked out the need to cover up mistakes, out of *fear* of the consequences on that individual, is not only not helpful but is obstructive and detrimental.

The objective will be the starting point whether a corrective action, current project needs or organization wide change, and care should be taken in the exploration. It is easy for preconceived notions of the true reason for the problem, and cognitive biases can get in the way of seeing the nature of the obstacles as well as determining a suitable approach to the problem. Although there is a crisis of sorts when it comes to replication, especially in the social sciences, that does not does necessarily mean that these social science statements are falsehoods. Replication, the ability to of an experiment to produce consistent results is fundamental to science in the establishing the veracity of the statements made or *truths* gleaned from the experiment results. These social systems can be quite complex and have abundance of parameters and variations that influence the results.

Root cause analysis and the subsequent corrective action require a methodical approach. Not all events are emergent, that is not predictable and seemingly spontaneous, neither are all things or events perfectly predictable. If you would like a glimpse of what is required to find the root cause, check out Air Disasters on The Smithsonian Channel. This methodical approach is best served to be recorded for a host of reasons. It should be acknowledged that some events are emergent and root cause is not easily ascertained.

This book provides an overview of the many systems, both social and technical, required to create a learning organization, as well as ways to capture and propagate learning throughout the organization. The longevity of the organization depends upon the ability of that organization to learn and propagate that learning throughout the organization.

Acknowledgements

We would like to thank those that helped with the generating of material and in providing stories of their experiences.

Steve Lauck

Steve Lauck is a retired Project Management Consultant who helped businesses solve project management problems, ultimately improving project delivery and successes. He was instrumental in developing and conducting Employee Goals training, CAPM, PMP training, and Employee Mentoring programs.

Before retiring, Steve's career spanned over 33 years in which he held titles of Machine Designer, Mechanical Designer, Department Manager, Procurement Leader, and Project Manager (PMP®PMI from 2003 to 2016). He delivered automated production operations, innovative machines, procurement supplier management systems, and vertical production startups.

Steve's experience focused on delivering solutions in Architectural Engineering, Commercial/Industrial Facility Construction, and Consumer Products Manufacturing.

Currently, Steve is contributing to Value Transformation, LLC through collaboration on developing training, books, and a monthly newsletter.

John Cutler

John Cutler is keenly focused on user experience and evidence-driven product development. He mixes and matches various methodologies to help teams deliver lasting outcomes for their customers.

"Team tetris and the feature factory will only take you so far. Cross-functional teams desire so much more, and my passion is helping them get there. It's a win/win for the front-line teams, the business, and the customer and user."

John currently works as a product evangelist at Amplitude. As a former UX researcher at AppFolio, a product manager at Zendesk, Pendo.io, AdKeeper, and RichFX, a startup founder, and a product team coach, John has a perspective that spans individual roles, domains, and products.

His viral enthusiasm has been heard through speaking/teaching engagements at Agile-Lean Ireland, UX Thailand, Front, Oredev, Mind The Product, Agile 2015, Heart of Agile Philadelphia (2016), and various ProductCamps (Vancouver, Los Angeles, Raleigh, NC) and MeetUps (Santa Barbara, Los Angeles, New York). John's talk on Feature Factories was voted one of the Top 10 Product Talks of 2017.

Mixing in some less-than-typical experiences — driving rickshaws in NYC, and touring the US with "five other weird creative people in a van playing music" — John blogs prolifically about collaboration, product development, diversity, UX research, lean startup, and user experience. Some notable posts include The Evolving Product Manager Role, Persona(s) Non Grata, 12 Signs You're Working in a Feature Factory, and Stop Setting Up Product Roadmaps to Fail.

Eric Weinberger

"Eric was born in England and studied Mathematics and Philosophy at the University of Bristol. He then moved to Germany to learn German and worked there as a translator and interpreter, traveling widely in the process. He and his American wife, whom he met in Germany, moved to America and put each other through school. Eric studied Computer Science at the University of Wisconsin, Nursing at Cardinal Stritch University, and Medical Informatics in a joint program put on by the Milwaukee School of Engineering and the Medical College of Wisconsin. He has been developing online database applications since early 2008 and is the author of Competent Company (www.competent-company.com), an application which is designed to help organizations ensure that their staff are always up to date on the processes and other rules that they are supposed to follow. He and his wife live in the beautiful city of Eau Claire, Wisconsin. He can be reached by e-mail at eukalemia@yahoo.com."

Thank you Ellen Raim, for the interesting discussion and the bad war story contribution on education.

Lastly, we also thank Nick from Fiverr [Nikolaypavlov25] for his help in getting InDesign set up and all of the coaching he provided.

About the Authors

Jon M. Quigley has three college degrees: B.S. Electronic Engineering Technology from the University of North Carolina at Charlotte, MBA in Marketing, and M.S. in Project Management from City University of Seattle. In addition to the degrees, he has the following certifications:

- Project Management Institute
  - Project Management Professional (PMP)
- International Software Testing Qualifications Board (ISTQB)
  - Certified Tester Foundation Level (CTFL)

In addition to the degrees and certifications, Mr. Quigley has a number of patents and awards:

- US Patent Award 6,253,131 Steering wheel electronic interface
- US Patent Award 6,130,487 Electronic interface and method for connecting the electrical systems of truck and trailer
- US Patent Award 6,828,924 Integrated vehicle communications display (also a European patent)
- US Patent Award 6,718,906 Dual scale vehicle gauge
- US Patent Award 7,512,477 Systems and methods for guiding operators to optimized engine operation
- US Patent Award 7,629,878 Measuring instrument having location controlled display
- US Published Patent Application 20090198402 Method and system for operator interface with a diesel particulate filter regeneration system
- Volvo-3P Technical Award for global IC05 instrument cluster project 2005
- Volvo Technology Award for global IC05 Instrument cluster project April 2006

Mr. Quigley has worked in a variety of capacities within the new product development organizations:

- Embedded product development engineer (hardware and software)
- Product engineer
- Test engineer
- Project Manager
- Electrical and electronic systems manager
- Verification and test manager

Mr. Quigley has taught at a variety of product development and management topics for technical schools, universities (City University of Seattle) as well as guest lecturing at Wake Forest University's Charlotte campus as well as Eindhoven University of Technology. Additionally, he speaks and teaches on product development topics to businesses. He has written scores of articles for more than 40 magazines and ezines and has a recurring column at Assembly Magazine. He presents at many technical, product development and project management conferences.

Shawn P. Quigley is the Area Improvement Coordinator and Program Exposure Manager at Nuclear Regional Maintenance Department Kings Bay Georgia, which is a remote branch of Norfolk Naval Shipyard (NNSY). Mr. Quigley retired as a Chief Warrant Officer after 30 years of naval service. He has experience managing projects for both the Navy and NNSY ranging from the refueling of a nuclear aircraft carrier (*USS THEODORE ROOSEVELT, CVN-71*), a fast attack submarine (*USS SAN FRANCISCO, SSN-711*), and the decommissioning of a fast attack submarine (*USS HAMMERHEAD, SSN-663*) and a destroyer tender (*USS PUGET SOUND, AD-38*). He has also trained and qualified hundreds of Naval Nuclear Operators over his career. He has been trained in and is currently teaching organizational learning, root cause analysis, and organizational development. He is also a recurring writer at several outlets including projectmanagement.com and many others on the topic of learning, learning, organization, and organizational development.

The Changing of the Work

Work has made considerable changes since the start of the industrial revolution. From the time of interchangeable parts in mass production on the assembly line, work has steadily and increasingly become more segmented. The principles of scientific management started with Frederick Taylor wherein work based largely on scientific principles that include measurements, analysis, and understanding of interactions of variables went a long way to quantifying the work. Administrative principles focused more on total organization and grew from insights such as Henry Fayol and his proposed fourteen principles such as each subordinate receives orders from only one superior, as well as concepts of unity of command, that is similar activities of the organization grouped under a common manager.[*] The list is provided below:[†]

- Division of work – the principle of specialization which can be seen in the functional organization even today.
- Authority and responsibility – the manager has both authority of position as well as authority of experience and intelligence.
- Discipline – respect for rules, hierarchy, and other outward marks of respect, good superiors, clear and fair agreements, and judicious application of penalties.
- Unit of command – employee only receives orders from one superior (unlike today's matrix organizations).
- Unity of direction – each unit has one head, and one plan.
- Subordination of individual interest – interests of the group supercede that of the individual.

---

[*] Daft, R. L. (1998). Organization theory and design. Cincinnati: South Western College Publishing. Page 21.
[†] https://www.managementstudyhq.com/henri-fayol-principles-of-management.html last accessed 3/27/2019

- Remuneration of personnel – fair payment and methods, maximum satisfaction of both employee and employer.
- Centralization – level of centralization or dispersion of authority in the organization, and the optimum solution is situational dependent.
- Scalar chain – the line of authority, the chain of superiors, or the corporate hierarchy from highest to lowest. No short circuiting of this chain.
- Order – material and social order for the organization.
- Equity – devotion from the employees, and a combination of kindliness and justice from the managers in dealing with subordinates.
- Stability of tenure – instability due to bad management, costly with unnecessary turnover of personnel.
- Initiative – thinking out and executing the plan; managers are to sacrifice personal vanity in order to permit subordinates to exercise it.
- Esprit de corps – union of strength and extension of the unity of command, the need for teamwork.

These models of the organization in terms of command and control and economics are helpful. There was still much that was not addressed or understood about the organization from these myopic vantage points, and this would be hit upon in the 1920's in the Hawthorne studies. This exploration led to the discovery that there was more to the organization than meets the eye. The studies showed that taking an interest in the employees and positive treatment of the employees resulted in increased productivity and motivation. In the 1950's through the 1960's, post-World War II, the competitive forces were not so strong as the world set about to rebuild the infrastructure and manufacturing capability that was decimated by the war. By the 1970's and 1980's it became clear in many organizations that the ratio of overhead workers for every worker was out of balance with some examples ranging from 1.3 overhead workers for every worker in the United States -based Xerox to 0.6 for Japanese affiliate.[*]

Over the years the authors have been tracking the annual studies by Gallup in the State of the Global Workplace[†]. This is one of the factors influencing the book. This series of global surveys of the workforce identifies the three categories below. We encourage all that read this book to check out the results of the survey, and consider the implication of this survey on the work world and business at large. For example, consider an organization that may have 30% of the employees actively engaged. This made us wonder how much of this engagement issue is due to the way the work is undertaken. One of us has personally experienced a serious impact on the motivation when it seems like the organization at large is incapable of learning,

---

[*] Daft, R. L. (1998). Organization theory and design. Cincinnati: South Western College Publishing. Page 21.

[†] https://nicolascordier.files.wordpress.com/2014/04/gallup-worldwide-report-on-engagement-2013.pdf accessed 8/20/2019

distributing that learning, or acting on this learning effectively during some future project. The result is experiencing the same failures, over and over even when some part of the project team may have experienced that the course of action planned has, in the past, resulted in failure. To be sure past failures of taking a certain set of actions are not perfect predictors of future results. However, it is at least an inkling or portend what may happen and summarily disregarding proves learning is very difficult.

1. Actively Disengaged
2. Not Engaged
3. Engaged

Modern work is now taking on a new flavor in many organizations, often described as a lean or agile approach to the work, that stresses learning throughout the project and product development effort. Software has been moving toward an approach that is often referred to as agile, with one version of that being scrum. These are both variants of lean, as well as an employee empowerment approach.

It is not the intent of this book to invent some new motivational technique, personnel/organizational development, or provide some guidance on how to manage either your people or a project, but to provide some insight into both and allow for self-development. There have not really been any new developments in any of these areas (motivation, personnel/organizational development, or project management). While there have been numerous new terms bandied about when explored they are or appear to be a rehashing of a previously discussed hypothesis. The term "Hypothesis" is used because when dealing with motivation and personnel development empirical data quite often contradicts itself from one group to another or in some cases. There is a replication crisis in psychology. In science, we perform multiple tests of a theory, the tests executed by others in other regions, using the same methods and arrive at another conclusion.*

> Psychology has recently been viewed as facing a replication crisis because efforts to replicate past study findings frequently do not show the same result. Often, the first study showed a statistically significant result but the replication does not. Questions then arise about whether the first study results were false positives, and whether the replication study correctly indicates that there is truly no effect after all.

This lack of repeatability means the assertions made as a result of the test are questionable. We have provided many theories in this work, many cognitively satisfying, and perhaps even supported by our experiences; however that does not

---

* Maxwell, S. E., Lau, M. Y., & Howard, G. S. (2015). Is psychology suffering from a replication crisis? What does "failure to replicate" really mean? American Psychologist, 70(6), 487-498.

mean these theories apply perfectly or at all. However, knowledge of these theories does provide a different perspective from where a better understanding may begin.

It is to that end why we have taken the approach of first reviewing several different people who have been key in the area of motivation, personnel/organizational development, and project management and their hypothesis and then showing how these hypotheses can be applied to working with a person, a group, a team, a department, an organization, and projects.

This book also explores the difference between learning and knowledge and how these two different mindsets are commonly misunderstood. This approach is instrumental in knowing the what, when, where, why, and how to plan and execute a plan for motivating your personnel, developing your organization, and using your project to obtain both. While we know from years of experience working as team members and team leaders, one size does not fit all and must be tailored to not only the people, but the organization and the project; that is why the approach is to show opportunities and allow you to determine the when and how of the application. As important as the application is, so is the execution and flexibility of the application. The ability to respond to a needed change based upon performance and the ability to understand how any change will be perceived and what outcome it will produce. There is little ability to fully determine the outcome of any proposed change. The priorities and the plan for the change will point the team members to specific metrics. These metrics (measurements and data) will serve as validation points, that is serve as a comparison of the actual results with the desired. This will inform those involved as to whether the planned actions taken are producing the desired results. In the event the actions are not moving these key metrics in the desired direction, the team can perform analysis on the results for the reason and adjust the approach to the objective.

While this book will discuss the aforementioned processes and their application it will have a slant toward project management. It will also discuss the different styles of project management and how each has some opportunities and pitfalls with these processes. Having previously stated that every situation is different from another, even repeat situations, we again will not offer some magic bullet, but attempt to provide some insight into the opportunities available to you because of the project itself.

Chapter 1

Introduction Learning and Thought

1.1 Importance to the Organization

Learning is important for the organization and especially when it comes to creating new things or product development where the constant learning mantra is not only oft repeated, but also essentially required. Yet, and you will see this throughout the book, the teams continue to take a course of action that has been taken before that had an unacceptable outcome. This is not the way to continuous improvement. Neither does an approach to the work that leaves the team members experiencing the same types of failures.

Stating "Importance to Organizations" is like saying, "see that?" It is an open statement that provides no background for deciding or way of assessing. Only the organization can determine what is important (specifically) and how and what to measure to ascertain how the results of the actions taken. The point behind starting with this topic is to aid in establishing the validity of the items determined important along with some mechanisms as to why it is important or how we know it to be so. We have all been part of organizations that have a mission or vision statement that says its people or innovation, or some other catch phrase, are key to their success, but when you delve into how these actually stack up in what and how the organization is run they are but curtains on a broken window: look nice but have little to do with how the organization actually operates. In truth all organizations, except for charity organizations, are in business to make money for their shareholders. While profit and organizational and personnel development are not mutually exclusive, these are commonly viewed as such when looking at the short-term return on investment (RoI) or other measure of economic gain.

Perhaps you have been in a project or organization that has a personnel development (training) plan to enhance its people and when there is a crunch—getting an item to the customer, job completed, or budget constraints, those are the first things to be reduced or stopped because these take time and money. The organization usually defaults to what is known as the tried and true, or how we've done it before to get through whatever situation is currently at hand, or the approach for the organization to survive, we cut spending on relatively unimportant areas. This type of operation is self-defeating in several ways: shows the individuals and team members that they are not as important as the organization often states, and it could erode the worth and meaning of the vision/mission statement of the organization. In line with the previous statement that personnel development plans and process improvements are usually the first items reduced or stopped when fiscal crises present, we all have seen or been part of organizations that have the motto, "Quality is our Job," or something of that nature. Yet when a project deadline is in jeopardy of being missed the testing to validate or the extra review is partially omitted if not completely removed. Having a good understanding of personnel and organizational development, and motivation will assist the organization in maintaining its training plans, its deadlines, and its profits and thus help maintain the motivation of its members. We are believers that embedding development: personnel and organizational, into everyday processes, in project plans and aligning this development with the mission or vision statement of the organization will reduce the chance of these items being reduced or even stopped during times of need.

A question to consider, "Do you know the mission/vision statement for your company or organization, and how does it align with the actions of the company

Figure 1.1 There are ways to communicate and each has a positive and negative implications.

or organization and even your daily actions?" If you do not know the mission and vision where you work how do you know the goal of the work or what constitutes success? Most would answer this question by saying, "I do what I'm told, or I know my job." How does your job affect the whole? Are you doing what is really needed? Perhaps worse yet are you contributing to an environment which erodes potential growth both for individuals and the organization? It is these types of questions that an affective member of any team should be asking themselves and that management should be promoting in their people. For it is these types of questions that when answered honestly that promotes a team mentality amongst the people in an organization.

1.2 Communication

Merriam-Webster defines communication as a process by which information is *exchanged* between individuals through a common system of symbols, signs, or behavior.* When discussing the learning organization, we will spend considerable time discussing communication as this is how perspective is shared. Communication, both informal and formal, is the mechanism we will use to both uncover situations that will enable the team to learn, as well as achieving the actual learning within the team and finally propagating what is learned to other parts of the organization. There are several communications models. These models depict some of the blocks associated with communication, but as we all know from attempting to communicate with others even when we think we are effectively communicating we can still miss the mark. While there is no one sure-fire method to ensure we have been effective in our attempt

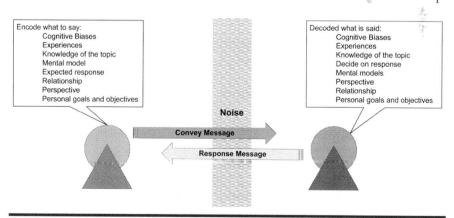

Figure 1.2   An example of communications model that illustrates some of the complications.

---

* Communication. (n.d.). Retrieved July 23, 2018, from https://www.merriam-webster.com/dictionary/communication

to communicate with someone or a group of people, asking the intended recipient(s) what they heard can help determine the effectiveness of your communication.

There are many forms of communication, face-to-face discussion, e-mail, phone, and so on; each one of these communication methods have benefits and draw-backs relative to effective to communicate. As with any form of communication, or even actions for that matter, attention to detail for both in both sending and receiving communication is critical. By attention to detail we mean only communicating exactly what is needed to be communicated while minimizing distractions that will allow for misinterpretation to occur. Distractions come in many forms and are part of any type of communication, from verbal to even an e-mail. E-mails have embedded distractions just by their nature. When most people read e-mails they are using their mental model associated with the individual who sent the e-mail to decode the e-mail. Mental models are how everyone views everything, as we have discussed already and will continue to discuss throughout this book. Experience is the gauge we all use to view current and potential future situations. While some organizations and projects use historical data to predict future work the difference is that historical data is neither right or wrong, it is merely data, but mental models are subject to emotional context of the individual or group. In Peter Senge's book "*The Fifth Discipline*" he states that Mental Models are one of the five core items of a learning organization.[*] In his book Mr. Senge describes Mental Models as:

> Reflecting upon, continually clarifying, and improving our pictures of the world, and seeing how they shape our actions and decisions.[†]

The continual modification of our mental model is due to the continual experiences we are going through coupled with past experiences. While he uses the term "Mental Model" we prefer the term "Open Mental Model." This is another one of those points that sounds like semantics but is very poignant. If our mental model is jaded by past experiences only it will determine what we hear and think before we have even fully heard or thought about the current topic or situation. Just

$$NumberCommunicationsChannels = \frac{n(n-1)}{2}$$

Figure 1.3 The equation for identifying the number of communcation channels in a project or group of people working together.

[*] Kleiner, A., & Senge, P. M. (1994). The Fifth discipline fieldbook. London: Nicholas Brearley.
[†] Kleiner, A., & Senge, P. M. (1994). The Fifth discipline fieldbook. London: Nicholas Brearley.

knowing that our and other people's mental model affects incoming and outgoing communication helps with communication in that actions can be employed to ensure this is minimized. Adding to that knowledge of perspective variation (the delta between reality and the perspective held by yourself and others) the desire to clarify and improve our perspective, we become more effective communicators and thus greater understanding of the situation.

In concert with the group size will be the number of communication channels. The larger the group, the more communications channels. Project managers must heed this and often take actions in the structuring of the project to ensure quick and accurate lines of communication, reducing some of the communication load via the multitude of channels.

From this equation it is easy to see that many individuals in the network will increase the communications channels. The reason for the large number of channels is that everyone can talk with any other individual. The size and conmplexity of these channels add complexity to the clarity and distribution of the information, message, or articulation of specific learning.

Later chapters will look at networks and specifically the distribution of information and learning throughout the organization. From this section you will see the larger the organization in terms of people, the more channels and increasingly difficult it can be to keep the message or information under discussion consistent throughout that network.

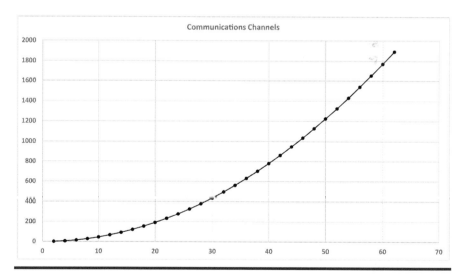

Figure 1.4   The number of possible communications channels with size of group is not linear.

1.3 Lessons Learned, or Re-learned

Experience plays a significant role in learning, as such, it would seem obvious that it is in our interest to make experience an integral part of lesson learned. However, if that were truly the case organizations would plan key points into their projects to both learn and capture that experience. While most organizations do have some form of lesson learned program it is commonly an afterthought or operated primarily when there is a problem. (NOTE: while all problems are said to be opportunities, they are not usually capitalized upon during a project due to time and monetary constraints.) Perhaps you have been involved with solving problems and capturing those answers into the organizations' lessons learned database that nobody knows where it resides or has the time to revisit, This historical record sits there until the issue is repeated and recaptured. This type of lessons learned program serves no actual purpose except to "check a box" and diminishes the organization, project's and individual development. While issues or problems cannot always be forecasted, they can sometimes be narrowed down (using historical data and or tactic knowledge) to key points of a process or project. This makes it possible to plan into the process or project thus allowing for a more structured and useful lesson learned program not to mention placing emphasis on learning. This would be an example of planning for an opportunity rather than reacting to a situation.

> Think of a project that you were involved with that you knew there were certain points (we will refer to these points from now on as: *Lesson Points*) that historically came with difficulties. Now think of what actions could have been added to the plan that would capitalize upon those lesson points. By capitalize we mean minimize or alleviate them all together and provide strategic information to verify the effectiveness of those actions.

If you had a project jump right to mind in the question above, that would mean you have experience with what we refer to as the Lesson Re-Learned program. As we alluded to in the beginning of this section most organizations employ a lesson learned program but have little to no follow through applying what was learned. It is this lack of follow through that de-motivates people and diminishes the development of the organization. Organizational and individual development, as well motivation, are proactive items that cannot be ignored or placated without diminishing their return, and thus, rendering them ineffective.

1.3.1 Burning Our Hand on the Same Stove and Motivation

Projects are unique, each present distinctive challenges, though these challenges may have a common theme allowing an extrapolation to other future projects. We can see in projects, functional areas, and business processes where this repeated

Figure 1.5   Burning our hand on the same metaphorical stove over and over again is not constructive.

failure to learn costs our organization dearly. Learning and adapting are hallmarks of good project management and of functioning organizations. Making mistakes is not an issue as that is how we learn.

> Good judgment comes from experience, and experience comes from bad judgment.
>
> **Rita Mae Brown**

However, we should not consistently burn our hand on the same stovetop and act surprised. If you find your project or organization making the same set of mistakes, you have a learning problem. To be sure not all can be known, but if you are learning every day, more is known every day.

> There is only one thing more painful than learning from experience, and that is not learning from experience.
>
> **Laurence J. Peter**

It may at times seem like the organization as an entirety is not capable of learning. Learning at the organization level is walking a tight rope. Learn something productive and necessary, while not excluding alternatives that may work next time. This requires understanding what matters and what may appear to matter but does not really.

> We should be careful to get out of an experience all the wisdom that is in it -- not like the cat that sits on a hot stove lid. She will never sit down on a hot lid again -- and that is well; but also she will never sit down on a cold one anymore.

Mark Twain

Each failure, each success provides us with an opportunity to learn. If we maximize that opportunity (spread throughout the organization) we become stronger as an organization. We learn more as a group about what works and what does not work. This is helpful for the product, service, process and for the project. This requires paying attention to what is going on and listen to those that have learned lessons that we have not yet learned, as well as teach (or coach) lessons to those who have not learned. Student and teacher are one and the same.

Our personal experience suggests repeatedly making the same mistakes, often results in employees suffering the same consequences every time does not improve morale. One of us worked at a company where another senior manager said, "it is okay to make mistakes, but can't we make new mistakes rather than the same old mistakes?" Decisions made by the management can have an impact on the employee, and poor decisions have consequences on the business's financial viability, but it does not end, there are consequences on the employees.

1.3.2 Lessons Learned and Organizational Development

To remain relevant, the organization must constantly work to understand and adapt to the external environment as well as improve the internal environment. Any talk about the organization learning really means the people learning both as individuals and as a group, and as group of groups. At first blush it may seem to be obvious how a learning organization would use lessons learned to create a continuously evolving and improving environment to meet the organization's objective, though what may be less obvious is the complexity involved in doing so. Even though it does seem obvious that a robust lesson learned program would be beneficial to just about every organization at many levels, based upon experience, it may seem lessons learned programs are not given the attention needed to achieve the maximum benefit. This could be for any number of reasons from the program being too cumbersome, insufficent time allocated for the work, to a lack of understanding on how this helps the organization over the long run. There is no wrong or right way to set up and run a lesson learned program because it must be tailored to the organization, its people, and its objectives, we will not discuss the setup or basic operation of a lessons learned program. We will, however, review some items that are needed to help make the program effective for everyone.

What is the objective of a lesson learned program as seen by the different levels (CEO, CFO, Managers, Supervisors, and Workers), departments, and people within your organization? Are these objectives at odds with on another? While you may intuit that the overall objective would be the same for everyone, it may not be. Even an individual's perspective may not be the same over the course of a project's life cycle. These disparate answers could be due to a lack of "Systems Thinking" or an individual's mental model. In *The Fifth Discipline,* systems thinking is described as a way of thinking about, and a language for describing and understanding, the forces and interrelationships that shape the behavior of systems.* The lesson learned program's objective may not change during a project's life cycle. It may change over time as the organization adapts to opportunities internal and external. Altering the objectives of learning has to balance between adapting and consistency that provides a foundation for the effort.

These are obstacles to success to be sure, however, there are other hurdles. For example, in the article Six Myths of Product Development† (fallacy 1, **High utilization of resources will improve performance**), shows companies tend to move to ensure the team members are engaged during most if not all of the hours they are at work or a high utilization. This leaves little time for learning or even adapting to circumstances presented to the project. Essentially this effort to improve throughput by accounting for all of the available hours, actually has the opposite consequence. Another fallacy of interest from the article, fallacy 3, **Our development plan is great; we just need to stick to it**. Believing your development plan is great, means you are not likely to be thinking of ways to make things better. This perspective means we believe we do not need to invest time in improving, this deters the need for learning. Lastly from the article, is fallacy 6, **We will be more successful if we get it right the first time**, this misguided belief prohibits experimentation our team members may be afraid to try new methods as any failure may come with some negative feedback from the management.

1.3.3 Why Lessons Learned Are vital

Competition does not get easier as the organization grows. If our industry or segment is profitable, we can expect other companies to nudge their way into the space. If the business is not profitable, then the organization either goes out of business or must find ways to become a profitable by adapting, or changing the business into something that can deliver value to the customer. This is in effect learning, and it is likely that projects will be the mechanisms for that change and learning. Even established profitable businesses must work to remain in business lest they fall into the previous category of a business on the edge of failure and closing. Success today does not mean success tomorrow. According to Forbes the expected return on investment in the stock market will drop from the 7% to a future of 3%.‡

---

* Kleiner, A., & Senge, P. M. (1994). The Fifth discipline fieldbook. London: Nicholas Brearley.
† Reinertsen, S. T. D. (2015, July 16). Six Myths of Product Development. Retrieved from https://hbr.org/2012/05/six-myths-of-product-development
‡ https://www.forbes.com/sites/baldwin/2017/10/27/stock-market-forecast-2018-2043/#71b355cc7c75 last accessed 7/25/218

Lessons learned provide a means to improve quality, schedule, and the overall effectiveness of an organization if employed properly. This does not infer that every lesson learned program will be run the same way, it is implying, however, the program run it must be modeled specifically for the organization using it. While the overall objective may be the same, how each part of the organization contributes to this objective may be different, consider an organization that develops and manufactures products as an example. There will be different ways in which the product development portion of the company will contribute than the manufacturing portion. However, there may be opportunities for learning via the shared work areas and work exchanges between these groups. For example, the design for manufacturing and assembly are areas the development staff will need to be part, as the development work delivers a product for manufacturing. The objectives may be different in support of the common organization goal, but collaboration is required for either to meet their respective objectives.

1.3.4 How Lessons Learned Apply

Learning provides the mechanism for improvement. We learn what does not work; we explore to find what may work, and experiment to ascertain what will work. We work to understand those things that limit our performance, hindering us from the objectives we wish to achieve, and then work with our team members to devise potential solutions to overcome these limitations. then experiment with these potential solutions, learning along the way. This continuous improvement is like the approach of Total Quality Management; though those books tend to focus on the technical portion of the work, this book will explore the employee and team aspects required to make something like Total Quality Management work, along with a review of the tools that can be used to help.

1.3.5 Inhibitors To Communication

There are many things that get in the way of communications. The structure of the organization as well as the organization's culture impact the level of open discourse and achieving the corporate objectives along with consistent learning. In this section we will delve into some of these obstructions to communication and how they are counter to Organizational Development.

1.3.5.1 Conflicting Priorities

One of the inhibitors to communications is conflicting priorities, objectives, and competing needs for resources of the organization, as well as an individual's personal goals and objectives. These conflicts are not necessarily team conflicts although these may be linked. These conflicts are not due to politics or team and us versus them root causes, but more a struggle for optimum use of resources and available talent, as well as an attempt to keep their respective priorities in front of the executives. Of course, these things set up the office politics aspects of working in the organization.

1.3.5.2 Office Politics Is defined as

> (business) (functioning as singular or plural) the ways that power is shared in an organization or workplace, and the ways that it is affected by the personal relationships between the people who work there*

Let us first state that Office politics is not personal interaction in the aspect of how we talk or act toward others related to the struggle for power or position. This can be ascertained from the definition above. Many people think that office politics are a required part of every business. We should ask ourselves, are they really? Why do office politics exist? Can the fact that your company has office politics be an indicator of your organizational health? To answer if these are a part of every business, we must first examine why these exist. To do that let us look at Organizational Politics Perceptions (OPP). OPP is a way of looking at the aspects and/or perceptions of people that cause them to see their office or business as a political one. Surprisingly enough with all the studies over the last 20+ years done on this topic very few have found any relationship between OPP and demographics such as age, race, sex, or tenure. The major drivers to perceiving an environment as political can be divided into three groups:

1. Personal Control and Certainty
2. Relationships and Opportunity
3. Conflict

If we were to look at these three areas closer, we would see that they are all functions of what is known as Stage three of tribal leadership. In the book "Tribal Leadership" it lists five stages:

1. Stage one: "Life sucks"
2. Stage two: "My life sucks"
3. Stage three: "I'm great, and you're not"
4. Stage four: "We're great"
5. Stage five: "Life is great"[†]

---

* Office politics definition and meaning | Collins English Dictionary. (n.d.). Retrieved August 6, 2018, from http://www.collinsdictionary.com/dictionary/english/office-politics
[†] Logan, D., King, J. P., & Fischer-Wright, H. (2011). *Tribal leadership: Leveraging natural groups to build a thriving organization*. New York: Harper Business.

The first two stages do not represent very much of the workforce, about 25 percent.* Stage three (the section where office politics occur) represents about 49 percent of the workforce.† This would explain why most people are familiar with office politics. Many of us are taught at an early age that knowledge is power. While it is true that knowledge can be perceived as power the reality is that until it is shared and put to use, knowledge holds no power, other than the perception of the person with the knowledge by the person who desires it. This would make the brokering of knowledge for power purposes flawed in its inception. So why does it continue as office politics? To answer that we must look to human nature and the desire to be needed and secure in the basic needs.‡ While hoarding knowledge or information does not provide either of these it may be the perception of the individual that it does. This perception, which was established from some experience, is what needs to be addressed and will likely require new experiences that would modify the response to alleviate this situation. This will need to be done if we wish to have an open sharing of knowledge at all levels of an organization.

1.3.5.3 Politics—Personal Control and Certainty

We will review personal control and certainty first because it actually plays a role in all the drivers we will subsequently discuss. An individual who feels that they have some control in the (their) work situation are less likely to view the office as political, because they do not perceive a struggle for power in their work. This also provides a feeling of certainty in their position and further reduces the perception of office politics. There is, however, an additional need to fully satisfy the certainty requirement and that is communication. Without good communication between parties about personal control, a perception of mistrust could foster the perception of a highly charged political environment. When we use the word "communication" it also refers to the communication we provide via the experiences we show others.

1.3.5.4 Politics—Relationships and Opportunity

Now let us discuss Relationships and Opportunity as they pertain to OPP. In the introductory paragraph we stated, "personal interaction and how we talk or act toward others is not related to the struggle for power or position." So you might be asking, "What is meant by the term relationships if it does not mean personal interaction?" In this context the term relationship means perceived positional

---

* Logan, D., King, J. P., & Fischer-Wright, H. (2011). *Tribal leadership: Leveraging natural groups to build a thriving organization*. New York: Harper Business.
† Logan, D., King, J. P., & Fischer-Wright, H. (2011). *Tribal leadership: Leveraging natural groups to build a thriving organization*. New York: Harper Business.
‡ Maslow's Hierarchy of Needs. (n.d.). Retrieved August 6, 2018, from https://simplypsychology.org/maslow.html

relationships. If an individual perceives their relationship to the structure of an organization or group (team) as non-contributive or inferior, then they may be more likely to perceive their environment as political due to a lack of control and/or contribution. As we discussed in the previous paragraph personal control is an important aspect in the perception of whether an environment is political or not. How are opportunity and relationships grouped together? Opportunity can be seen as the ability for growth and development both on a personal and professional level. If someone sees that they have the opportunity for growth and development within a team or organization, they perceive that they have some control, if even in a small way, of the situation and better yet their own personal growth. Again, we see how personal control comes into play with the perception of office politics.

1.3.5.5 Politics and Conflict

Conflict is the third aspect that contributes to the perception of a political environment. Conflict is defined by Webster as:

> *a: competitive or opposing action of incompatibles: antagonistic state or action (as of divergent ideas, interests, or persons) // a conflict of principles*
>
> *b: mental struggle resulting from incompatible or opposing needs, drives, wishes, or external or internal demands. // His conscience was in conflict with his duty.*[*]

There will always be some level of conflict within any team or organization. While Webster's definition of conflict would seem to indicate some form of impasse we know that there would be no change in anything without conflict. Changes are caused from the dynamic tension (conflict) between one's current situation and a desired situation. If the tension is slight the desire to change is also slight; if the tension is large a change is more likely and perhaps more extreme or radical departure from the present situation. While change management likes the term **tension** versus **conflict**, they can produce similar results if employed in productively. It is the nature in which conflict is resolved that creates the perception of a political environment. If we approach conflicts using the five disciplines of a learning organization, we can minimize the potential for creating a political situation or environment. It is when the conflict turns away from a team solution; you're wrong and I'm right, that power comes into play. As every leader can attest there are times when this answer is required. However, when time permits a discussion as to why it was done this way should follow to show all parties involved that their contributions are important, but the situation was such that this discussion could not be done. During this

---

[*] Conflict. (n.d.). Retrieved August 6, 2018, from https://www.merriam-webster.com/dictionary/conflict

discussion input as to how to best handle the situation next time could be discussed to minimize or even prevent repeating it, and this is part of learning. The irony of this is that unless the situation is some form of causality, not something that arises from a typical business project, there is frequently time for a discussion and this discussion would lead to a more thorough answer to the situation.

1.3.5.6 Summary

During our reviewed the confluence of these three drivers, we have touched on some of the basic principles of a learning organization, change management, and motivation. Therefore, we can use this information to explore how having a perceived political environment could diminish the productivity of our people and thus our organization. Something we should note about our review, is that we consistently use the term "perceived." The reason for this is that every individual will perceive a situation differently, at least initially. It requires constant effort (**communication**) and attention (**involvement**) to maintain and develop a clear and accurate team perspective.

1.4 Enhancement to Communication

1.4.1 Corporate culture

We see the complications with communications and those things that can degrade communications. Fortunately, there are things that improve communications or make clear communications possible. Our corporate culture can be an enhancement to the communication within the company. A corporate environment that fosters or holds clear communication in high regard improves the possibility of effective communication happening. That does not countermand earlier observation where the corporate environment could be an inhibitor to communications.

1.4.2 To Dyadic or Not (weak ties)

A large portion of corporate communication can be considered dyadic, that is between two people within the organization. However, when we think about knowledge and the organization, it is only as good as the distribution network that pushes what has been learned throughout the organization. "It turns out that most useful information comes from the individuals in a person's extended networks, casual acquaintances and friends of friends. This information is the most useful precisely because it comes from infrequent or weak contacts. Strong contacts are likely to be people with whom there is a constant sharing of the same information. As a result, individuals within these groupings have come to have the same information base and similar perspectives. However, information from outside this base gives unique perspectives, and in some instances, strategic advantages over competitors in a person's immediate network."*

1.4.3 Communities of Practices

The organization can create an atmosphere in which communities of practice can organically spawn, worse case, set about developing these communities within the organization. Communities of practice can bring about an accretion of our team members or key skill sets of the organization. This gathering of common interests can create an atmosphere of learning along with distribution of that learning throughout the organization. Knowledge of these collections of skills are a resource for the rest of the organization - provided others know this. In addition, this collection of expertise is now in a position to share what each of the individuals know with each other, increasing the expertise and capability of this group's ability to be of service for the rest of the organization. This will be discussed at length in the book. At this point is suffices to write that a single point source of knowledge then becomes a single point of failure. To that end communities of practices can help in developing or cultivating and nurturing specific knowledge that can be advantageous to the organization.

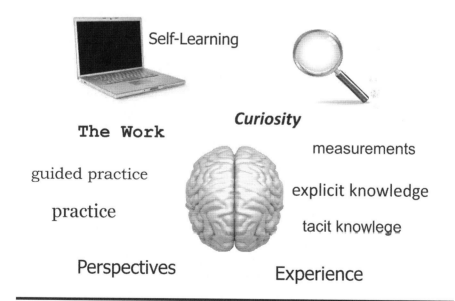

Figure 1.6　There are many ways to learn.

---

* Johnson, J. (2009). *Managing knowledge networks*. Cambridge, UK: Cambridge University Press, p.36.

1.4.4 Types of Knowledge

Now that we have looked at **learning** we need to define a few more terms, such as knowledge. Knowledge is defined by Merriam-Webster as "the fact or condition of knowing something with familiarity gained through experience or association, the fact or condition of being aware of something, the circumstance or condition of apprehending truth or fact through reasoning, the fact or condition of having information or of being learned."* Learning and knowledge share a commonality, experience, that will be instrumental throughout our discussions. This explains why two people can see the same situation and arrive at different conclusions with this information. They also differ with the use of the terms "truth or fact." Learning does not use these terms, but knowledge does. This would make it seem that knowledge is a concrete concept. We know from the test of time that this is not always the case as knowledge of many things are constantly evolving. It is to this end that we will say that *learning is how we gain knowledge* and that knowledge is the logical application of what we have learned. This makes these two concepts just sub-sections of one project: development. There are two categories of knowledge, **explicit** and **tacit**, as noted by scientist and philosopher Michael Polanyi. Tacit knowledge is embedded in the human mind through experiences and jobs and explicit knowledge is codified and digitized in books, documents, memos, etc.†

1.4.4.1 Explicit

Explicit knowledge is knowledge that is captured in some form: a book, a procedure, a process, etc. Its capturing of knowledge gives it strength because it can be shared freely. However, it is also the weakness of explicit knowledge, in that it has been codified in some manner, its global evolution can and commonly is constrained in one way or another, additionally, it is not possible to ask questions of the documentation. Since we know that no single process fits every situation and even when repeating a task, it may not unfold exactly as it has int he past. To have a ridged structure can be self-defeating, and since we know that knowledge (understanding) is ever evolving explicit knowledge is best employed as a guidepost to shed light on the constraints. Since explicit knowledge is written or captured in some manner it allows for a review of its evolution over time, if we have been exploring and recording. This review can show trends which can be used to develop growth and development of plans and provide process and procedural lessons learned.

There are some instances where explicit knowledge, solely by its nature, best fits a situation. An example of these types of situations would be the specifications of an item, or the testing requirements to validate those specifications. However, as alluded to earlier, this is not always the best fit for a project in that a rigid structure "MAY" not allow for development of an approach that fits the range of

---

* Merriam-Webster, Knowledge, 2018.
† TLU, Key Concepts in Information and Knowledge Management, 2018.

variations to which a project may be subjected. To provide an example let us look at a multi-divisional or departmental instruction. For the sake of discussion, we will say that 4 department heads have approved (signed) the instruction and one of those departments decides to modify one of its processes contained within the instruction. They must obtain the approval of the remaining three department heads prior to that instruction modification. This delay could be both good and bad: **bad** because it may not occur in sufficient time to apply to a specific project, or **good** because the initiating department may not have thought out the effect of their desired change on the other departments. This type of situation can be minimized by the use of a "Living Document or Procedure." An example of a living document is The Constitution of the United States because it was written knowing that it would have to be continuously updated. When we write a procedure or process guide we should keep in mind that it will not be able to apply to every situation and will require changes as our people, processes, and organization develop and write and maintain it as a living document, subjected to the rules of configuration management. Writing a document in this manner will require more time and attention to the details, but in the long run will shorten the revision or modification process.

1.4.4.2 Tacit (Tribal Knowledge)

Tacit knowledge being embedded in the mind and not written and is sometimes referred to as tribal knowledge as it is often specific to an organization (tribe as opposed to industry). By that we mean that there are things that are not written down or are contrary to the written guidance that are done to complete a task. This knowledge is sometimes passed from one individual to another, but may also be held by its owner. This could be an example of stage three of tribal leadership, I'm great— you're not,* or it could be a function of the individual attempting to feel needed. For as long as the individual is the sole source of the information, they hold some power within the team and feel needed. This false sense of need erodes the team structure and promotes the same action within others. When this "I" mentality is overcome the tacit knowledge can become explicit knowledge and used for further development. Since tacit knowledge is acquired through experience it can also be related to lessons learned, even when informal. WE will elaborate on lessons learned in the next section.

To take this idea a step further let us look at the words **thought** or **think**. Merriam Webster defines think as "to form or have in the mind; to have as intention, to have as an opinion, to regard as; to devise by; to have as an expectation."† If we take our previous two definitions, learning and knowledge, and relate them to think and thought we can see that they are predecessors to our first two. This concept can be related to the first phase or project development: initiating. All of these definitions leave room for subjectivity from the individual's (group) participation

---

* Logan, D., Fischer-Wright, H., & King, J. (2011). *Tribal leadership: Leveraging natural groups to build a thriving organization.* London: Harper & Row.
† Merriam-Webster, Think, 2018.

in that activity. It is this subjectivity that is a common source of confusion when allowed to remain open to further subjectivity from others involved within the project. This is one reason we will be discussing communication and expectation management later in this book.

1.4.5 Common Lessons learned Mistakes

There are many reasons for failure of the company to learn from the work. The corporate culture influences the ability of the organization to make the most of these mistakes. We hear people in the company say things like "it is okay to make mistakes, but can't we make new ones" in our organization. In fact, that was directly from a senior manager at a place I once worked.

- No organizational plans for learning (not a priority)
- Failure to exploit opportunities
- Silo and other communications challenges not addressed
- Errant proximity and cause
- Corporate culture
- Complex lessons learned program(s)

1.4.5.1 No Plans for Learning

Many organizations have some form of plan for learning, the priority is commonly the bottom line. While few to no organizations are more concerned about learning to become better over making a profit, it is this very mentality that can and usually does have a drastic effect on profit. The improvement of processes that will allow an organization's people to more effectively achieve their goal will assist in increasing the profit margin. While this is usually the type of issue that is a longer-term return on investment it is still a return on investment. A lesson learned program will not achieve its true value until something more than window dressing has been invested. It is this very approach that commonly condemn the lesson learned programs.

The complexity of the databases associated with lessons learned programs is legendary. The complexity of data entry is most only surpassed by the complexity of how to retrieve the information from the program in a useful manner. While there is no one best way (must be a tailored fit for the situation, personnel, group, or organization) to set up a lesson learned database, minimizing the main topics and more veneering the second and third topic lines can be most useful. Some lessons learned will fit into more than one category or are and most commonly do. Where they differ is what the assorted explorers garner from the lesson learned. If something different was learned by let's say the three disparate department involved, all three items should be linked in such a manner that each department can see the other departments lesson learned because it could and commonly will affect the actions or plan of the other.

Let's go back to the tribal mentality for a second (I'm great and you're not).* Another issue that weakens the lesson learned program(s) is who does what from a lesson. Most lessons learned have some form of follow on corrective action to attempt to prevent reoccurrence and the action may or may not be directed toward the group that noted the lesson learned. When a root cause analysis or causal mapping are associated with a lesson learned it may branch beyond what is may be considered the lead department. When an item branches beyond to other groups the response is quite often "that's not my issue." This is commonly referred to as "my rice bowl mentality" and shows a lack of systems thinking/understanding in most cases.

1.4.5.2 Failure to Exploit

Going in hand with no plans for learning failure, comes the failure to exploit. The hyper focus on the bottom line impacts the actions that can restrict some of the actions that are deemed appropriate, allowable, or even prudent. Failure to exploit are times when there are opportunities for the team to learn but rather than take that learning possibility, and the risk, a safe approach is taken, that fits within what is already known by the team. This is effectively passing on the opportunity to extend what is known, which is learning. In the agile community (a form of project management for software) there is a saying, fail fast, and fail often. There are many variants of this saying, the point being that nothing new can be learned without risk, and we should not fear failure, but take calculated risks that advance learning and not let failure erode the possibility of learning. This learning mindset is influenced by the corporate culture.

1.4.5.3 Corporate Culture

This book will constantly bring up the corporate culture. The culture of the company will set the environment for how people treat each other and how and what the management values in the employees. The corporate culture defines what behaviors are acceptable and this will impact the learning that may be possible an example of which is described in the previous section. Another example, is a command and control culture, from experience, will impact the learning in ways, starting with exclusion of those doing the work or not be actively involved in the learning, rather will receive direction from the management and leadership functions.

1.4.5.4 Why Organizations Fail to Exploit Opportunities

We can sum most of the failures to exploit learning opportunities as the corporate culture and prioritization of learning and distribution of that learning. Learning

---

* Logan, D., King, J. P., & Fischer-Wright, H. (2011). Tribal leadership: Leveraging natural groups to build a thriving organization. New York: Harper Business.

takes time, and distribution of that learning likewise takes some time. It is not just the time and effort to draw out what has been learned, but also time to distribute that learning not just to the immediate team, but to the entirety of the organization that could benefit of this learning.

While most organizations understand that in today's environment change is inevitable, they do not relate this change to what is being learned or the need for learning, but to what new technology is available. Technology is not necessarily the savior of the organization. Organizational development is a manner to bring about planned change.* This would seem to be contrary to what we obtain from lessons learned because most lessons learned are not planned, but the response to some failure. However, what we do with the lesson learned should be both planned and new; not the same action that taught us the lesson to start with expecting a different result.

Yet another possible reason that an organization fails to use lessons learned to their fullest opportunity could be they have an existing lessons learned program that they believe works. While this may seem to contradict itself maybe you have seen this type of lessons learned program. While the program is great for helping solve short term problems the solutions it provides do not meet their long term objective. Since this type of setup commonly provides a quick return to the task at hand and the long term objectives will not be seen (missed) for some time it meets the goal of getting the project back on schedule. This getting back on schedule for the one part of a project becomes the price of another part or project being delayed by the same or similar lesson learned.

All in all, most organizations fail to exploit their lessons learned because their focus is on the now instead of the long term fix. This could be because they believe the situation will continually evolve and the answer for the first lesson learned will not fix the next extended lesson learned. This assumption is flawed in its inception because any new change will not be based upon a firm starting point if past issues (lessons learned) are not fully understood. These things are nuanced and have many variables that interact.

1.4.5.5 Proximity and Cause

Any discussion of lessons learned will need to include things like root cause analysis or determination of the true cause of the observable symptom. In our experience, there is a tendency for humans to see the immediate preceding action as the cause of the observable symptom. Seldom is that the real cause of the disturbance. Hanging all of your business resources on this supposition as the root cause, in our experience, is a waste of time as we solve the thing that had nothing to do with the resulting observation. There are many things wrong with this approach besides the wasting of time solving minor problems that likely had no impact, but this rush to judgment

---

* Cummings, T. G., & Worley, C. G. (2016). *Organization development and change.* Toronto: Nelson Education.

Figure 1.7   The sky is the limit if we open our mind and collaborate.

can reduce the learning. With a rush to determining the cause we reduce the time available to evoke the possible causes of malady from the team, which is opportunity for learning and sharing knowledge from within the team members. This type of decision making commonly leads to one of the archetypes we will discuss later in this chapter: unintended consequences.

1.5 Motivation

Motivation is what moves a person from one condition, to another. The uncomfortable dissonance, or tension, between where we want to be as individuals, a group or as an organization to the desired condition. This tension moves us to take some action to move us to this new desired state. We have been in Twitter discussions with people that believe motivation is an extrinsic event, a manipulation of one person by another person to get them to do what the first person wants. As we indicated on Twitter, we disagree with this characterization of motivation. As an organization goes, it is in the best interest to ensure the people we hire are well motivated and intrinsically so, that is, they do not require disproportionate cajoling, but want to make their mark and do things that are in line with the business in ways that are consistent with the business's philosophy.

1.5.1 What Is Motivation

While we use Merriam-Webster for most definitions in this book, we will use the Oxford dictionary to define Motivation:

> A reason or reasons for acting or behaving in a particular way, Desire or willingness to do something; enthusiasm. A set of facts and arguments used in support of a proposal.*

Motivation can be both internal (Intrinsic) and external (Extrinsic). Internal motivation is from within an individual and can be closely related to personal mastery, another one of the five disciplines written about in Peter Senge's book "*The Fifth Discipline.*" He describes personal mastery as:

> Learning to expand our personal capacity to create the results we most desire, and creating an organizational environment which encourages all its members to develop themselves toward the goals and purpose they choose.†

There is a connection between motivation and personal mastery. These are aligned via the desire to obtain some goal or objective (tension) and action taken is taken to close the gap which will require personal mastery.

Figure 1.8   What moves you?

---

* Motivation | Definition of motivation in English by Oxford Dictionaries. (n.d.). Retrieved August 7, 2018, from https://en.oxforddictionaries.com/definition/motivation

† Kleiner, A., & Senge, P. M. (1994). *The Fifth discipline fieldbook*. London: Nicholas Brearley.

External motivation comes from external forces such as rewards, a paycheck, and/or even just encouragement. This type of motivation can and is commonly confused with manipulation. While attempting to motivate an individual or group could be considered manipulation, this is not necessarily so. A relationship between the objective and required activities and the individual or group's internal motivation can be established with truth and that is not manipulation but **buy-in**.

1.5.2 The Motivation Masters

For decades, there has been considerable research into motivation. Trying to make an environment that maximizes human potential, is important for businesses, In many industries the human talent can be a significant business cost, and more importantly, it is the source of creativity and the propulsion of the of the organization towards its objective. It should be clear then, that to maximize this effort it is important to understand motivation. Well motivated individuals and team members will be productive, not so motivated, will be a drain on the teams and the organization.

1.5.2.1 Maslow and Ziglar

When most people think of Maslow, they immediately think of a triangle that is built of blocks representing human needs and desires. While Maslow did arrange human needs in a hierarchy of pre-potency he also stated that the order of these needs and the amount needed to be satisfied before the next need emerges is individually driven and the order he listed them in was just a basic outline. This basic outline was generated to provide a framework for future research in the absence of any

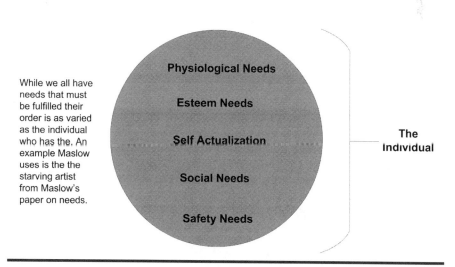

While we all have needs that must be fulfilled their order is as varied as the individual who has the. An example Maslow uses is the the starving artist from Maslow's paper on needs.

Physiological Needs

Esteem Needs

Self Actualization

Social Needs

Safety Needs

The Individual

Figure 1.9   Maslow's hierarchy of needs is cognitively satisfying.

other theory at the time.* One might think that this is an unusual way to start a conversation about the Theory of Human Motivation and how it applies to people, projects, and organizations, but it is a prime example how everyone, group, or group of groups have their own hierarchy of needs related to their specific motivation and needs.

What we can garner from Maslow's work is a basic outline of things that provide motivation to people? He does not delve into how this works with groups or groups of groups, but we know from studies done of "group think" there is some shift in an individual when they are part of a group, both good and bad. Managers and project managers need to understand the basic drivers for motivation on individual and group levels, before we can effectively apply actions to influence the situation. When we talk about Maslow, we like to link him with Zig Ziglar because Ziglar believed that to motivate you needed to know what the other individual or group goals and desires are and show them how what needs to be done will help them reach that objective. Zig Ziglar did not dissect the specifics about what motivated people, but focused on the relationship between seller or buyer, worker, and manager (project manager). Looking at these two together gives both the what and the how for a basic motivation framework.

One of Ziglar's best quotes is, "You can get everything in life you want if you will just help enough other people get what they want."† This may not sound like what a manager, project manager or company should think because it sounds like it could cost either time or money, and probably both. This type of thinking is predicated on an assumption that helping others get what they want or desire to achieve, does not actually align with the project's, group's, or organization's goals, or is not worth the time and effort spent.

1.5.2.2 Herzberg and Festinger

Herzberg's two-factor theory is also referred to as the hygiene factor due to its split approach to motivation. Herzberg theorized that satisfaction and dissatisfaction were affected by different factors and thus could not be measured on the same scale.‡ Hygiene factors were those that pertained to the job and were comprised of supervision, interpersonal relationships, work conditions, salary, and company policy. It is easy to see how these items are primarily physiological but have some extension into the psychological realm. The motivational factors were such items as recognition, a sense of achievement, growth or promotion opportunities, responsibility, and

---

* Barnes, M. (n.d.). A. H. Maslow (1943). A Theory of Human Motivation. Retrieved August 15, 2018, from http://psychclassics.yorku.ca/Maslow/motivation.htm

† Zig Ziglar - 91 quotes. (n.d.). Retrieved August 15, 2018, from http://www.great-quotes.com/quotes/author/Zig/Ziglar

‡ Herzberg, F. (1965). The New Industrial Psychology. Industrial and Labor Relations Review, 18(3), 364-376. doi:10.2307/2520909

Figure 1.10 Motivation may errode over time, like taking a shower, we must take recurring action to make things smell better.

meaningfulness of the work itself. The motivational factors discussed by Herzberg are of a psychological nature only. According to Herzberg's theory, hygiene factors cannot produce motivation, only satisfaction or dissatisfaction.[*]

If we apply the two-factor theory to a work environment we can see how we could have a satisfied worker that is not motivated or a dissatisfied worker that is motivated or for that matter any combination of these variables. The point behind this is to know that there is a difference between the two (motivation and hygiene) and identifying specific actions that affect, providing focus, for example, to not work on a hygiene issue when it is motivation issue. We would recommend two YouTube videos: **Jumping for the Jelly Beans** a discussion with Fredrick Herzberg through the BBC part one and two.

Motivation can also be facilitated through actions taken by the organization, setting the work environment in a way that encourages the team members. This is discussed at further in the section on learning with B.F. Skinner.

1.5.2.3 Festinger

Festinger is associated with the development of **cognitive dissonance** theory, which states a situation that involves differing attitudes, beliefs, or behaviors produces discomfort and this discomfort leads to their alteration to restore balance.[†] This sounds like the theory of change where there is tension between the current state of a situation and the desired state of that situation causing some action to bring the situation more in line with the desired state thus alleviating the tension. When you

[*] Herzberg, F. (1965). The New Industrial Psychology. Industrial and Labor Relations Review, 18(3), 364-376. doi:10.2307/2520909

[†] https://www.simplypsychology.org/cognitive-dissonance.html

examine the study done by Festinger in which 71 people were assigned a dull and meaningless task and then paid either one dollar or twenty dollars to inform a second party that the task was interesting, those paid only one dollar to lie experienced dissonance and the only manner to overcome this was to believe the task was really meaningful, whereas the people paid twenty dollars had more of a reason to turn the pegs and thus had less or no dissonance.[*] Applying this theory we can see how many decisions may have some form of dissonance, the manifestation is different, and the manner in which these are resolved (internal or external) is what we are looking for with people.

We will also look at another part of dissonance called "effort justification." This is when it is easier to convince ourselves that a task we have been employed to execute, actually holds meaning or worth even when it is determined to hold less value or meaning than we originally surmised. To minimize or alleviate the dissonance we convince ourselves of the activity's worth.[†] This attempt to remove or reduce the dissonance (effort justification) causes people to fight against change or to hinder communication as different archetypes or logical fallacies are employed to justify the position and reduce the dissonance. The key is to not cause more dissonance, but to show the individual or group how their effort has allowed for the change or improvement thus providing them a different form of justification instead of rationalization and resistance to the change.

1.5.2.4 Kurt Lewin

In 1936 a group of researchers led by Kurt Lewin developed many different aspects pertaining to leadership. For the **leadership equation** we are attempting to show that the experiences provided to the employee are a significant driver for behavior. Motivation and behavior are inexplicably linked through the experiences of the individual. This is predominately because everyone uses past experiences to initially assess most situations because unfamiliar situations commonly cause some form of reticence or anxiety. Therefore, to elevate this anxiety experiential association is employed.

1.5.2.4.1 Leadership Equation

$B = f(P, E)$: where **B** is behavior, **P** is person, and **E** is environment.[‡]
This should clear up all our questions about leadership and project development, right? What if we further dissect Lewin's equation?

---

[*] https://www.simplypsychology.org/cognitive-dissonance.html
[†] https://study.com/academy/lesson/effort-justification-aronson-mills-study-examples-applications.html
[‡] Lewin, K., Heider, F., & Heider, G. M. (1936). *Principles of topological psychology*. United States, NY: McGraw-Hill.

If we say that $P = f (Exp) (MM) (A)$: where **Exp** is the individual's personal experiences, **MM** is the Mental Model of the individual, and **A** is the individual's Attitude.

And then we say that $E = f (P_2) (GB+GT^X) (WC)$: where P_2 is other people influences, **GB** is Group Behavior, **GT** is Group Think (^{X} is the number of people in the group), and **WC** is the actual working conditions.

Having stated all this, we can now modify Lewin's equation to be:

$$B = f \{f (Exp) (MM) (A)\} \{f (P2) (GB+GTX) (WC)\}$$

Now we can further break down some of the person portion of the equation if we assume:

1. Mental model is a function of experience (Exp), attitude (A), and desire to learn (D_L):

$$MM = f (Exp) (A) (D_L)$$

2. Attitude is a function of experience (**Exp**), environment (**E**), and treatment (**T**):

$$A = f (Exp) (A) (T)$$

Therefore, we can say: $B = f \{f (Exp) \{(Exp) (A) (D_L)\}$
$\{(Exp) (A) (T)\} \{f (P_2) (GB+GT^X) (WC)\}$

Or $B = f \{(Exp^3) (A^2) (D_L) (T)\} \{f (P_2) (GB+GT^X) (WC)\}$

So thus far we could surmise that behavior is predominately experience and attitude. What if we go further? Consider your experience, for example, have you noticed how people respond to group behavior and group think? Are these responses based mainly upon experience and attitudes?

Experience is a long term or require considerable time to develop and therefore we will call that a slowly sloping curve. However, attitude is a rapid response item, a quick changing curve, directly tied to treatment, therefore a change in treatment, causes directly proportional to motivation. Desire a quick change (relatively speaking) we should focus on improving the treatment (perceived or real) of our personnel, but for the long haul we should focus on developing good experiences for our people.

We are sure this clears up any questions you may have had about leadership, right? This is why people have studied what makes a good leader and why they are successful for so long. There is no simple answer, but there are commonalities, most of which we can gather from the equations above.

1.5.2.5 Alderfer

Like Hertzberg, Alderfer grouped Maslow's hierarchy of needs into large sections: **Existence**, **Relatedness**, and **Growth (ERG)**. Even though Maslow did not believe that the lower needs must be satisfied prior to the next higher need becoming a new motivational factor, though many people believed that was the intent of his work based upon how he had laid out his theory. However, Alderfer clearly stated that at any point, any need could be satisfied and the driving point behind motivation is the obtainment of one if not more of these needs. Whether the division is five, like Maslow, two, like Hertzberg, or three like Alderfer each comes with their own specific issues for validation or rebuttal, is not the point of this book to discuss. The key point is that needs, hygiene, relatedness, or motivation are subjective to the individual, and it is only through knowledge of the individual and their specific hierarchy of needs will any true motivation occur.

1.5.2.6 Vroom

Unlike the people we have previously discussed Vroom looked to the cognitive side of the motivational process with the **Expectancy theory** of motivation. In his theory the motivational factor (unfortunately abbreviated **MF**) for behavior is based upon the individual's perception of obtaining the desired outcome.[*] The equation he devised is:

$$\text{MF} = \text{Expectancy} * \text{Instrumentality} * \sum (\text{Valence(s)})^{\dagger}$$

Expectancy is the individual's perception of the relationship between their effort and performance. This perception is primarily based upon the individual's experiences, personality, self-confidence, and emotional state.[‡]

Instrumentality is the individual's assessment of the probability that they will obtain a performance level that will facilitate some reward.[§]

Valence is the value the individual associates with the outcome.[¶]

---

[*] https://www.leadership-central.com/expectancy-theory-of-motivation.html

[†] Lunenburg, F. C. (2011). Expectancy Theory of Motivation: Motivating by Altering Expectations. *International Journal of Management, Business, and Adminstration*, 15(1), 1–6. Retrieved August 20, 2018, from http://nationalforum.com/Electronic Journal Volumes/Lunenburg, Fred C Expectancy Theory Altering Expectations IJMBA v15 NI 2011.PDF

[‡] https://www.leadership-central.com/expectancy-theory-of-motivation.html

[§] https://www.leadership-central.com/expectancy-theory-of-motivation.html

[¶] https://www.leadership-central.com/expectancy-theory-of-motivation.html

Vroom's Expectancy theory of motivation is based on research done at the University of Michigan in 1957 by Basil Georgopoulos, Gerald Mahoney, and Nyle Jones that focused on the conscious and rational aspects of motivation.* Using their findings Vroom theorized that this was a manner in which an individual could logically ascertain the probability of a need being met through the effort they were exerting toward a specific task.

1.5.2.7 Summation

There are countless theories surrounding motivation and other psychology based theories, some of which have passed the test of time and some that were debunked.† We have attempted to show a link between the experiences that are provided to people through the workplace and their level of motivation. We also explored the "Leadership Equation" to show how the significance of the experience factor. This was done to emphasize that the experiences provided in the workplace have an enormous impact upon motivation and leadership qualities, and the perception that people have of both.

1.6 Learning

1.6.1 What Is learning

In our experience, and much of what this book is about, communication is a significant component to learning, project management and any organization's endeavor. Words have meaning, and left unquestioned, that meaning between two people may be radically or slightly different and we may never know. Therefore we start our discussion, by establishing an understanding of some of terms and concepts. Most of the terms we will be using are common. Additionally, to ensure appropriate conveyance of the ideas is facilitated through a common lexicon. For example, *learning*, it is defined by Merriam-Webster as, "the act or experience of one that learns; knowledge or skill acquired by instruction or study; **modification of behavioral tendency by experience**."‡ This definition suggests there are many ways in which we can learn and this learning will affect our behavior depending upon our level of openness and this is a constant process. We may believe we are all constantly learning, and likely so. We should know that the application of what we learn is subject to questioning and is the true test of learning. Adequate application of what is learned is a demonstration of that learning, and in fact, is an opportunity to spread learning and learn more. This answers the question whether we have

---

* https://www.leadership-central.com/expectancy-theory-of-motivation.html
† https://nobaproject.com/modules/the-replication-crisis-in-psychology
‡ (Merriam-Webster, Learning, 2018)

actually learned anything. In the realm of motivation, organizational development, and project management a deep understanding of these things make a difference. If we all have different perspectives, and we do, communication and coordination can be less than affective, but if we establish some key points where we agree on a perspective, especially on what needs to be learned, we start with a more stable foundation, and this enables learning across the group.

In Webster's definition of learning we see the statement, "modification of behavioral tendency by experience." There is an old adage that experience is the best teacher, but do we actually behave in a project or as an organization in conformance to this principle? Everything that we do creates a situation wherein someone else can experience something and therefore learn. Is the experience we present others promoting one experience (lesson) and expecting a different result (learning result)? As we have briefly touched on in this chapter and will additionally in the later chapters, experience plays an instrumental role in both motivation and development. This is not to say that we should always provide people with what would be considered a positive experience, we should prove or facilitate the experience that is related to the modification of behavior that is desired. On its surface this sounds like manipulation, but if this is done with an open dialog between the parties involved it is not manipulation, it is mentoring. Mentoring is thought of as from a senior individual to a more junior one, but when we apply how experience teaches it must provide all people involved some form of development.

1.6.2 Methods of Teaching

What comes to mind when you think of teaching: a PowerPoint, a classroom, homework? While there are many ways of conveying information such as PowerPoints or general instruction which are not teaching, anymore than conveying an experience to others? If we take the experience idea to the next level for teaching we might see that the different styles of leadership are very similar, if not identical, to teaching. For what is a leader, but someone who provides experiences to an individual or a group of people - and that is what a teacher does. The experiences provided by a leader or teacher can be both positive or negative and both are expected to produced the desired results. However, the effect of either positive or negative experiences should be understood by the individual employing them to avoid any unintended consequences that may result. Essentially, set the experience to be congruent with the learning objective or the expected competency developed.

According to a paper published by Concordia University Portland and written by Eric Gill* there are five effective methods for your classroom: Authority (or Lecture), Demonstrator (or Coaching), Facilitator (or Activity), Delegator (or Activity), and

---

* Gill, E. (2018, June 13). Teaching Styles: Different Teaching Methods & Strategies. Retrieved July 23, 2018, from https://education.cu-portland.edu/blog/classroom-resources/5-types-of-classroom-teaching-styles/

Hybrid (or Blended). While the workplace is not a classroom per say it is a place where people learn, similarly, the reason for a classroom.

As we can see from comparing the two: Methods of Teaching and Leadership Styles, there is distinct overlapping of methods and principles in teaching and leadership and both are based upon providing some form of experience to the individual or individuals being taught or led. While both the articles that are referred to provide some insight into when each style might be used and the potential overall effect of that style's employment every situation and the individuals involved are what and who will determine the effectiveness and overall impact of the style used. It is to that end that both the teacher and/or leader must know those being led and this can only be achieved through open communication and that is why we say that the teacher or leader is also provided some experiences by the student or employee and thus is learning as well.

All parties involved, teaching or working; leading or employed; students, or teachers, are being provided some form of experience by each other. What we choose to do with these experiences is the next logical question. As with the measures and controls section of project management checks and/or validates what is done or being done we must also determine if the experiences being acquired are effective toward their goal. This question would seem to create its own question, "How do

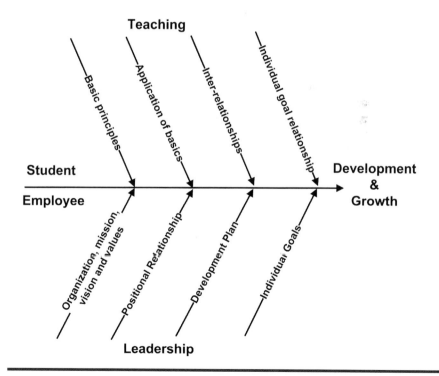

Figure 1.11   Leadership and teaching are connected.

you measure experience?" If learning is the modification of behavior and teaching is what causes that modification, then determining if the behavior has been modified as desired or needed would be the validation of the effectiveness of the experience and thus the teaching.

Considering both time and monetary constraints that most organization have experiences cannot be provided for every situation. This would seem to lead to problems in that people would be expected to do activities for which they have not been trained. Sharing of experiences via the open dialog between people and establishing key points for review or discussion to ensure the desired progress is being achieved could help bridge these gaps. Also the capturing of the lessons learned (discussed later) from these situations could be useful for later similar endeavors.

1.6.3 The Learning Masters

To be able to influence the organization's ability to learn, it is necessary to have some background in learning and teaching. This includes limits to learning and especially the environment conducive to learning. What do we need to know to create an environment that is conducive to learning in the organization? What actions can we take to encourage learning and facilitate dissemination of what is learned throughout the organization. Otherwise the organization may end up with pockets of understanding with the bulk of the organization not learning from these mistakes, essentially required to make those same mistakes over and over again with different team members to learn.

1.6.3.1 B.F. Skinner

B.F. Skinner was an American psychologist whose contribution to learning cannot be denied. Skinner coined the term operant conditioning. Operant conditioning is learning that is facilitated through rewards and punishments. In this case, rewards and punishments are deliberately used to alter behavior to that which is acceptable or even desired.

Skinner believed that there is no such thing as free will, we are all the product of experiences and those experiences have had consequences on our behavior. Essentially, those experiences represent stimuli that **trains** the individual to act in new and different ways. The stimuli have altered the way the person responds or thinks. In this way, we do not have free will, but are the results of this conditioning. He referred to this conditioning as operant conditioning, essentially, learning. This conditioning consists of both positive and negative approaches. Positive approaches are often referred to as rewards, and negative approaches are referred to as punishments. Positive reinforcement seeks to evoke a specific or increase the

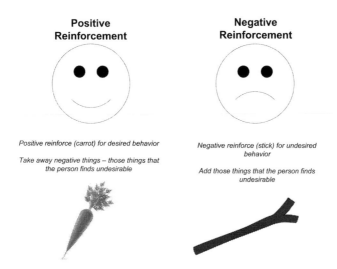

Figure 1.12 BF Skinner describes how behavior can be changed or learned via positive and negative reinforcement.

frequency of a specific behavior. Negative approaches seek to eliminate or reduce the frequency of occurrence of a specific behavior.

Positive reinforcement is the quick application of the metaphorical carrot for behaving or performing in ways that the organization approves. We may provide the person with more time off or other reward mechanism after accomplishing some objective of the company.

Negative reinforcement is like positive reinforcement, only rather than providing the metaphorical carrot for the action of which we want to see more, we take away some aspect of the environment or job that the individual finds unpleasant. Perhaps, the person has to this point been required to attend a specific meeting because of their actions, they may be excluded from this in the future or at least a respite for some short period of time.

Punishment is the opposite of reinforcement. Punishment seeks to make the behavior disappear, as we are working to reduce the occurrence of the behavior, and to that end we provide a negative condition often referred to as punishment. A positive punishment is the application or addition of a condition that is unpleasant upon the occurrence of the unwanted behavior.

Negative punishment is like negative reinforcement, as it is the removal of something desired by the individual no Wii for 2 weeks because you were late.

For this conditioning to work, the stimulus must be near (in time) to the behavior we wish to either increase or eliminate, and it must be perceived by the recipient as the appropriate one of these categories.

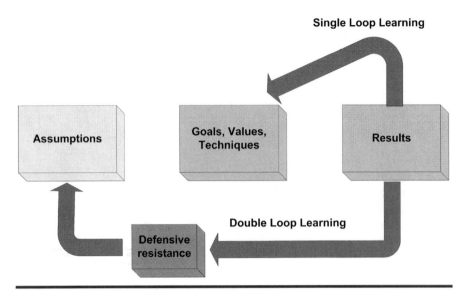

Figure 1.13   Argyris loop learning.

1.6.3.2 Argyris

> Why are employees reluctant to report to the top that one of their company's products is a "loser" and why can't the vice presidents of another company reveal to their president the spectacular lack of success of one of the company's divisions? The inability to uncover errors and other unpleasant truths arises from faulty organizational learning, says this author. Such habits and attitudes, which allow a company to hide its problems, lead to rigidity and deterioration. The author describes how this process can be reversed by a method he calls double loop learning.[*]

In this paper by Argyris, he states, "Organizational Learning is the process of detecting and correcting error."[†] He counsels that this correction is done either via single or double loop learning. Single loop learning is where information is gained that allows correction to a situation and double loop learning is when the second order questions are asked such as what is the goal or policy of the task with the error, and is it valid. Double loop learning is based upon the theory of action which has three main requirements according to a paper written by UC Davis in 2014;

---

[*] Argyris, C. (2014, August 01). Double Loop Learning in Organizations. Retrieved August 28, 2018, from https://hbr.org/1977/09/double-loop-learning-in-organizations

[†] Argyris, C. (2014, August 01). Double Loop Learning in Organizations. Retrieved August 28, 2018, from https://hbr.org/1977/09/double-loop-learning-in-organizations

1. The theory of action must begin with a statement of a causal relationship.
2. It must be empirically falsifiable.
3. It must be open-ended.*

Double loop learning is also related to **reflective learning** in that reflective learning is based in action learning. With reflective learning it is diagnosing, testing, and belief in personal causation.† Whether it is double loop or reflective learning we see that there is a gap between personal beliefs and the actual actions conducted, this is maybe why Argyris related the point of view of most people as actors.‡ In either case, double or reflective loop learning, the primary outcome is personal change directed at professional development. When we look at them in that context we can see how they are related to the five disciplines: Personal Mastery, Mental Models, Shared Vision, Team Learning, and Systems Thinking, discussed by Peter Senge in *The Fifth Discipline.*§

1.6.3.3 Vision and Mission Statements

Vision and mission statements have been around for a little while now, and over the years these have been comically regarded at best. These are important statements about the organization (or they can and should be) to help focus the work, as well as create an environment in which the individuals can use these statements to make decisions and prioritize actions. Instead, the mission and vision statements have become a list of buzz words, jargon, folderol that is referred to by the employees when they need a good laugh.

1.6.3.4 Vision Statements¶

Ideally, the vision statement describes where we want to be as an organization. It articulates the organization's ultimate purpose. It describes the aspirational objectives of the organization, informing those associated with the company (inside and outside) what a successful **future** of our company resembles. The vision is a future focused statement. This is not a dynamic or changing statement about the company objectives.

---

* What Is a Theory of Action? (2014). Retrieved August 28, 2018, from https://education.ucdavis.edu/post/what-theory-action

† Smith, P. A. (2001). Action Learning and Reflective Practice in Project Environments that are Related to Leadership Development. *Management Learning, 32*(1), 31-48. doi:10.1177/1350507601321003

‡ Last Updated March 31st, 2018 11:28 pm. (n.d.). Double Loop Learning (C. Argyris). Retrieved August 28, 2018, from http://www.instructionaldesign.org/theories/double-loop/

§ Kleiner, A., & Senge, P. M. (1994). The Fifth discipline fieldbook. London: Nicholas Brearley.

¶ https://www.diffen.com/difference/Mission_Statement_vs_Vision_Statement last accessed 9/30/2018

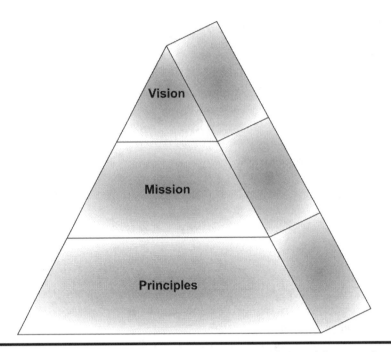

Figure 1.14   Vision, mission are connected to the principles of the organization.

1.6.3.5 Mission Statements*

The mission statement describes how we will get to that future we desire. The mission statement starts from now and carries us into the future. The mission statement connects to the values of the organization. The mission statement articulates the reasons the organization is in business (not for a paycheck). The mission statement is for those within the company as well as those that invest in the company.

1.6.3.6 Value Statements

The value statement articulates the specific behavior expected from those employed by the company.   This will culminate in a specific lists of behaviors expected by those in the employ of the organization. The values will be a short list of what is deemed fundamental to ensure the company culture is put into conditions that are deemed desired. An example of one statement in the value statements would be "we promote honest and clear communication."

---

* https://www.diffen.com/difference/Mission_Statement_vs_Vision_Statement last accessed 9/30/2018

1.6.3.7 Summation

While the first section of our journey may seem to have started with a mixture of motivation theories, behavioral theorist, biases, learning, teaching, and so much more that all seem relatively disjointed, when you reflect back upon each section with the collective in mind you can see a common line to it all. We touched slightly upon this thread in the previous section, Argyris. We did not, however, show how all these topics and theories string together as that is something that each individual must develop for themselves. We also did not overly discuss some topics as the idea is to merely promote the reader to reflect and develop their own assessment to share with others. The relational development of these topics will, as most individual and organizational developmental items, be a continually evolving (LEARNING) experience. We also did not claim to have some magic answer nor did we use new terms to explain a theory that has been around since the industrial revolution. We are merely proposing that these are proven items which can be applied to most projects and organizations to facilitate growth and development of their people.

Chapter 2

Organizing Learning for a Purpose

We want to eliminate or at least reduce impediments to our learning. As a company, we would like to do things to create an environment for learning, as well as capture that learning in some effective way and find ways to encourage this learning to be distributed throughout the organization.

The organization has objectives both long term and short. Competition and a constantly evolving technical landscape require adapting and this adapting is best met through growing competence in the organization. Competence can be developed through providing an environment that recognizes the importance of learning, not just for the individual, but for the organization. This environment of learning can only be developed through the effective sharing of knowledge obtained by all its members.

Organizations that are unable to share the learning of teams beyond the individual learning, can find a company work environment wherein project failures have a recurring theme, or failure mode. This happens, in part at least, because different teams work within the organization. Failure to learn is costly and is not the most productive way to grow teams or a company and is counter to a high or positive morale a learning organizational environment.

2.1 The Organization

There are many factors that influence the organization and how it operates, none of this larger than the impact of the structure and culture of the organization. The organization is subjected to chaos theory, that is, the randomness and uncertainty

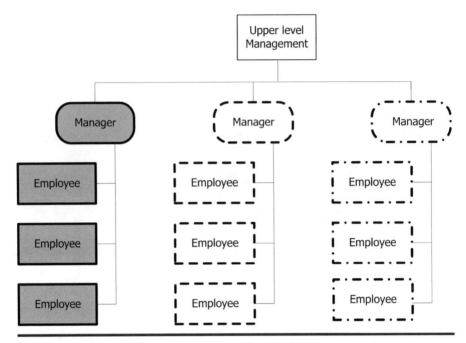

Figure 2.1   An example of the structure of a functional organization.

to which everything is subjected. These can be unknown (and often are) and, even when known, difficult to measure, consisting of unknowable inputs or stimulus.

There are many types of organization structure types. Generally speaking, each structure type comes with strengths and weaknesses. We start with the functional structured organization; it is a collection of special skills. For example, we may have an organization that produces vehicle electrical/electronic systems and have a collection of groups that could look like this:

■ systems engineering
■ embedded software engneers
■ embedded hardware engineers
■ wire harness
■ project managers
■ test department

Each of the groups has specialized skills, work with tools specific to their domain, and have processes unique to their respective work. The advantage of this structure is in this focus on the required knowledge and tools to be successful in each of the respective domains. This focus on individual competencies, from experience, comes at the expense of lateral communication and understanding how the parts connect to make the whole.

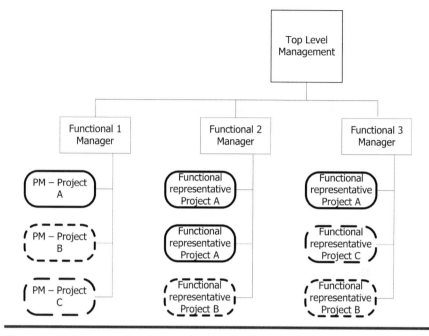

Figure 2.2 An example of a matrix organization.

There are many other types for an organization beyond the functional; some other examples are matrix and project structured which are some of the more common. Modern work now has the organizations distributed all over the world, and even when co-located, there are fabrications beyond these typical ones. For example, there are modern examples that lack structure. Some software development organizations opt for the team members to be in a group that is self-directed, and that have a variety of skills to undertake the work. This self-directed teaming and a reduction of hierarchies that manage the work flow provide some advantages as well as disadvanges. This book does not address the optimum organization structure, only to point out that the structure of the organization and the environment in which it exists will influence learning and distribution of that learning through the organization.

2.1.1 Structural

The structure of the organization consists of many elements and influences. Below is a short list of the sort of things that influence the organizations structure:*

---

* Daft, R. L. (1998). *Organization theory and design*. Cincinnati: South Western College Publishing.

Formalization – refers to the amount of documentation such as process documentation, procedures, work instructions, company regulations, and other policy manuals.

Specialization – refers to the degree to which the organization divides the work, sometimes referred to as functional organization, that allows for specialization in each of a variety of disciplines. For example, in the automotive product organization, there will be mechanical engineers, electrical engineers, power train specialists, test engineers, procurement personnel and much more. This specialization often means these unique areas will have a high level of expertise, including the tools for the work, but this comes at negative consequences of depending upon communication throughout the organization.

Standardization – refers to the degree to which the company's work activities are uniform, businesses like restaurant chains. These organizations detail how the work is to be accomplished that will apply to all locations of the organization.

Hierarchy of authority – refers to the reporting structure of the organization, often displayed as boxes with horizontal and vertical boxes showing individual titles and people, connected to other positions up (reports to), lateral (peers), and lower (reports to). In this structure, an individual has a collection of people reporting to

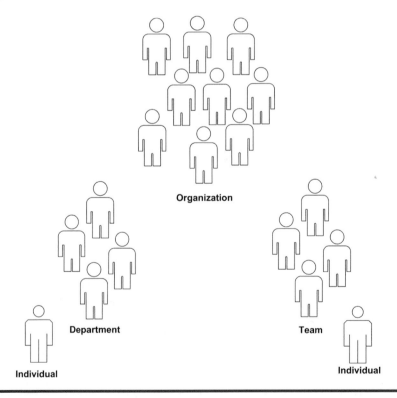

Figure 2.3   **Team sizes and distribution vary through the organization.**

them; in other words, the person these people report to is responsible for that part of the work and those individuals reporting to that part of the hierarchy.

Complexity – refers to the number of systems and subsystems of the organization; within the organization. Things like the number of layers of the hierarchy, as well as the horizontal span of those layers, number of departments, the global distribution of the departments, and the expected interactions of these layers, departments as well as the geographical distribution.

Centralization – refers to the decision-making authority of the organization; centralization is when decisions are made at the executive or management levels. Decentralization is when the decision making is made at the lower organization levels; sometimes this is referred to as empowerment to the organization.

Professionalism – refers to the amount of education and training of the employees. Does the organization work require that much of the staff be highly trained with university degrees and perhaps advanced degrees and certifications? Professionalism is often measured by the average number of years of education for the employees and staff.

Personnel ratios – refers to the deployment of people to the departments and functions of the organization. This includes things like the ratio of the administrative staff to the functional staff in the case of an engineering or product development organization, for example, the number of engineers to the number of administrative personnel.

2.1.2 Team Size

It likely is not very surprising to find out that team size significantly impacts the work and how the team works together. There is more to this than randomness, but some evolutionary biology associated with the limits that Malcolm Gladwell referred to in his book Tipping Point, as social channel capacity.* The case for a social capacity has been made, most persuasively, by the British anthropologist Robin Dunbar. Dunbar begins with a single observation. Primates, monkeys, chimps, baboons' and humans – have the biggest brains of all mammals. More important, a specific part of the brain of humans and other primates, the region known as the neocortex, which deals with complex thought and reasoning, is huge by mammal standards. Dunbar argues that group size correlates with brain size. Dunbar's arguments are that brains evolved, getting bigger in order to handle the complexities of larger social groups. In fact, Dunbar developed an equation, that works for most primates. The equation looks at the neocortex size, specifically, the the ratio of the neocortex size to the size of the entire brain. With this ratio the maximum group size can be derive and that is the Dunbar number. For humans, this calculation renders approximately 150 connections. This represents the maximum number of individuals with which a genuine social relationship can be developed and maintained. Dunbar goes on

---

* Gladwell, M. (2014). *Tipping point.* Place of publication not identified: Little, Brown.

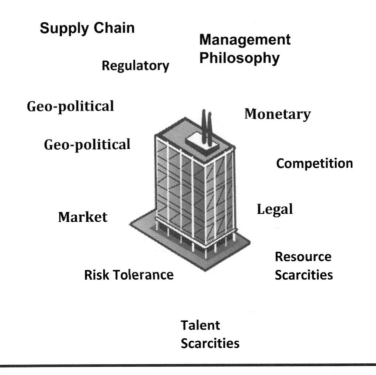

Supply Chain

Regulatory

Management
Philosophy

Geo-political

Monetary

Geo-political

Competition

Legal

Market

Resource
Scarcities

Risk Tolerance

Talent
Scarcities

Figure 2.4   The organization must contend with many external influences.

to explore hunter gatherer societies and finds that the average number of people in a village is about 150. The work even cites a religious community (Hutterite) that has a strict policy that every time a colony approaches 150, they split into two and start a new one.

Even exploration of military hierarchy yields a maximum size not to substantially exceed 200. Larger groups require increased regulation and formal measures to maintain command and control. At 150, orders can be implemented, and unruly behavior controlled on a basis of personal loyalties and direct man-to-man contacts.

So what does all of this mean for the organization? The larger the organization the more command control processes; additionally, this limit can be an impediment to dispersion of information and learning. Large companies will have to contrive other ways of spreading the learning, as the personal connections and social limits will be impacted.

2.1.3 Environmental

The company may be inundated by many external stimuli, ideally identifying those things that can be the most damaging and the most promising of opportunities to avoid the pain from the damaging events and risks, and to capitalize on the opportunities. Since the businesses are unique, these challenges and opportunities are also different, for example, an automotive design and manufacturer company will have risk associated with product, material, and legal issues. A bank, on the other hand, may not produce material parts, but may have internal systems along with legal requirements that have no resemblance to that of the automotive manufacturer. A software gaming company, which has no hardware, perhaps the game is online, and requires no personal information to log in such as real name, credit card, and similar type of inputs, will be in an entirely different category of risk and so the approach to the work will likely be different.

The significant stimuli may originate from outside of the organization, but not be relegated solely to that. A large organization will likely have considerable internal dynamics as well. For example, consider the churn of the talent within the organization. At any given time there may be some loss of key personnel within the company. There may be change initiatives within some groups within the organization that will alter the operations of the company and how the individual units work together.

2.1.4 Contextual

Each of the other characteristics, structural and environmental, are implicated by the context of the company.

Size – refers to the number of people in the organization, and this measurement may be by specific division of the organization or for the entire organization. The size of the organization can make communication and distribution of things learned.

Organizational technology – refers to the level of technology required to transform the inputs to the organization to the outputs of the organization. A manufacturing line employs some levels of technology as well as a product development, but these are likely not the same level nor type of technology.

Goals and strategy – refer to how the company intends to achieve the goals and objectives of the organization. These are often documented articulations of the aspirations and the constraints within which the company wishes to abide, for example, social and environmental aspects of the goals and strategy.

2.1.5 Culture

The culture of the organization is elusive to describe and includes a mix of a variety of attributes. This includes, but not limited to, the guiding principles of the organization, the beliefs, the aspirations of the organization, as well as priorities of how the organization will go about working and the behaviors expected to achieve those objectives. Everybody is touched by the organization's culture, but culture is not really noticed or easily articulated by those in the organization beyond perhaps some parroting of the formal documents. That is not to say that the organization's culture consists of a set of documents, on the contrary. The overt articulations of the culture are but a small aspect of the corporate culture. Organizations generally teach new members about the culture via formal training and ceremonies. The culture of the organization provides an identity and commitment to the beliefs and mission of the organization.

- Symbols
- Ceremonies
- Behaviors
- Stories, legends, myths
- Language

We can plan, and create, an organizational environment to influence or drive the culture where it is desired to be; however the culture of the organization has significant emergent properties. That is, it is influenced by many variables much of which will be random, unknown, and therefore unplanned. The culture is more easily influenced early in the organization's life. This cannot be overstated. The biggest ability to influence the culture is at the start of the organization, before bad habits have been formed, with no need to overcome the inertia of a pre-existing culture. In addition to the culture being emergent, so too can be the strategies.

First, we should start by saying changing the organization's culture is not so easy. In fact we cannot really predict how the culture will alter. Culture is emergent. That is, it is not the sum of the individual actions we take nor the sum of the individual interactions within the organization. We can take actions that we believe will help create the culture we desire, and we may plan carefully; however, culture is not the sort of thing on which we can exert perfect influence, all the more reason for being persistent and consistent in our organization culture change efforts. Any change that runs contrary to the corporate culture will meet the headwind that is the present corporate culture. Change at the organization level is large scale change, and changing the organization's culture is like changing the direction of a wheel with considerable inertia (mass and speed).

2.1.6 Learning Organization

Management has shifted from the Frederick Taylor approach, often referred to as scientific management. Instead of looking at the organization as a purely economic model, there is a recognition that the organization is an economic and social model. Management's role, at least in part, is to make the most of the organization's resources and talent. That is, to set the operating environment of the company in such a way as to maximize the results. There has been a shift from the command and control approach to management typical of Frederick Taylor to an empowerment approach.

This management shift has been prompted by two accelerating trends. The first is the increasing rate of change brought by global competition. Organizations must adapt faster and be able to do more things well. The second trend is a fundamental

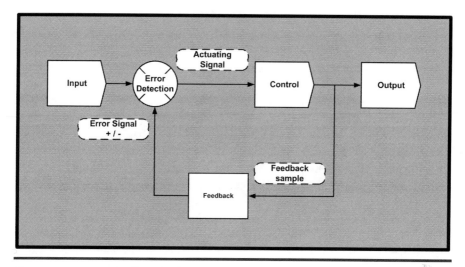

Figure 2.5   Process diagram is a way to illustrate the process and the control mechanisms.

change in organizational technologies. Traditional organizations were designed to manage machine-based technologies, with a primary need for stable and efficient use of physical resources, such as mass production.*

In certain areas of the world, the work has moved from the mechanization or manual manufacturing line type of work, to knowledge intensive. For an organization to be an effective global competitor, it will require the constant learning by the individual team members that enable the organization to become increasingly competent and efficient and able to discover new opportunites and effectively take advantage of these. This ultimately requires more than the individual to learn, but team learning, and learning that spreads through the organization.

2.2 Processes, the Building Blocks for a Better Project

Processes are not just for manufacturing. Consider a company that develops electronic control units for vehicles. There may be requirements written, hardware, software, and verification tests. The organization may have associated processes for each of these.

There are many a bad thing said about processes. Some say these processes and procedures constrain adaptation to circumstances. We may hear complaints by those in the organization that there are too many processes, but experience shows that few if any are actually followed. Processes seldom can be created or crafted to address all situation variations, especially if the key parameters and variations are unknown.

---

* Daft, R. L. (1998). *Organization theory and design.* Cincinnati: South Western College Publishing.

There are complaints that the processes are too complicated, or unknown, even when the organization has introduced these processes through formalized internal training. This lack of understanding of the structure of processes, its intent, or even its existence calls into question the effectiveness of the formalized internal training. This is yet another reason find another way to do this and specifically embed learning and development into the organization's projects. This will aid in understanding of processes and the principles associated with them. This understanding should connect the relationship to the objective, congruent with Systems Thinking which was discussed in Chapter 1. This distrbutes expectation as well as defining the expected manner to achieve those expectations.

Processes are most commonly considered explicit knowledge covered in Chapter 1. We say explicit, in that these are recorded in some form. As we discussed explicit knowledge is best employed as a guidepost rather than constraints, but this requires an understanding of the objective of the process. While there are some instances that require strict adherence to a process or procedure—safety of personnel or regulatory requirements—most processes are or have been developed with the intent to allow repeatability of an action or item with minimal variation and/or the collection of information which could facilitate an improvement to a process or procedure.

The expectation of minimal variation in inputs of a process may be one reason people consider it constraining.

Variation applies to both the inputs to the process, and the ability of the process to adapt to the range of inputs. The latter is the output, or how much control we

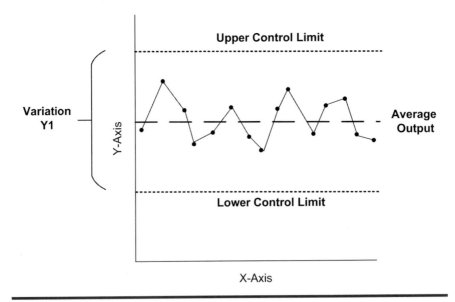

Figure 2.6 Control charts help us to understand the process capability and range of variation typically seen.

are able to exert onto the variables and the system output. We wish to understand the output of the process and therefore understand the limits, looking to be able to predict the system and the results. Understanding the system and the ability to predict both inputs and output make possible improvements in the system.

There are two categories of origin of variation, common cause variation and special cause variation. There is variation in everything, and when we have studied and have mathematical models of the system, we then have some data from which to be able to differentiate between these two causes. **Common cause variation** is predictable; our data collecting and analysis inform us of the range possible or probable. **Special cause variations** are not able to be anticipated. This variation is not part of the system or the incoming material as we understand it from our previous analysis and mathematical models. This variation is outside of our data and our experiences. This variation is not able to be predicted and essentially is a surprise that will require exploration into root cause.

We can use control charts to record the performance of the system over time. These types of charts are used for manufacturing processes, but there is no reason for these charts to be used only for manufacturing processes. The examples shown are referred to as X-bar R chart, though there are a number of other options. Any process with idenitifed metrics can be recorded in a number of ways, to include the control chart. This chart illustrates the range of the variable under scrutiny over time. Over time, we see the process capability, and this will become the baseline, giving us a point from which we can explore improving the process with some level

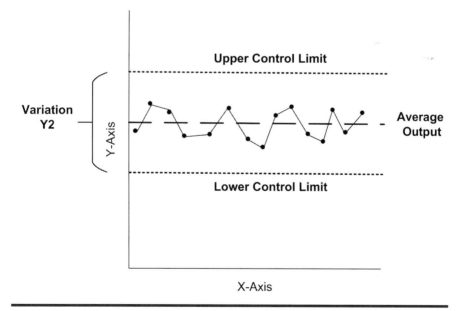

Figure 2.7   Knowing the performance of the present system allows us to conceive and contrive ways to reduce the variation in the system.

of confidence. Perhaps we do not like the variation and we will be well equipped to take action to reduce the variation.

Those using the process will likely have some productive commentary on the process from which we can begin this exploration. Tacit knowledge and processes, as reviewed in chapter 1, tacit or **tribal knowledge**, could be considered the opposite of processes or procedures in that this type of knowledge is not captured in any written form and may be even contrary to the organization's documented procedures and processes. This tribal knowledge is most commonly a function of the belief that these procedures and processes are rigid and cannot be changed.

For processes and process changes to be successful requires our team members to understand the reason for the process. Why do we perform this specific step or process? What are the objectives of this work? What problem does this work solve or issue does the process address? Not knowing why the process is there reduces the work to a checklist, and is not a way to make the most for the organization with the team members. This approach neither sets the organization up for growth, nor the team members.

There are many reasons for this approach to processes in the organization, some of which are connected with the organization's philosophy and management style, while other reasons can be caused by any number of the myriad of logical fallacies, or cognitive biases by the personnel using the processes. Another reason for the belief that processes are rigid that promotes tribal knowledge is the selective application of processes by senior personnel or executives during key points of a project due to schedule or budget constraints, perceived or real. For example, our organization may provide propaganda that stresses the importance of processes at times, then, at other times, places expectations on those doing the work that process will not impact scheduled delivery. This contradiction can cause consternation from those doing the work. There may be times when the organization's words do not align with the deeds, for continuity, this should be very infrequent and followed quickly upon an explanation as to why we are behaving contrary to our principles. We would not this exception to be misconstrued as the norm. Further, we should follow up with a project review to determine why the process could not be followed. Additional, as part of this discussion, a determination of specific indicators should be identified to that decision point so we can ascertain the appropriate course of action to meet the objective. This gives the team the opportunity to experiment with an adaptation that may both meet the needs of the organization, and provide an improvement to the process. Any project after action examination, even when processes are followed, should consider the performance of the processes and especially any need to adapt that arose from that project work. This type of review, **root cause analysis**, will allow the tacit knowledge to be incorporated into the process or procedure, i.e., made **explicit knowledge** and thus reduces its potential use as political leverage or stage 3 tribal leadership; see chapter 1 section on politics.

Why do we have processes and procedures? What is the underlying need that drives their creation? If this need is valid why do we commonly see deviation from

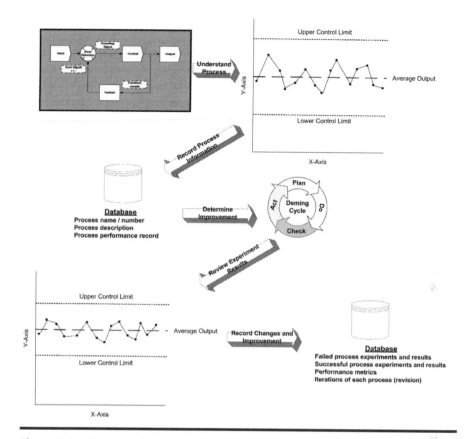

Figure 2.8   An example of how we learn from the process and store the results.

the processes and procedures? Improvement, repeatability, and planning are the most common drivers for processes and procedures. We will discuss this and the relationship to learning in the next section.

2.2.1 Relationships, Projects, Processes And Learning

Projects have processes associated with them; to see this list one need only check out The Project Management Institute (PMI). According to PMI, there are 5 process groups. In each of these groups, there are a number of processes. The 5 project process groups according to PMI are:*

1. Initiating
2. Planning

---

* https://projectmanagementacademy.net/articles/five-traditional-process-groups/ last accessed 8/30/2019

3. Executing
4. Monitoring and Controlling
5. Closing

There is much more to consider in the interaction between the objectives of the company, the work, the project, and the company processes. To best discuss this, we will divide into sections as we do with most of our discussions, to allow for a more in-depth look at the parts that make the system. Understanding the building blocks of any system allows for a better understanding of the whole and thus better application of said system towards the goal at hand.

2.2.1.1 Why Do We Have Processes And Procedures

First we must establish what we mean when we say process or procedure before we can fully discuss the why of having them. Process is defined as a systematic series of actions directed to some end and a continuous action, operation, or series of changes taking place in a defined manner.* Procedure is defined as an act or a manner of proceeding in any action or process conduct or a particular course or mode of action.†

Applying these two definitions we can make a few determinations. At the root of all of this, the most detailed are the work instructions. The work instructions are the detailed results from the procedures. The aggregation of a specific set of procedures are used to build processes and used by those working the project.

Now that we have set a starting point, we can begin our discussion as to why we have processes and procedures. Since work instructions are the basic building blocks for processes, we will start with them. There are numerous reasons for having work instructions for conducting work in a way that has a high degree of repeatability. Not working from a common set of instructions means the outcome would not have much of a chance of repeatable outcome, nor will we have an effective starting point from which we can improve; everytime is like the first time, and any data collected cannot be readily associated with a method of conducting the work. With random range of execution of the work, we have a random range of outcomes not traceable to a specific set of actions, nor can we calculate the variation as a range of possible outcomes, due to conducting the work in a specific manner. There is no baseline from which differentiation of the various ways of conducting the work is possible.

---

* Process. (n.d.). Retrieved September 26, 2018, from https://www.dictionary.com/browse/process
† Procedure. (n.d.). Retrieved September 26, 2018, from https://www.dictionary.com/browse/procedure?s=t

Another limitation brings the question of how would you train the work force to conduct a task if each time was different? Consistency allows for a training to be conducted effectively because you can not only train on the work instructions but more importantly, the underlying principles. What is the goal of this work? Why are we doing it this way? When a team member knows why a set of work instructions and procedures are in place, it is possible for the team members to contrive improvements or make a rational, well-thought out decision to eliminate a specific procedure from a specific project because it does not apply. This type of training can be directly related to organizational learning: in chapter 1 and Argyris.

Yet another gain from work instructions and procedures is development. A process is broken into work instruction; these smaller parts can often apply to other processes and or projects. This minimizes the need for developing completely new work instructions, procedures, or processes.

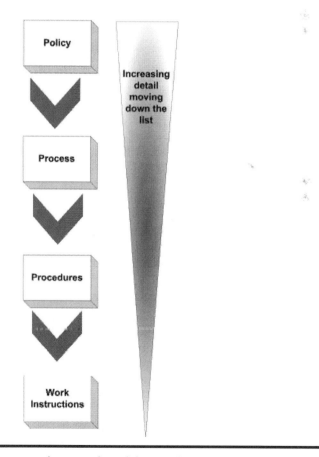

Figure 2.9   Processes, procedures, and work instructions are connected.

Processes are more fluid than procedures in that they are made of or consist of many procedures and even more work instructions, and must account for any discrepancies between those procedures. As a mechanic I view procedures as the valves or piping of a system and the process as the dynamics of the system when assembled. That is to say that the system as a whole does not exhibit the characteristics of any one component (procedure) or the total of said components collectively, yet establishes its own dynamic based upon those pieces. Having said that, there is a point of diminished return if the system (process) is comprised of too many components (procedures). Therefore most processes have been developed to maximize the ROI while simultaneously improving the outcome of the work, and maximize the repeatablity or replication of outcome.

2.2.1.2 How do Processes and Procedures relate to Learning

Processes and procedures serve as a baseline to make the output and outcome repeatable and is predicated on the belief that input variation can be accounted, but that is not all. If we operate according to these processes and procedures, and take key measurements of the process, most notably the outcome, we are now armed with more than anecdotal information about the process, and with a little bit of effort, statistical information on how the process performs. This statistical analysis of a repeated approach to the work will enable us to learn more about the process or procedure. We know if you do these things, the outcome range will look like some measured outcome. We can then review at the process, procedure, or

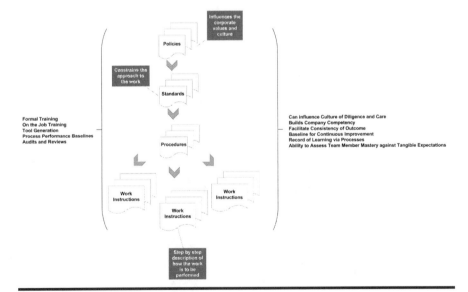

Figure 2.10 Our work documentation provides a framework and input for learning.

work instruction level, with our team exploring those areas we believe that have the largest impact on the variation of output or outcome. We plan an approach that would theoretically change the process or procedure and run an experiment using this newer slightly altered approach to the work. Then we would look at the results of that outcome of this new approach determining if this temporary modification should be enacted within the process or procedure documentation, not just on a temporary and exploration scale and rewrite the process or procedure documents. This approach to process improvement is described in detail in Total Quality Management.

How do we learn? A difficult question to answer, as each person values learning differently. People are motivated by different things, and have different attitudes about learning. We have to balance the structured environment with flexibility to be able to meet the learning needs as these arise. When we understand the best delivery method for our people, at times individually or as a group, we then must determine the method to provide that opportunity within our project(s).

This requires clear understanding what an individual already knows (as much as possible), along with what they need to know, and then find specific ways to build this into the project activities to which this individual will contribute. Knowing these things, we can better build it into the project plan and when we cannot provide it in the best fit, we can enhance it with other techniques such as teaming. Having stated all this, we can now address how processes and procedures are related to learning.

In the first part of this section we stated that a procedure is a specific course of action or way of proceeding forward. While the term procedure commonly prompts a vision of a rigid structure that has no room for deviation, one would think that that leaves only specific ways, times, and/or opportunities for training or learning. While most procedures have key points that must be met or followed, they rarely forbid training or learning or adaptation to circumstance as these are presented. With the ever-advancing technological environment and the need for organizations to constantly evolve any structure that does not allow for growth and development of its people, processes, and procedures is destined to be left behind.

2.2.1.3 Measures to ... Processes, Procedures, and Learning

As noted earlier, processes and procedures facilitate repeatability and we can measure inputs and outcomes from processes and procedures to ascertain their effectiveness via the recorded performance (for example, provides an established baseline) which over time, will provide clues as to the natural variation in the system. We are then able to compare the impact of any changes we make in the process, establishing some cause and effect via the pre- and post-change measurements. While these measurements can be very valuable to the change process, we must ensure that the measures are understood, valid, and relevant. In today's society we collect information on everything, and this information is used to sell things, determine product development directions, location of stores, and so much more, but how much of this information is real? For the most part the information developed by marketing teams is very real and yields companies' returns on their investment. However, it seems that some other fields, like project management, either game the information or hide/don't understand the true meaning of the data collected or its object.

2.2.1.4 Modularity Within Project Management Processes

Modular manufacturing has been around for a long time and is one of the methods that makes mass customization possible along with shortening product development and manufacturing in general. As we discussed in the previous section, the building blocks can be the same for many projects with either variation in their assembly, addition of new, subtraction of previous, or a combination of both. If the basic understanding of the building blocks are formed, then the way they are structured only changes the product outcome, not its building. To provide an example of this both a small house is built of bricks as well as a mansion. The way the bricks were laid did not change nor the way they were held together. However, the outcome is quite different. We may learn new things in the brick laying for the mansion, and this would be recorded in our process documentation creating a new track of learning for this new variable.

2.3 Limiting Factors

2.3.1 Law of Diminishing Returns

Before we move through the things that can help, a review of the law of diminishing returns is in order. The law of diminishing returns will first require we talk about marginal or increment of some variable. Let's say we have a field of wheat and we have no automated equipment, so the field needs to be harvested manually. We gather up our friends and commence harvesting and we average 10 bushels of wheat per person, per day. We add one more person to our harvesting team, and we again see that the amount we are harvesting per day is 10 bushels of wheat per person per day. That additional person is an increment, and that increment of labor was still able to harvest 10 bushels of wheat. With the need to get the fields harvested, we get one more person to help work the field, and at the end of the day we then have an average of 8 bushels of wheat per person per day. This incremental addition of labor does not yield the same results as the previous increments. This is a demonstration of the law of diminishing returns and it is an important thing to know as we explore the actions we need to take to improve our organization.

The reason we need to know about the law of diminishing returns is that there are times when the course we are taking to improve the organization will come to an end. There are limits to what can be achieved with one approach.

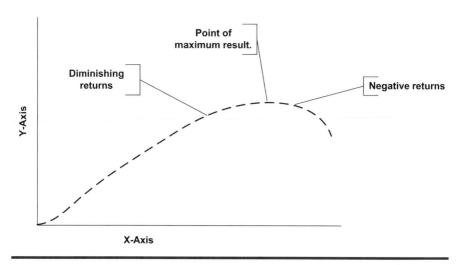

Figure 2.11   Adding resources adds output until a point where it adds less output, diminishing returns.

2.3.2 Theory of Contraints

There are limits to any system, and businesses are a collection of systems. These systems interact with each other, a system the consists of subsystems. This system is only as capable as the slowest or weakest point. This is why local optimization is not the answer. It is important to understand the entirety of the system: where are the constraints then address those limits, continually moving to the next limit. In the graphic below, x is the starting point, followed by 2, and then maybe 3 will be next depending upon where 3 fits in the system flow. When we make decisions about the organization's way of working we must decide what to prioritize. If we are

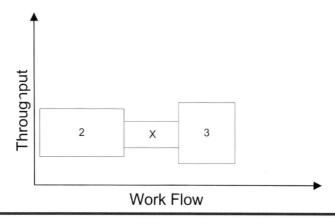

Figure 2.12   Care should be taken not to dwell on local optimization.

prioritizing the correct thing, we improve throughput and capabilities, but only to find there is another restraining factor.

The first step is to recognize that every system was built for a purpose. We didn't create our organizations just for the sake of their existence. Thus, every action taken by any part of the organization should be judged by its impact on the overall purpose. This immediately implies that, before we can deal with the improvement of any section of a system, we must first define the system's global goal; and the measurements that will enable us to judge the impact of any subsystem and any local decision, on this global goal.*

To improve the capabilities or throughput requires a systematic approach to the constraining factor at any given time in the organization's process or organization's structure. According to Goldratt, there are five steps to addressing these constraints.

1. Identify system's constraints
2. Decide how to explore the system's constraints
3. Subordinate everything else to the above decision
4. Elevate the system's constraint
5. If in the previous steps a constraint has been broken, go back to step 1

In this way, whatever the constraining factor is for the organization is constantly explored to find ways to elevate the constraint's impact on this attribute on the entire system. At some point, what was a constraining factor will eventually not be the limiting element. Then the new constraining attribute will need to be under this recurring scrutiny.

2.4 Processes Make the Best Lessons Learned Repositories

When done well, process management, especially the documentation portions of the work, make great lessons learned repositories. We move from the anecdotal, not knowing what set of circumstances precipitated that observable result. We may see that either a project or set of tasks produced a win but have no idea what was done nor how it may have been done to any level of detail. What can we say about that specific approach, when we do not know how or what set of circumstances?

We also discussed that processes require system knowledge to be effective as the procedures which build them are only small; this begs the question of why processes make the best repositories for lessons learned. To answer that question, we must look at the application of the lessons learned. When you apply any lesson to one small part it is trapped to that part, but if you can show the relationship to the greater

---

* Goldratt, E. (1990). *Theory of constraints: What is this thing called and how should it be implemented?* Great Barrington, MA: North River Press.

function, the process, it can be associated to several other items (the procedures) within that group. This provides us with some recorded history and associations limiting reliance upon human recall that is plenty fallible. This is both an example of systems thinking and true root cause analysis.

2.4.1 Benefits of Capturing

To provide the maximum benefit, lessons learned need to be captured in a manner wherein data is is easily deposited and equally easily recovered. This is commonly a function of either understanding the true issue(s) which caused the lesson or the ability to look at how the system as a whole could gain from what was learned. While these two hurdles inhibit using lessons learned to their full potential the most common failure of applying lessons learned is tribal knowledge and information brokerage. Tribal knowledge and information brokerage both go hand in hand as is discussed in the book "Tribal Leadership."* As we discussed in the section on **Inhibitors to Communication** and in **Tacit (Tribal Knowledge)** we can see how the control of information is or can be used to support the position or perceived position of the individual. This type of office politics is without a doubt the largest inhibitor to an effective lesson's learned program as the sharing of this information would diminish the position or perceived position for some people. At this point you are probably asking why we keep saying, "position or perceived position." That would be because if the individual's position was based on reality rather than perception, the sharing of this information would be automatic. It would be what is discussed in stage 4 tribal leadership, "We're Great,"† rather than the sporadic dissemination of information as with most office politics. Elimination of this malady will lend to codification of learning and, therefore, become explicit knowledge.

2.4.2 Organizing Lessons Learned by Process Helps Codify Knowledge

Processes are not stagnant, as we do the work; we learn and try permutations or wholesale modification of the process or processes based upon prioritization and objectives - process improvement. We begin with the review of the process data, that is, the metrics generated by the work. Armed with performance metrics and the specific methods (the process documentation) we can start to work through any connection (correlation) between the process and the results. We will perhaps use a process similar to the **Deming cycle** to work through these improvements. The **plan** step is where we identify the area for improvement and the experiment we want

---

* Logan, D., Fischer-Wright, H., & King, J. (2011). *Tribal leadership: Leveraging natural groups to build a thriving organization.* London: Harper & Row.
† Logan, D., Fischer-Wright, H., & King, J. (2011). *Tribal leadership: Leveraging natural groups to build a thriving organization.* London: Harper & Row.

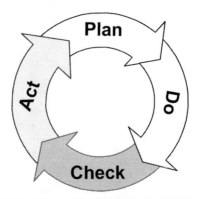

Figure 2.13 The Deming cycle is a structured way to continuous improvement.

to conduct to make that improvement. The **do** phase, we execute the experiment recording the results. Upon completion of the do, we will **check** the data generated from the experiment: Did what we thought would happen actually happen? If not then we need to rework our experiment. If things are better and we know why, we will **enAct** the change to the process across the organization.

Understanding how we got the results, a track record of the the adaptations we made, culminating in the understanding of the process limitations and the range of variation that the process as it presently exists produces. If the organization does not like the variation, or finds the variation impacting in ways that are not acceptable, then it is time to adapt the process. These processes are then tested out (via TQM tools for example), and if the tests prove the adaptation is the way for the organization to move, then the process documents are updated, thereby codifying the learning at least on paper. This type of action—evaluate, change, evaluate—can be viewed as either single loop, double loop learning, triple loop learning, or organizational learning.

2.4.2.1 Single Loop Learning Theory

Single-loop learning is the most basic type of learning and behavioral change that can take place within a system and is also described as incremental learning. Single-loop learning describes the type of learning that takes place when the objective is to fix problems within the present organizational structure so that the system will function better and does not attempt to alter the structure of the system.*

---

* Graybeal, L. (2017, February 22). Single-Loop Learning Key Terms. Retrieved November 7, 2018, from https://www.business.com/articles/single-loop-learning-key-terms/

You will note that in the description of single loop learning, it states that the objective is to "Fix Problems."* While problems will always arise, even within a learning organization, a proactive stance of seeking the problems before they become a physical manifestation is the true goal of a learning organization. From experience, we note that fixes to problems are focused on the end result or the manifestation of the problem, rather than proactively exploring improvements before the poor performance is visible. In that we mean that a fix is determined to allow progression of the tasks or item and little thought or concern is given to the long-term effects of that action or its ramification on other projects using the process or procedure that was modified to restore operations.

2.4.2.2 Double Loop Learning Theory

> Double-loop learning, also known as reframing, contrasts with single-loop learning by questioning the purpose and function of work being done within an organization and does not take existing organizational structures for granted. Double-loop learning is concerned with understanding the basis for the tasks being completed, rather than a more efficient process for completing them.[†]

This approach is more refined than single loop learning because it looks into the basis of the actions undertaken, which promotes systems thinking, an important part of a learning organization as discussed by Peter Senge in his book *"The Fifth Discipline."* This understanding of the basis of an action allows for a deeper understanding of how changes could affect the process as a whole and thus reduce the potential for untended consequences, an archetype which we will discuss in the appendix. The double loop learning theory as stated in the above quote is not focused on the efficiency of the process upon which the evaluation is being completed. Thus this type of learning is more informational than active. However, the information garnered using double loop learning almost always facilitates enough information to initiate some form of change action.

2.4.2.3 Triple Loop Learning Theory

> Triple loop learning is the third type of learning that is compared with single-loop and double-loop learning. Also known as transformational learning, triple-loop learning involves the questioning not just of work

---

* Graybeal, L. (2017, February 22). Single-Loop Learning Key Terms. Retrieved November 7, 2018, from https://www.business.com/articles/single-loop-learning-key-terms/
† Graybeal, L. (2017, February 22). Single-Loop Learning Key Terms. Retrieved November 7, 2018, from https://www.business.com/articles/single-loop-learning-key-terms/

processes and the basis for tasks within an organization, but also the reflexive examination of the individual's attitudes and point of view.*

It is not until we get to triple loop learning that we see the inclusion of the individual's attitude and view point. It is this dynamic shift that brings the individual into the equation and appears to start the valuation of the people conducting the tasks. While this addition may seem small in nature it plays toward many of the motivational theories in the respect of individual's value or self-worth, a key component in motivation.

2.4.2.4 Organizational Learning

Organizational learning (OL) is the broader field of study in which single-loop learning was developed. OL has been defined in multiple ways over the past several decades by organizational theorists. The most basic definition of organizational learning is the process of finding and correcting errors in organizations, but organizational learning also has come to include other processes for understanding the culture and behaviors of organizations.†

Last but not least, we come to organizational learning. This approach is more a summation of all the different types of loop learning with a slant to cultural and behavioral aspect that are fostered within the organization itself. The cultural and aggregate behavior of an organization is not the sum of its personnel, but something with a life of its own. While it is comprised of the aspects of all its members, the results presented are not always demographically divisible into its components: the people who comprise it.

2.4.2.5 Theory of Action

Argyris formulated single-loop and other learning theories based on his theory of action, which claims that individuals have a theory or mental map for the actions they perform. These theories are enacted in an unspoken way through theories-in-use, or in a verbalized way that is used to explain actions to others through espoused theories.‡

---

* Graybeal, L. (2017, February 22). Single-Loop Learning Key Terms. Retrieved November 7, 2018, from https://www.business.com/articles/single-loop-learning-key-terms/

† Graybeal, L. (2017, February 22). Single-Loop Learning Key Terms. Retrieved November 7, 2018, from https://www.business.com/articles/single-loop-learning-key-terms/

‡ Graybeal, L. (2017, February 22). Single-Loop Learning Key Terms. Retrieved November 7, 2018, from https://www.business.com/articles/single-loop-learning-key-terms/

Espoused theory according to Argyris and Schon is the world view and values people believe their behavior is based upon.*

Theory-in-use according to Argyris and Schon is the world view and values implied by the behavior of people, or the maps they use to take action.[†]

As we saw from our discussion of triple loop learning and organizational learning, the aggregate of the organizational perspective that is the sum of the individual's perspective has come into play. Since perspectives can be some measure of distortion from the actual, it is important to understand the underlying sources for any distortions. We would not want to undertake unreviewed assumptions and perspectives as doing so starts the exploration falsely. Communication is how we get past the facade that is perspective, and explore the true circumstances. This open and truthful discussion brings us to mental models, part of the learning organization as discussed by Peter Senge in his book "The Fifth Discipline."[‡] While he calls it a "mental model," we prefer to call it an "Open Mental model" as this better infers a willingness to listen and change based upon information gathered during the discussion and other perspectives.

2.4.3 Downside of Capturing Lessons Learned in Processes

While we have just spent the last portion of this section discussing why processes make a good repository for lessons learned we must also cover the potential drawbacks of that action. As most of us know from working any project or being a member of any organization the only constant is that there are few constants and almost no absolutes. Even when organizations are basically structured in the same way, independent of geographic location, that does not mean the different locations capture lessons learned in the same way and same place. It is those slight variations in structure that shift the system dynamics in such a manner that capturing information, such as lessons learned, and its best repository could vary extensively. However, when you apply the theory of diminished returns the prime location for capturing such information is at the apex or when put in organizational terms the mid-level which is most commonly the process level.

---

* Anderson, L. (2014, August 19). Argyris and Schon's Theory on congruence and learning. Retrieved November 7, 2018, from http://www.aral.com.au/resources/argyris.html
† Anderson, L. (2014, August 19). Argyris and Schon's Theory on congruence and learning. Retrieved November 7, 2018, from http://www.aral.com.au/resources/argyris.html
‡ Kleiner, A., & Senge, P. M. (1994). *The Fifth discipline fieldbook*. London: Nicholas Brearley.

2.4.3.1 Organization Structure—Localization

When a process is captured within one department it can diminish both the sharing or the lesson learned, and the potential enhancement of that lesson learned. As with most changes, which is what a lesson learned promotes, perspective plays a major role and thus obtaining a second perspective, especially from an external source, can assist in determining the true usefulness of said lesson learned. If we look at Kotter's 8 step change model in steps 1 and 2 he discusses communication and the make-up of the team/group being from different departments and when we look at the McKinsey 7S step change model, we see the emphasis placed on knowing the current state and understanding the desired future state.* In both Kotter's 8 step approach and McKinsey's 7 step change model there are steps that work to identify the scope of the change including the required participants. Thus consider the present organization's structure and breadth of the focus of the change event.

2.4.3.2 Process Restrictive

Process restrictive is the focus of the improvement on a single process or component of that process. While this type of dilemma is not restricted to just processes, when process exploration is solely captured within the process and not shared with others for evaluation of applicability, then it will only serve the process owner. This hiding a lesson learned is yet another example of information control. If lessons learned are captured within any procedure, process, or even a functional area a brief overview should be provided to at least one or two other equal areas for an application review: this constitutes knowledge sharing.

Many processes are structured such that if they are a standalone they are still a part of a system or organization. Knowing how and where the processes fall within this system, its predecessors and depending functional relationships will aid in reducing the process restrictive effect caused by the lack of system understanding.

2.4.3.3 System Effect Restriction

In this case we make alterations to the process based upon what we learn, without considering the entirety of the system, having impact on depending actions and processes. Similar to the discussed process restrictive, but with the key being solely on the system dynamic of the lesson learned is what is meant by "System Effect Restriction." Unlike in the process restrictive section, the lesson can be shared, but the actions developed from it have little to no evaluation of the overall dynamic of

---

* Using the 7s model to increase the chance of successful change. (2017, February 10). Retrieved November 15, 2018, from https://www.educational-business-articles.com/7s-model/

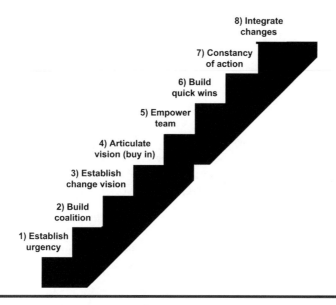

Figure 2.14   Kotter's 8 step approach.

the whole. This type of pinpointed assessment usually leads to corrective actions that contain unintended consequences as we discussed similar to the proximity and cause discusion in Chapter 1.

2.4.3.4 Lesson from Lessons Learned

We have discussed some of the places to deposit lessons learned and why they might or might not work for an organization, but one thing we have yet to discuss is the lessons we learn from what we have learned or think we have learned. This is two different topics and we shall approach them in the following sub-sections. However first we should look at what is a lesson learned from what a lesson is; to best understand this we must review actions we employed from what we thought we learned, the results we expected from those actions, and how those actions related to the genesis of the lesson learned.

2.4.3.4.1 Measures of Actions from Lessons Learned

Correlation of lessons learned with the data captured is essential to longevity and effectivity of any organizaton or project improvement endeavor to be able to build some measure of crediblity how we handle the lessons learned. The approach should be congruent with the scientific method, which enables us to make some definitive statements, within the context of the experiment, about what is observed.

1. Identify the problem
2. Research and Hypothesis
3. Experimentation
4. Data analysis
5. Conclusion
6. Repeat

The actions we take generate measurements, or they should. These measurements will be compared to specific goals of the organization or the project. Therefore it is important to develop metrics that are associated with the goals of the project and the organization. This is not a trivial activity, and we must remember that metrics or measurements tend to drive individual behavior.

2.4.3.4.2 Correlation of Lessons Learned for Data Capture

It is not uncommon to find that the lessons we have learned do not apply toward the actual change that is needed. This is why we are of the opinion that when an issue arises and is covered by a basic root cause analysis or team learning session, the outcome is neither long term nor sustainable. Most root cause analysis and team learning sessions performed by companies are superficial and, from experience, often driven by those with a political agenda, whereas in a learning organization the issues that produce lessons learned are actively sought out and checkpoints along the path are inserted to verify if a directional change is needed in the process, project, or organization.

For example, while heading across the Atlantic it is noted the course is off by 3° at the beginning, so a 3° correction is made. The reason for the difference of the desired course and the actual course is not determined, but a validation point is set for a certain number of miles to ensure the correction is effective. At the validation point it is noted that a minus 1° from the desired course is being made. At this point an evaluation of cross currents is done and noted as shifting along different points on the path taken to our destination. This produces the action of setting the course based upon the different areas of cross current and establishing more validation points where corrections are needed to be made.

Above is an example of stacking a lesson learned and its collective application. Often, we learn a lesson, and there are follow on lessons directly related to that lesson. The manner in which these lessons are captured is just as important as the original lesson itself, perhaps more so as this lesson is linked to other lessons. If these lessons are captured as several different lessons learned the overall point will likely be missed and thus the actions will more than likely be disjointed and ineffective. However, if we capture them as they occur and link them in such a way as to show the evolution and the actions that developed them along the way we can better see the direction and the effect upon the system as a whole.

2.4.4 Summation

Organizing lessons learned by process helps codify knowledge, in a way in which there is a measure of confidence in the results (not anecdotal stories). The processes provide a starting point and baseline for future learning. While most people look solely at the actions taken or done, it is best to know the why behind the actions as well. If an action or reaction to something is based upon a flawed assumption, it will not lead to our goals and most likely lead to secondary issues, even if the initial action proves successful—accidentally. When there is a secondary issue from this type of logic they are commonly attributed to some unrelated event because the action or the first issue was successful and thus is incorrectly removed from the potential cause of the second issue. This type of logic is only compounded if the action from the first issue was also successful on some other action as well thus further reinforcing the logic flaw. As we discussed in this section we can see how as the loops increased, single, double, and triple, the likelihood of this type of flawed assumption is diminished. Knowing this and then applying the Action Theory we can or at least should be able to determine if some form of personal bias is affecting the outcome and/or analysis and thus diminish its effect on developing the best solution as well.

2.4.5 Sharing Lessons Learned across Processes

From experience, we can say spreading the learning is one of the more difficult tasks that an organization will attempt to execute. There are numerous obstacles to the sharing of knowledge. They range from indifference, the manner in which the lessons are captured to lack of information or concern of office politics. As we can see from most of the references on organizational learning and leadership the political aspect is the most difficult to overcome followed not so closely by understanding or informational application. In this section we shall discuss how sharing lessons learned across processes could help negate at least two of these three issues: understanding and informational application. The political aspect, I'm great and you're not,* is discussed in section on Office Politics subsections.

Processes are a collective of several different procedures and can span across several departments of an organization. While this possible multiplicity could potentially cloud the gain of a lesson learned it in fact aids in the understanding and could assist in the propagation of the lesson and if conducted in a manner to promote understanding between process owners and thus better systems understanding. The

---

* Logan, D., King, J. P., & Fischer-Wright, H. (2011). *Tribal leadership: Leveraging natural groups to build a thriving organization*. New York: Harper Business.

fact that sharing a lesson across processes could open the lines of communication and promote understanding of the processes end to end rather than as a discrete activity, including another process owner and vice versa should be reason enough to approach it in this manner.

2.4.6 Limits of Lessons Learned through Processes

Any learning from the process is only in the context of the process. It is not possible to say anything beyond the process or variations of inputs that are not accounted for in the process. Additionally, because we may sometimes not be aware that the process was not followed, we cannot say the veracity of the individual contributes to the data.

There can be issues with the data collection in general if it is not automated. You may be (or may not be) surprised how often self-preservation or company politics creep into metrics and the data is manipulated or twisted to not look so "bad" which leads to ignorance of a problem, and as an executive I worked with once called it, a cancer on the organization.

We have touched on this earlier; lessons learned from processes may not have adequate mechanism and methods for articulating this beyond the process area and those that immediately use the process. That is, the learning may be scenario specific.

2.4.7 Distribution of Knowledge

If learning from the work is difficult, distribution of that knowledge requires even more consideration. Once we know we have something that we can classify as knowledge, what do we do with that? How do we propagate that through the organization? We will need some either formal or informal or even both approaches to knowledge distribution, to ensure that what one area of the organization learns is available to all that need to know and in general, everybody in the organization at large.

Recording learning in books may not be an effective way of knowledge distribution, including process metric tracking sheets. In our experience, very few people spend any time looking through books for this information, and when they do considerable time is spent reading things that may not matter.

2.4.8 Database

Databases can help with at least the recording and searching ability via tags and metadata that makes it possible to search without having to read large volumes in the hope that one will stumble upon what is needed. We have seen these types of tools used to store lessons learned about the product over the course of the product life cycle. As the product makes it through the life cycle, especially those things we learn during the development of the product, followed close behind by those things

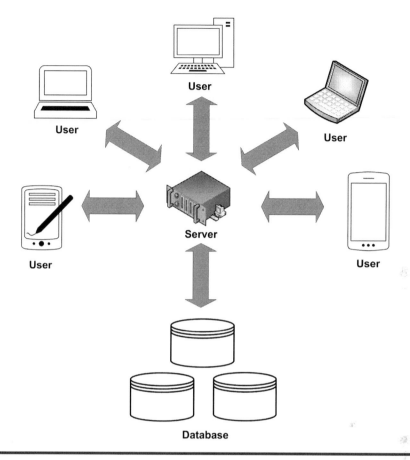

Figure 2.15   Databases are not new and have been used for decades in business.

found in the field after launch. We have seen companies employ the system found at http://www.wjjsoft.com/innokb.html set up for each of the products the company develops and tracks changes over time.

There are several different databases that are currently in use for lessons learned repositories and most of them are effective in some way or another, but are they right for your organization? The trial and error method of going through all these databases can be very expensive and again run through time that probably doesn't exist to start with. So what do we do? We will not even beging to suggest that a specific database best for your organization. That statement does not seem helpful, does it? Let's look at it another way. What are we expecting to gain from employing this tool; how do our people want and need to see the information captured and why; can we use the database chosen across different shops, teams, and projects (i.e., is it a good fit for the whole organization). So we are back again to establishing an understanding of the objective and why it is the objective before we proceed.

2.4.9 Community of Practice

Communities of practice are collection of specific areas of talent. For example, in our company we can have a community of practice focused on software testing, or configuration management, or even a larger focus area such as specific type of product development, for example an Advanced Product Quality Planning expert. These people have an interest in specific subject areas, and perhaps have additional training and certainly more and varied experiences.

2.4.9.1 Self-Organizing

Self-organizing groups are not orchestrated by the organization but are a natural accretion of specific talents by willing association or by invitation from some already existing talents. There are benefits to this self-organizing, first and foremost that those that are part of this group are not coerced or bribed to participate. They are involved with this subject matter and the other members through their own decision and motivation. Next, since there is no connection between the organizing of this group and the organization beyond the fact that the organization is the employer, there is perhaps reduced chance for this group being distracted for political intent or propaganda rather than the focus on the topic that the individuals bring to bear on the topic out of genuine interest.

2.4.9.2 Organization Selected

The organization selects the individuals that will be part of this group. We have seen a company that created specialized and temporary positions that they called senior specialists. These specialists would serve a defined number of years and would be part of a group of other individuals that have similar talents and experiences. There are downsides to this form of selection.

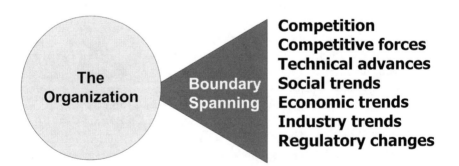

Figure 2.16 Boundary spanning is gathering intel from the outside world to help the organization adapt.

First, the selection of the right person can turn into a political boondoggle, not necessarily the best person for the job, but the person that has a similar perspective as those selecting in such a way that they can guarantee the selected individual will come to conclusions that the management will find satisfying, not necessarily moving the direction or the organization in the direction that the facts take.

2.4.9.3 Boundary Spanners

Boundary spanners are those that have the expertise and interest that put them in positions of discovery and transforming of that discovery to others, essentially propagating this information to others for them to act.

Boundary spanners are a rare breed, however, and few networks have many of them. That's primarily because most people don't have the breadth of intellectual expertise, the wealth of social contacts, and personality traits necessary to be accepted by the vastly different groups.*

Boundary spanners are typically associated with information gathering from external sources and usually associated with innovation. However, this type of exchange can be seen to occur between departments and other parts of the organization as well as spreading discovery and learning through the organization. However, as the reference above indicates, the people who fill these roles have very specific attributes and are generally few in the organization as this is a strong mix of a variety of subject matter expertise, inquisitive nature, as well as a well-connected social network that allows action to be taken based upon this information.

2.4.10 Networks

When we consider the distribution of the knowledge throughout the organization, we are at least in part referring to the interactions of people that form the network. Much of this network forms organically, and probably because developing these networks is not really something that can be formally done. There are two types of relationships, contextually determined and actor determined, each with their own dynamics and outcomes.

Contextually determined relationships are associated with situationally or culturally determined roles. Contextual properties are intimately associated with asymmetry. Essentially asymmetry means that a relationship is not the same for both parties. This is an important property of organizational network since there are a multitude of differences between organizational members, especially in terms of status and direction of communication.

Actor-determined relationships reflect the idiosyncratic bonding that characterize relationships between interactants. For example, importance, a

---

* Cross, R. and Prusak, L. 2003. The People Who Make Organizations Go – or Stop. In R. Cross, A. Parker, and L. Sasson (eds.), *Networks in the Knowledge Economy*, Oxford University Press

variable that has traditionally been examined in network studies (e.g., Richards 1985), provides a direct assessment of the tie between an informal communication relationship and work performance. It can be associated with the more access individuals have to needed task related information (Johnson and Smith related advice (e.g., Blau 1954). These peers are not formally assigned by the organization; rather, these relationships develop informally often as a result of friendships. Thompson (1967) asserts that these work-dependent relationships determine communications channels in an organization to a greater degree than such factors as affiliation, influence, and status.*

Reciprocity is another concept associated with these networks and associations. Reciprocity is the degree to which both parties in a relationship similarly characterize the relationship and is a measure of the strength of the relationship.

2.4.10.1 Nodes and Links

Networks can be documented or recorded in a way that illustrates the organization as a collection of individuals and their respective contacts within the organization, resembling a net. The individuals are represented as nodes or circles (or bodies), with connections to other nodes via links. This provides graphical representation of how the people of our organization are connected, which provides a glimpse into how the parts of the organizations communicate. The links are the communications or interactions between the individuals providing the viewer with some small measure as how information moves through the organization or pathways in which information and knowledge can be shared.

Not only do we see how the individuals of the organization connect, but we can see where the individuals fit into the dispersion or conversely the accretion of knowledge. For example, an individual may be located on the edge of this net, or the individual may be in the center of the network with multiple contact points.

This is not the same as an organization chart that demonstrates the functional areas of the organizations and reporting structures as well as the management distribution for the organization. This does not illustrate the interactions beyond that of the command and control attributes of the company, even when the functional areas are broken down into respective individuals within that function area; we have no connection or inference to the ways and connection between these individuals illustrated.

In the graphic, the nodes represent individuals and the links represent the relationship between the two or more nodes or people. These nodes and interconnections are not necessarily symmetrical, that is, sometimes information is not disseminated in both directions equally, these would be referred to as asymmetrical, the graphic illustrates this via the arrow directions. Command and

---

* Johnson, J. D. (2009). Network Analysis. In *Managing Knowledge Networks* (p. 37). Cambridge, UK: Cambridge University Press. p 33

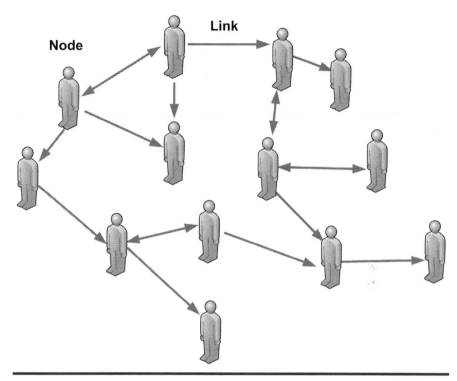

Figure 2.17   We can model the individual as a network into nodes and links.

control mechanisms are often associated with the organization's hierarchy can be asymmetrical in the communication can be more top down than bottom up.

2.4.10.2 Strong and Weak Ties

In network theory we have a concept of strong ties and weak ties. Each of these have their respective benefits.

- Essential for sharing of tacit knowledge*
- More stable and reliable than weak ties
- Constant sharing of the same information

The strong ties have constant contact, sharing of knowledge within the group, and repetition and as such are higher trust environments. The limitations are also due to this limitation. For example, the perspective of our team is of a similar perspective. A team solely consisting of strong tie inputs will miss information from

---

* Johnson, J. D. (2009). Network Analysis. In *Managing Knowledge Networks* (p. 37). Cambridge, UK: Cambridge University Press.

outside of this realm; therefore these teams are missing information from outside their group that may improve or certainly influence how their work gets done. Their learning is limited to that of the immediate team.

Notions about weak ties originate from research on how people acquire jobs, and the ties that hold the disparate functions of the organization or silos together in a cohesive and effective entity.* The strength of weak ties is perhaps the best known concept related to network analysis. It refers to less developed relationships that are more limited in space, place, time, and depth of emotional bonds. This concept has been intimately tied to the flow of information within organizations and by definition is removed from strong social bonds, such as influence and multiplex relations.†

Weak ties may be useful for discussing things one does not want to reveal to one's close work associates; providing a place for an individual to experiment; extending access to information; promoting social comparison; and fostering a sense of community.‡

2.4.10.3 Three-Way Network

Perhaps some of you may have heard the acronym SIPOC, Supplier, Input, Process, Output, Customer. This is the chain of events that can describe both external and internal customers. Consider a company that has divided the work according to functional specialties. We will likely find that the work is passed from department to department; for example, requirements are written by a department that specializes in obtaining these from the customer, the product development happens in other department(s), and the testing of the product in yet another department. This is a rudimentary description of what is often referred to as a functional organization. There are benefits and drawbacks to having such a structure, just as there are benefits and drawbacks to other structures.

With this arrangement, the connected departments can understand how the parts are used in the chain of the work, along with how the work and work results impact the others in the chain. Working to understand this chain of events provides fodder for a continuous improvement of the processes of the organization. This is a good way to evoke the opportunities for improvement in the value chain, and we can use techniques such as value stream mapping and work flow charts to demonstrate the way the work is accomplished and model the way we think the work could work better, from which we can devise actions to determine if our improvement thoughts

---

* Granovetter, M. S. 1973, The strength of weak ties. *American Journal of Sociology*, 78: 1360-1380.
† Johnson, J. D. (2009). Network Analysis. In *Managing Knowledge Networks* (p. 36). Cambridge, UK: Cambridge University Press.
‡ Adelman, M. B., Parks, M. R. and Albrecht, T. L. 1987. Beyond close relationships: support in weak ties. In T. L. Albrecht and M. B. Adelman (eds.), *Communicating Social Support*: 126-147. Sage.

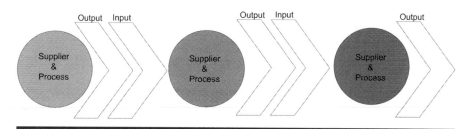

Figure 2.18 Input, supplier, process output, is a change even within the organization.

are valid through exploratory techniques such as Total Quality Management (PDCA).

2.4.10.4 Cliques

We may all have experienced cliques in our high school years. These are groups that have some tangible congruent interests that connect these individuals into a group. In a company, for example, we may find people enjoy bike riding over long distances. These people may not have anything else in common, and perhaps do not work in the same department, but this common interest binds these people to exchange ideas and learn from their experiences and studying.

How people categorize their social world into affiliative groups is critical to how they go about searching for information, since the first step will often embed certain assumptions about the types of people likely to have certain kinds of knowledge. Highly dense, relatively isolated cliques can be expected to have high levels of tacit knowledge, while overlapping is critical to sharing of knowledge and the development of common perspectives throughout an entire organization.*

What we need to learn from this is that cliques, when centered around a specific area of the company, will have strong tacit knowledge from the sharing of findings and learning by the individuals from within the clique. To distribute this learning to other parts of the organization we must find mechanisms to share this knowledge which can be through mechanisms that develop common perspectives about the work and that includes a common lexicon.

* Johnson, J. D. (2009). Network Analysis. In *Managing Knowledge Networks* (p. 36). Cambridge, UK: Cambridge University Press. page 53

Chapter 3

Learning from Experience, Experiencing to Learn

While we have all learned from experiences, what does it mean to create experiences from which to learn? In this context it carries the meaning of planning to gain something that allows for growth and development from every action undertaken, or at least from the sigificant actions undertaken. While we have all learned from doing something the first time, we commonly do not actively look to learn more after we have conducted a task numerous times. It seems many projects performed within a company in a speicifc industry, for example, there can often be a common restructuring of past activities or sub-sections of previous projects. This type of mental model encourages recycling which can discourage learning. This approach, when not coupled with a continous improvement approach, actually diminishes the growth potential for our personnel and our organization. We see this type of activity in organizations and it is evident when you hear someone say, "That is always how we done this or that." In today's ever-changing technological world statements like this is most certainly a condemning strategy that cannot be allowed to flourish.

There are many things to learn from doing the work. Learning better ways to accomplish the work is important. The level of competition in the field may vary from industry to industry, but the fact is to remain in business requires constantly working to improve the way the work is done, as well as improving any product that is the result of the project. Both have implications on those doing the work as well as the customer or client of the organization.

Figure 3.1 Field failures can be painful for the project and the organization.

Figure 3.2 Learning over time will show up in how the work is done as well as the product.

3.1 Learning from Experience

Any ongoing concern, and especially early in the organization's life, there will be many challenges and opportunities to which the organization would like to advantage. A company that inspires the team members to experiment, has many minds working on its behalf. These experiences are the sort of things that help us build our people, departments and organization at large. This learning is not limited to process improvements, or corrective actions, but also opportunities for generating new ideas for new products that may end up in the product portfolio. Consider the story of 3M, providing employees with 15% of the work time to **explore, experiment** and **experience** things upon which a future can be built.*

> In 1948, 3M introduced a unique program that quickly became one of the signature elements of the company's reputation for innovation. The 15% program, which continues today, allows employees to dedicate up to six hours a week to their own projects, to range beyond the responsibilities of their job, hatch their own ideas and see what can become of them. The program is a perk that delivers benefits both to the individual and the company. Among other innovations, the company attributes the invention of Post-it® Brand notes to 15% time.

3.1.1 How Can We Get Good Judgment (Learn)?

Projects are unique; each present a distinctive challenge, though these challenges often are constant in theme allowing an extrapolation to other projects. We can see in projects, functional areas, and business processes where this failure of learning costs our organization dearly. Learning and adapting are hallmarks of good project

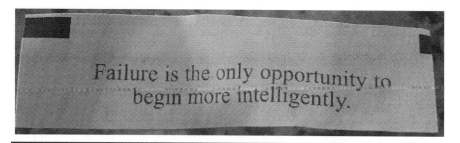

Figure 3.3 There is a connection between failure, learning and success.

---

* https://www.3m.com/3M/en_US/sustainability-report/all-stories/full-story/~/15-percent-time-innovation/?storyid=c871812b-1aec-45c3-9b1f-79104cf82f78

management and of functioning organizations. Making mistakes is not a problem as that is how we learn.

> Good judgment comes from experience, and experience comes from bad judgment.

> **Rita Mae Brown**

3.1.2 What Happens When We Do Not Improve Our Judgment (Learn)?

However, we should not consistently burn our hand on the same stovetop and act surprised. If you find your project or organization making the same set of mistakes, you have a learning problem. To be sure not all can be known, but if you are learning every day, more is known every day.

> There is only one thing more painful than learning from experience, and that is not learning from experience.

> **Laurence J. Peter**

3.1.3 What Are "the Limits of Learning?"

It may at times seem like the organization as an entirety is not capable of learning. That is one of the reason we have hyperfocused on the learning organization. Learning at the organizational level is walking a tight rope. Learn something productive and necessary, while not excluding alternatives that may work next time.

> We should be careful to get out of an experience all the wisdom that is in it — not like the cat that sits on a hot stove lid. She will never sit down on a hot lid again — and that is well; but also she will never sit down on a cold one anymore.

> **Mark Twain**

Each failure, each success provides us with an opportunity to learn. If we take and maximize that opportunity (spread throughout the organization) we become stronger as an organization. We learn more as a group about what works and what does not work. This is helpful for the product, and for the project, but we must pay attention to what is going on and listen to those that have learned lessons that we have not yet learned, as well as teach lessons to those who have not learned. Student and teacher are one and the same.

Learning from failures is important, because not learning from the failure is costly, corrosive to the project and the company's reputation, and equally important

Figure 3.4 Learning happens anywhere, labs, classroom and doing the work.

is not likely to be very motivating for the team members that are repeatedly suffering the same consequences of the same recurring failure.

3.1.4 Planning Experiences to learn

Planning to learn from an activity (experience) is something that needs built into as many activities as possible to get away from the "that is how we have always done it" state of mind. Additionally, any continuous improvement initiative of the organization will require a constant and consistent application of effort into improvement. Additionally, when you plan some form of improvement from an activity it inherently implies that a deeper understanding of the activity exists and is beneficial to acquire. While this might not actually be the case, it will become evident when we assess what is learned against what was expected to be learned. Either way, the planning and the activity will produce some form of knowledge via individual experiences. Whether we are after a better system understanding, or an improvement in an activity or even better, both. This is a prime example of a learning organization: planning to learn. While many organizations are reactionary using cause mapping and critiques to *hopefully* correct issues, a learning organization seeks opportunities to learn from activities rather than waiting for issues to arise. However, not even the best learning organization is immune from an unforeseen development (specific risk), but the more that is known, the easier it is to identify risks to the project and the organization. While a non-learning organization commonly seeks a rapid restoration to business as normal, not really exploring the root cause, a learning organization will seek the true underlying issue to allow a more effective solution. These will ideally culminate in checkpoints for validation to ensure those things learned are applied and produce the desired project effectiveness or need of modification.

3.1.5 Lessons Learned and Lasting Impact

It is one thing to learn at the individual level, it is another to learn at the organization level. An organization has multiple departments, disparate and often competing focus and objectives, and hierarchial structure.

The second step to developing a lasting change from a lesson learned is to understand what was actually learned and how that applies to the system (organization) as a whole. While you would think that what was learned from a lesson would be quite obvious, the lesson learned is commonly jaded by position protection. This single point perspective also effects the ability to determine the impact on the system as a whole and all but completely negates the possibility of a lasting change. While office politics are hard to overcome there are ways to reduce their effect on lessons learned. The most common way is to employ cross functional area group review of lessons learned. This is to say that interrelated departments discuss the lesson learned and how it relates to their processes as a group promoting communication between groups, a better system understanding, and a more effective and lasting change.

3.2 Learning Behavior

From our previous discussion in an earlier chapter, you may remember the leadership equation: $\mathbf{B} = f\{(\mathbf{Exp^3})\,(\mathbf{A^2})\,(\mathbf{D_1})\,(\mathbf{T})\}\,\{f(\mathbf{P_2})(\mathbf{GB} + \mathbf{GT^X})(\mathbf{WC})\}$, which was derived from Lewin's equation of B = f(P,E)*, (Lewin, 1936). Since we have discussed all of these concepts before it is time to work toward understanding their interrelations.

The most logical starting point is personnel behavior (***attitude***), there may be some common ways in which we act when we start a task or job. This starting attitude is usually based on being unsure of position and little to no perception of how things are done within the organization. This, coupled with the recollection of the situational leadership curve, leads us to surmise that most individuals start with a positive attitude.

Usually during the introduction phase to a new job or task, communication is at its highest. This usual high level of communication has an effect on the perception the individual has of their situation. The manner and message being communicated will

---

* Lewin, K. (1936). Principles of Topological Psychology. In K. Lewin, *Principles of topological psychoogy*. New York: McGraw-Hill.

determine what effect it has on perception. Then the perception of the situation will affect the type of experience the individual gains from the task. This brings us right back to the behavior/attitude of the individual. As the number of good or not so good experiences buildup over time they start feeding back on perception. We all refer to this as therefore been there done that or that is what we always do in these situations.

This internal feedback of experience to perception has a **log-rhythmic** for negative experiences and is therefore hard to overcome after just a short period of time.

3.3 Change and Learning

Learning and change, as well as motivation are connected. We are motivated to change because of some gap between our present state and desired state, a physical or mental discomfort. When the tension between the two become so great, action is taken with the goal of releasing this tension. The action, when it comes to projects, organizations and businesses, often shows up as process and procedure and is also the act of learning. The tension can also be released by a shifting of the thought that gave rise to the tension (i.e., what was once thought to be not acceptable is now either accepted or less unacceptable). This change of thought can either be brought about via a shift in the socially accepted norms (of the project or organization) or a generational change in the construct of a work force. There will be a deeper exploration into change management, we just want to highlight a desire for change has a role in learning. Additionally, it should be noted that change we must learn about what we desire to change and why we desire to change, as well as learning required to make the change. These are fundamental to an effective change, for without the knowledge of what we are changing and why we are changing the change will neither be effective nor lasting. It is to that end we will briefly discuss some of the change models as they relate to learning.

3.3.1 Lewin's Planned Change Model

Lewin's Planned change model consists of three sections: Unfreezing, Movement, and Refreezing.* During the "Unfreezing" section the organization, its behaviors, and structures are examined and why they must change is communicated to the employees.† The Movement section is when the change is enacted.‡ The final stage of Lewin's Planned change model is freezing or re-freezing depending upon the point

---

* Cummings, T. G. (2018). Organization Development and Change. S.l.: Cengage Learning.
† Lewin's 3-stage Model of Change. (n.d.). Retrieved December 26, 2018, from https://study.com/academy/lesson/lewins-3-stage-model-of-change-unfreezing-changing-refreezing.html
‡ Lewin's 3-stage Model of Change. (n.d.). Retrieved December 26, 2018, from https://study.com/academy/lesson/lewins-3-stage-model-of-change-unfreezing-changing-refreezing.html

in time for the effort. This is where he surmised the change was fully established and the new norms or status quo was established.* While Lewin's change model is commonly used and has been further expounded upon (***action research model***, as a Positive Change Model), it lacks any true depth and would appear to be based upon an autocratic style of leadership[†] as the change is not developed by the organization, but set down by leadership personnel (a top down approach to change management).

At this point you are probably asking, "What does this have to do with learning"? While we can learn from any changes, planned or not, how do we know if the change is going to get us to our objective? Lewin's model makes no mention of quality or assessment points along the course of the change. These sample points or quality check points, provide feedback that would be used to adjust the course of action. As we all know very few changes are instantaneous; therefore sampling of the result of those actions are required. This will serve as input for the next set of actions,

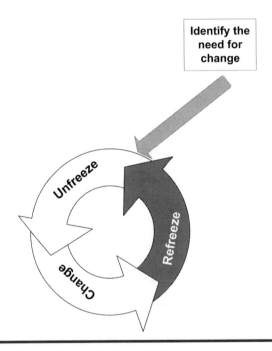

Figure 3.5 The phases of Lewin's planned change model.

* Lewin's 3-stage Model of Change. (n.d.). Retrieved December 26, 2018, from https://study.com/academy/lesson/lewins-3-stage-model-of-change-unfreezing-changing-refreezing.html
† Nayab. (2018, November 18). A Critique of the Autocratic Leadership Style - Characteristics. Retrieved December 26, 2018, from https://www.brighthubpm.com/resource-management/75715-a-critique-of-the-autocratic-leadership-style/

building upon what was learned much like an airplane samples present position and makes flight adjustments to accommodate for the external forces impacting the aircraft direction..All of this is part of the learning cycle.

3.3.2 Action Research Model

An Action Research change model differs from Lewin's Planned change model in that there is a pre-assessment (initial research) and the actions are assessed to provide information to guide follow-on actions.* While this change model promotes learning the learning is post-action due to having no predetermined quality points along its path. This type of change model is developed more toward increasing the general knowledge (systems thinking) that can be applied to other settings.[†]

3.3.3 Positive Model of Change

While Lewin's Planned Change Model and the Action Research change model are primarily based on needed improvement the Positive change model primarily focuses on what actions are positive within an organization and attempts to capitalize on those items.[‡] While this type of change management focuses on positive aspects of an organization, which aids in the morale of an organization, as with the previous two we have discussed it is a quantitative feature. This type of change model would be helpful with the experiential aspect of leadership as seen in the leadership equation from Kurt Lewin, in that it would provide positive feedback and promote an environment that promotes productive actions that facilitate continuous improvement.

3.3.4 Summation

Change and learning are, or at least should be tightly connected systems, they should be bound together in such a way that one cannot truly occur without the other and produce any lasting results. In chapter two we discussed lessons learned; if we combine that discussion with how change and learning work together, we find ourselves learning and planning changes on a continual basis. This would be the very academic definition of a learning organization. A learning organization neither waits of an issue to implement change nor waste an opportunity for change even during a change itself. As with double loop and triple loop learning the cycle of learning and action are consistent and part of the organization's structure itself.

---

* Cummings, T. G. (2018). Organization Development and Change. S.l.: Cengage Learning.

† Cummings, T. G. (2018). Organization Development and Change. S.l.: Cengage Learning

‡ Cummings, T. G. (2018). Organization Development and Change. S.l.: Cengage Learning

3.4 Data Sources

To set the groundwork for how to proceed requires exploration of what we presently have in capability, compared to what we need to have to remain competitive or grow. We have already discussed this tension between present state and desired state, but now we need to learn what the present state is along with how we will know if we are on the path for the future state. A brief list is provided below:*

- **Hard data** - these are hard numbers, metrics that are already or can easily be gathered. The lenght of time it takes to do a certain task, the defect rates, manufacturing parts per million and first pass yeild, are all hard data.
- **Soft data** - employee attitude surveys are examples of soft data. The information gathered, probably some Likert scale of magnitude is not really data that links to physical phenomenon but something less tangible though perhaps not likely less important.

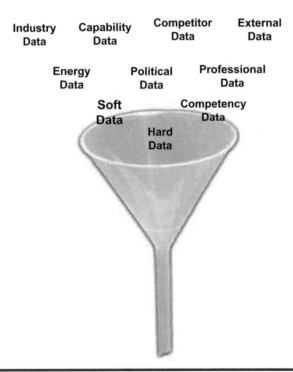

Figure 3.6 To get a clear picture often requires multiple data streams.

---

* Cheung-Judge, M., & Cheung-Judge, M. (2016). *Organization development: A practitioners guide for OD and HR.* Place of publication not identified: Kogan Page Stylus.

- **Energy data** - measures of the work or initiative being explored. This can be applied to projects as well as change initiatives that alter the way the company accomplishes the work.
- **Readiness and capability data** - do we have the requisite skills on staff to meet the objective, can we manage and effect the desired change.
- **Political data** - is there backing for the change initiative from the organizations power structures.
- **Competency data**-are the groups that are involved in the initiative able to meet the demands both in the short term as well as sustain.
- **External data** - the perspective of the team members or organization at large of external entities
- **Competitor data** - what are the competitors doing, what does this mean for the work we are doing and how we set about doing it.
- **Professional data** - depending upon what we seek to change we may need other professional resources and subsequent data.

3.5 Understanding Process Information

It is not enough to invoke a process where one is needed. Data collection from the process is how we understand the relevancy of the process as well as the competency of that process. How do you improve a thing when it is not known how a thing

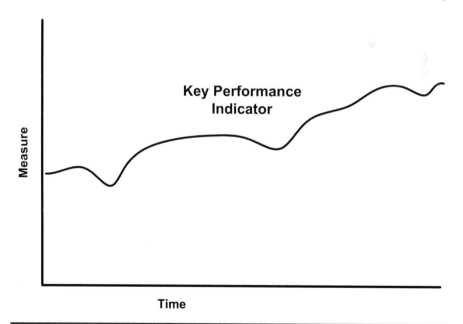

Figure 3.7 Define what matters and track through the changes to assess effectivity.

performs or question what impact our changes have on the item under scrutiny? What needs to be changed? Why does it need to change? To do this, an understanding of this process, the inputs as well as outputs to the next depending work, This is done through something often referred to as **Key Performance Indicators** or **KPI**. Notice next depending work, improving this specific process may not be the end goal. For example, perhaps the portion of work presently under review is enough, but the entirety of the work chain is not as it needs to be for the organization.

Understanding the present process capability (in some numeric and measured way) and the desired end state of this process (and the final output of the process chain), it is possible to ascertain what to change to meet this KPI improvement target. However, we need not wait for the output of the entire process chain to determine if the changes being made are having the desired impact on the process stream. To do so requires identification of leading indicators, metrics that make possible a reasonable attempt at prediction. Besides the process information that is available to help understand the situation, and perhaps more important, is that of those using the process. In fact, it is a good start to take time to ensure those that are performing the work understand the tools that follow. This combination can help drive improvement and facilitates a high degree of participation by the team members.

Leading indicators are predictive measurements. There are attributes, typically to inputs, that, when present, will allow us to predict in advance the outcome. For example, consider being on a diet; a leading indicator for weight loss would be caloric intake, below a certain number coupled with an exercise regimen that burns some defined number of calories. When set up correctly, that is the calories burned is greater then caloric intake over time, we can predict weight loss.

Lagging indicators are output focused. In the case of our diet example, a lag indicator would be the weight at any given time or the rate of weight loss over time. Lag indicators require a wait to the final attribute of the system; it is a more certain number, but there is a time dependency and associated investment in the work or effort. Metrics that are predictive may be more difficult to determine but offer the benefit of prediction.

3.5.1 Shewhart and Deming

If done well, our processes will provide us with tangible information regarding our ability to execute or deliver to meet the customer's expectations. The work will produce data or metrics, that is if we are attentive and realize the importance, that we will subsequently compile to produce information. For example, we may be interested in how long it takes to perform a specific process or achieve the output of a specific process, so we can better predict this in our project schedules. This prediction will have an impact on our project plan. We may not like what we find regarding the process output or performance. Our organization may not be satisfied with the performance of that specific process and we will need to understand what we have and why it produces the results it does to be able to determine what we need to change to perform as we desire. Of course, to know if the process is performing as we wish, we need to have some expectation from the output or outcome of that process. All of this will inform us as to the data and information we will need from the process. If we are interested in time and throughput, then we will measure things associated with time. If it is waste, we will look at the repeatability of the outcome for example, how much rework, or the amount of material that is disposed. If the variation of the output is too wide, then we will look for ways to improve this process by reducing the variation of the process output. There are a multitude of approaches we can take for the plan and physical work. We can use the simple Shewhart or Deming cycle earlier reviewed, or a project can be set up to take on these changes and that project can either be executed via a more formal or lean approach like Kanban.

There are four steps in Deming or Shewhart Cycle and these are fairly easy to understand. The first step is the **Plan** the improvement. In the course of doing the work, we may have been collecting data, and interviews with those doing the work to understand the limits of the system. What matters in the work? How can we make this better? How much better would make the system better? Knowing this allows us to formulate an approach, specific steps that will be employed in what will be a mini experiment, that is well understood by the team, not just the management.

Step two, is the **Do** phase. The do phase is where we invoke the steps in the plan. Along the way will be data collection. This Do phase is essentially the controlled experiment that we devised in the plan phase, this is not an across the board change, but an incremental change that allows exploration. What happens if we take this action? The results of this experimentation will inform us of the next steps.

Step three, is the **Check** step. In check, we compare what just happened in this experiment with what we believed would happen. If the prediction matches the outcome, there can be some confidence in that outcome and correlation to the actions taken. If the outcome is better than we thought, we should revisit the preparation and the experiment performed in the do phase, along with the post experiment analysis. We need to understand why things turned out the way they did for this experiment. Being wrong, either in predicting the outcome to be better, or worse, in either case, we are incorrect and need to know why.

Step four is the **Act** step, this really means enAct, as in institute the change across the board. We know the results of the experiment and now we are confident that this change is an improvement. This change is then articulated to other teams and other projects.

No matter the results of the experiment, we should record both the experiment details (what was done and how) and the results of the experiment. The positive results are typically recorded via updated process documentation updates. We question whether only updating the process documents are enough, as we then have no documented experiments recorded that gets us to this new version of the process. Those not involved in the process will not see how we arrived at this

Figure 3.8 There is much to Total Quality Management.

state. Thus, the learning should be recorded beyond that of the subsequent process updates. However, in our experience often the unfavorable experiment results are not recorded. Capturing the failed experiments are additional methods for learning. Not capturing these failing experiments will likely result in our conducting this experiment again. Now performing these past experiments once again, is not necessarily a bad thing, It is another opportunity to explore, ideally the results of any subsequent experiment, assuming the same set of experiment methods, will replicate the previous results.

3.5.2 Total Quality Management

One of the first things for our team and the organization at large to recognize is data is dispersed. There is variation in all things. This is also true for our process work and is one of the reasons for using tools to understand this dispersion. In addition to this dispersion, there are two types of variation.

Chance cause variation also called unavoidable causes, or chance causes or the randomness that is expressed and are the consequences of the system in its present incarnation. These causes are not yet under technical control but are present in

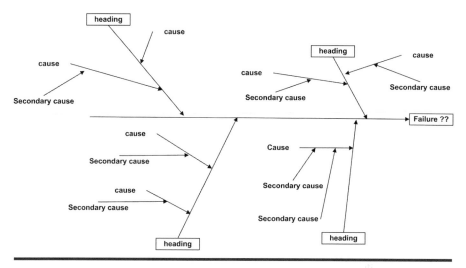

Figure 3.9 Ishikawa or fisbone diagrams are useful to generate ideas.

theoretically almost infinite numbers. They are unavoidable causes or chance causes and the variation produced by them is called "controlled variability. As managers, we cannot blame our workers for them based on existing work standards and drawings.

In contrast, the other type of variation known as special cause and is the type that produces some abnormality in the process and results in a particularly large variation, e.g., when something not covered by the work standards happens or the work standards are disobeyed. Such causes can be eliminated through team understanding of the reasons for this variation and cooperative effort; they are called avoidable, or "assignable causes" and the variation due to the miss called uncontrolled variability.*

Altering the system can alter the range of variation in a way that we desire. Additionally, this exercise of taking measurements and reviewing to understand the process capability (and get clues as to where improvements may reside) are opportunities for team learning.

We will use the tools associated with Total Quality Management (TQM) approach and tools can help us understand the situation and then be able to take some prudent action. In fact, we would want our team to be experienced with these tools and techniques to use in the context of the team and on their own, learning and propagating that learning throughout the organization.

---

* Ishikawa, K. (10601). *Introduction to Quality Control*. White Plains, NY: Kaoru Ishikawa. Pa 107

3.5.2.1 Cause and Effect Diagram

The cause and effect diagram, also called fishbone diagram, or Ishikawa diagram, is a tool for brainstorming or generating ideas that are associated with some phenomenon or symptom or improvement area. The large bones on the diagram are the hierarchal attributes we believe could cause the issue we see at the head of the fish, for example, these bones could be labeled measurements, materials, methods, machines, and personnel and environment for a manufacturing setting. Then we brainstorm ideas that fit those categories of major bones on the diagram, that would give us the symptom or performance we are seeing in the system.

To get the most out of this tool, those closest to the issues at hand, either a failure or specific area of desired must be part of the exploration. Experience using this technique indicates the open discussion required genearates many ideas as to why the system performance or outcome is the way it is. These exchanges build other ideas or thoughts for improvements. In classes we have conducted using this tool to explore the project management knowledge area has been productive with the students, where the arrive at the correct conclusion that these knowledge areas represent a collection of systems and the prediction of what system fails and produces the observed failure or phenomonon is much more complicated than originally thought.

3.5.2.2 Check Sheets

Check sheets are used to identify physical manifestations of a not understood process or interaction. For example, we may have some smudge show up on a quarter panel of a vehicle. We would make a graphic of this quarter panel, and every time we find a mark on the panel, we replicate that mark on the paper drawing. This shows the team where the anomaly manifests which can be used to understand the source of the anomaly and as such the root cause and subsequent resolution.

3.5.2.3 Control Charts

Variation, or variation that is not understood, is the bane of effective and efficient organizations. Everything from the processes of the organization, to schedules, and

Part Number
Date:
Data collector:
Inspection Station

	Monday	Tuesday	Wednesday	Thursday	Friday	Saturday	Totals
Cracking	1	1	1	1		3	10
Chamfer	3	1			2		6
Finish	2	5	1	3	8	5	24
Chipped		5	1	3	7	5	21
Void		3	1	10		4	18

	Totals	79

Figure 3.10 Check sheets can help us discover patterns.

costs is subject to variation. Not understanding variation in general often results in unrealistic plans. The things that matter to the organization especially require an understanding of these areas. For example, consider a test department that performs a set of steps in preparation for the testing. If this preparation is important, understanding the variation of this preparation work, the distribution of time in hours or days required to adequately prepare would be interesting for planning purposes as well as understanding the source of this variation in such a way to be able to influence this variation. Specifically, understanding the variation is the starting point for identifying the sources of that variation, and the determination of specific actions that can be undertaken to reduce that variation.

Control charts present the rate of performance of a process compared to the upper and lower control limits. This graphical representation of specific parameter performance makes it possible to see when performance of the system or process is moving from that which is within control to performance that is outside of control. The upper and lower control limits are calculated from measurements of a key attribute or parameter. In this way we see exactly how the process performs and can likewise see how things changing can make the process better or worse.

Distributions tell us something about the measure of control we can exert, as well as the range of possible outcomes from the effort. Gathering data will allow us to perform statistical analysis on the data, giving us the range of possible outcomes for the item under consideration. We can calculate the upper and lower control limits; this is the ***normal*** operating conditions, or common cause variation. Common cause variations are those things within the system that produce a consistent and random variation. Common cause is what we see when the control chart data performs within the upper and lower control limits, and the associated rules. Common cause variation is what remains after we have

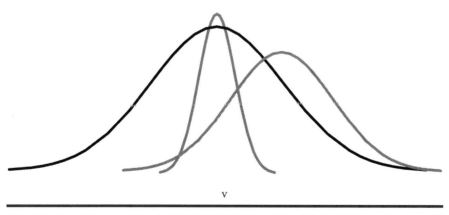

v

Figure 3.11 Understanding the variations in the system help us with prediction and future improvement.

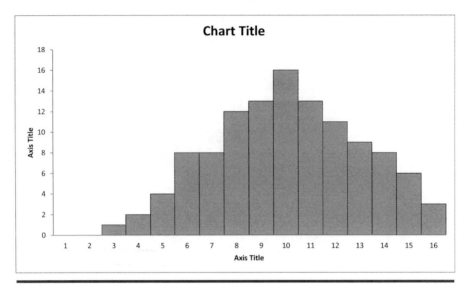

Figure 3.12 Histograms are also a good way to present distribution.

removed the special cause variation. This variation is not caused by the natural variation within the system, but some other exogenous change. For example, processed material comes into the manufacturing facility where the properties of that material are beyond that of the expected variation due to the process that is produced.

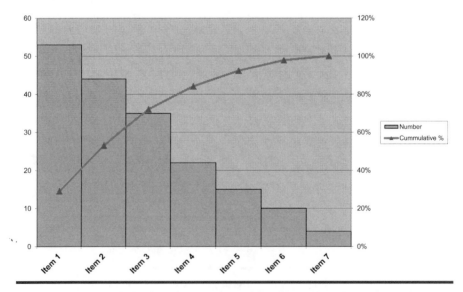

Figure 3.13 Pareto helps in prioritization of the things that should be addressed.

3.5.2.4 Histograms

Histograms are used to understand the distribution of a parameter, for example, we can review the time it takes to perform a certain function, or some other distribution of some variable. The histogram allows us to see the variation in that variable. Knowing the distribution of this variable enables our planning to be more accurate instead of guessing we have the range of possibilities. If we do not like the distribution, we can conjure up ideas to explore that would make this distribution more as we need it to be rather than what is presently demonstrated.

Histograms can help us see if there are a cascade of variables that may be impacting the final curve results. The graphic above is slanted or skewed left and not a normal distrbution. Histograms can be skewed left, or multiple peaks, referred to as bimodal. The appearance of the distribution are clues to the sort of things that may be impacting the distribution. For example, bimodal distribution indicates that there is more than one variable impacting the distibution.

3.5.2.5 Pareto Charts

When we want to prioritize what we undertake to improve, we will likely use a Pareto chart. This chart is a stacked histogram from larger to smaller, along with a separate line graph that demonstrates the cumulative percentage of the contribution of each bar in the histogram. This gives us the 80% 20% rule, wherein 80% of the problems come from 20% of the causes. This provides us with a prioritization scheme, where we have many issues to undertake. We want to apply our efforts to fix the biggest of our problems and work down to the lower sources. No sense in trying to solve the problems that only has a minimal impact on the project, and organization Pareto helps us determine either the volume of problems, or the cost for each of those parameters on the x-axis.

3.5.2.6 Scatter Diagram

The scatter plot (or scatter diagram) helps to visualize correlation between two variables (not causation). This can be used to understand the connection of one variable with another variable, that may aid in making the system more predictable. This is not causation, in that some other third element (or perhaps even there is cause and effect, but this method does not prove that) may be making both of these variables behave the way they do. The tighter the scatter the closer the correlation, wider patterns, the more loose the correlation. There are also positive and negative correlations, that is as one variable increases so too does the other (positive correlation) and as one variable decreases, the other variable increases. The tighter the collection of dots, the stronger the correlation, the more disperse, the less correlation. In the graphic we see that that the positive sloped (positive correlation) is a tight pattern, and therefore has a high degree of correlation. The

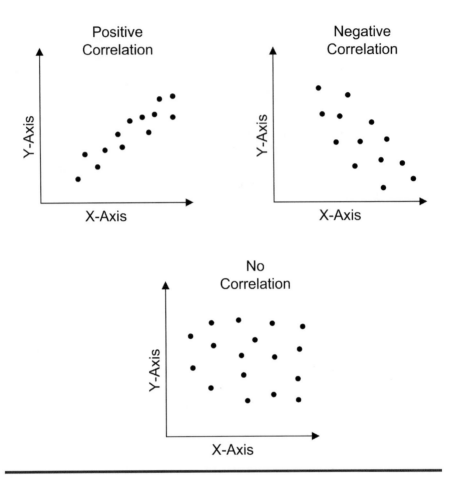

Figure 3.14 Scatter plots help to unover any correlation (not causation) between variables.

negative correlation, has a wider pattern and therefore it is said that the correlation is weak.

3.5.3 Other Tools

There are times when these tools usually associated with total quality management are not able to help the team and the organization to ascertain the source of the difficulties. This is especially true when it comes to creative thinking. Tools can help us to evoke connections between concepts, ideas, or material associations. Other tools help to ascertain the best decision out of several possible decisions. In each of these tools, a team approach can be employed, evoking connections that may not be readily seen by any one team member.

3.5.3.1 Mind Mapping

Mind maps are ways to explore ideas building the structure as we build associations. In this way the result is a graphical representation of ideas without a rigid structure at the start, facilitating brainstorming and discovery of ideas that we have not previously considered. Mind mapping is a more structured way of brainstorming, and can be done alone or with a team on a whiteboard.

3.5.3.2 Decision Matrix

We can use decision matrix to help us decide among alternatives, and these techniques lend to team discussion and therefore facilitate learning. In fact, these tools are not of much use for single person exploration. There are unweighted and weighted examples of decision matrix. The unweighted decision matrix is a list of attributes against which the decision alternatives under consideration are compared, with each attribute being equal. The Pugh matrix is an example of a weighted decision matrix, in that we prioritize the most prized attributes by assigning a number. Either of these can be used to evaluate a variety of possible decision alternatives against a common set of desired attributes.

First, it is important to note the team members when making any assessment or comparison of ideas. Noted throughout this material, is the need for more than one perspective. In fact, this differing of perspective opens the idea for true scrutiny as well as the possibility of generating more ideas or some amalgam of the ideas that are under consideration. These variety of perspectives are helpful when it comes to optimization, that is discovering the trade-offs for subsequent decisions. This perspective is generated from a cross-functional group of people that can articulate their perspectives, things like evaluation criteria as well as decision possibilities. This requires and environment that encourages engagement and is safe for the team members to speak their mind. We are not looking at the attribute from a single perspective, such as that of the development group; the expectation is there are discussions among the team members as the evaluation is underway, articulating why each team member thinks the way they do for each attribute evaluation. Decision matrix tools help us evoke these tangible

Next, weighted means that all the attributes we are considering are not of equal value when it comes to the decision. We will compare the strategies or ideas we generate against these attributes; some of these attributes we have a greater desire for than others. For example, perhaps we value cost attributes over some of the feature content, throughput or maintainability. If that is the case, the emphasis on the cost variable will be addressed in the matrix and the final number presented by the matrix will include the ranking of this desire.

This weighting (priority) becomes a multiplier for the rating and produces the end value for the attribute. For example, we would expect a **priority value of 5** to produce some weighted value of 20-25 as that would mean we have found a good

Pugh Matrix

2007-09-06

Evaluation criterias	Priority - 5 is high	Reference Design Rating	Reference Design Weighted	Concept 1 Rating	Concept 1 Weighted	Concept 2 Rating	Concept 2 Weighted	Concept 3 Rating	Concept 3 Weighted
Quality									
Maintenance support	5	0	0	-1	-5	-1	-5	3	15
Quality and Reliability	5	0	0	0	0	1	5	2	10
Complexity - user friendly	4	0	0	-2	-8	2	8	1	4
Assembly process	5	0	0	-2	-10	1	5	1	5
End of Line diagnostics and troubleshooting	5	0	0	1	4	1	5	1	5
Parts availability	5	0	0	-1	-5	-1	-5	-3	-15
Cost									
Product cost	4	0	0	-2	-8	1	4	3	12
Development cost	3	0	0	-1	-3	2	6	3	9
Assembly time	5	0	0	-2	-10	3	15	2	10
Maintenance	3	0	0	-3	-9	1	3	1	3
Repair time	5	0	0	-1	-5	-3	-15	-1	-5
Training / Education	5	0	0	-1	-5	-1	-5	4	20
Feature									
Product expandibility	3	0	0	-1	-3	-1	-3	2	6
Scale-ability	5	0	0	-1	-5	-1	-5	1	5
Feature flexibility	5	0	0	0	0	0	0	1	5
Configurability for second life application	4	0	0	-1	-4	-1	-4	-2	-8
Special tools	5	0	0	-2	-10	-1	-5	4	20
Field replaceable	5	0	0	-1	-5	1	5	2	10
Backwards compatibility	3	0	0	-1	-3	0	0	1	3
Delivery									
Development speed and flexibility	5	0	0	0	0	4	20	3	15
Total Score			0		-94		29		129

Leader:
Engineering:
Aftermarket:
Product Planning:
Product Planning:
Marketing:
Eng. PM:

Figure 3.15 The Pugh matrix is an example of a weighted decision matrix.

solution for the highest priority attribute (our solution then holds a ranking of 4-5, also the top end of the scale). If our priority or weighted level 5 produces a 10 (a rating of 2) then we have not matched the design to this objective very well.

3.5.3.3 Brainstorming

Brainstorming is a technique developed by Alex Osborn in 1941 and has been successfully applied over the many decades by many organizations. With brainstorming, we are tapping into the hive mind or the genius of the group. There are few rules to successfully conduct the brainstorming event.

- **Quantity**: The more ideas the better; the more ideas, the more probable that the list of ideas will include some very valuable gems from which we can take advantage. The key is to generate ideas, not to develop any of the ideas.
- **No criticism**: There will be no criticism of the ideas generated; critiquing the ideas can dampen the enthusiasm and the pace of ideas coming from the team, and we seek to generate many ideas.
- **No constraints**: To ensure the maximum ideas we likewise will not consider constraints upon the ideas, for the same reason there is not criticism. The intent is to bring a mass of ideas.
- **Combining ideas**: During the generation of ideas, the team is encouraged to build upon the ideas generated from the other team members. That is one of the benefits of this type of idea generation; the other group members hear the idea and that brings other related or extensions of that idea.

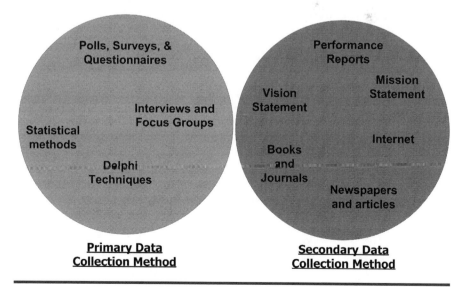

Figure 3.16 Data can be found in many places to help us understand the situation.

Experience suggests the exercise with the team can generate new ideas for doing the work, new sequences for doing the work, or elimination of unproductive work and even new products. Additionally, we have the collection of individuals contributing and exchanging ideas, which can expose them to different perspectives and mental models upon which the work can build.

3.6 Communicating the Goals of Collecting Information

Communicating the goals and methods of any data collecting effort is important because this sets the stage for all subsequent events and efforts. Collecting the wrong data will confound our improvement effort. For example, consider an airline that wants to understand the actual arrival of the aircraft against the expected or documented arrival time. Which is better, to measure the time the aircraft gets to the gate? Or is it better to set the time of arrival as the aircraft touches down for landing? The customers will likely call on time arrival something different than wheels down at the destination airport. This discrepancy will be pronounced on those landing where the aircraft sits on the tarmac due to traffic for several minutes causing missing connecting flights. The goals or objectives are important in selecting the attribute or data measured. It is important to collect the right or correct measurement or data. It is equally important to collect the measurement correctly.

Collecting data wrong will lead us to conclusions that may not be true. Collecting data wrong can be found in the data selection methods: what parameters are valid, what data is valid. For example, we collect specific process data, but the event for which we are collecting that data did not adhere to the defined process. Does this data mean anything when it comes to deciding about the process?

There are also unintended consequences possible when we do not articulate the goals and the use for the data we are collecting. This next problem is a combination of corporate culture and lack of transparency in the data gathering objectives and is best demonstrated in a story. Consider a fast food restaurant that is collecting data regarding the speed at which the customer order is made and subsequently concluded. Cars come through the drive-through and then move to the paying window. Upon paying, the vehicle is asked to move forward, away from the window, even though there are no cars behind; there is no line. We are given the illusion that the customer's order has been quickly dispatched, but the customer is still waiting. The measurements from this event, or similar events, then skew the reality of the data.

3.7 How to Analyze through Root Cause Analysis

This is not a book about root cause analysis, however there is much to learn from root cause analysis, and it is possible to come to errant conclusions when performed poorly. The root cause analysis effort is used to correct results from the various parts of the organization. These explorations are initiated from some performance malady or desired improvement area. The formal exploration into the root cause is a mechanism for team members to learn, along with improvements in the organization. Formalizing root cause analysis ensure some measure of rigor and repeatability, or repeatable outcome. Approaches to root cause are important, we do not want to randomly associate cause with effect. Root cause analysis is not near as easy as some seem to believe. If you really want to see what complex root cause analysis really looks like, check out the ***Smithsonian Channel's Aircraft Disasters***. This provides a glimpse into what it takes to truly arrive at a conclusion that can help us improve the organization. Errant root cause analysis will lead us to wrong conclusions, then corrective actions that do not mean anything, then improvements that do not improve anything at all. This will be a waste and more importantly at the end of the effort we may walk away believing we actually improved the situation. At the end of this, eventually, the problem will once again rear its ugly head, leaving us to go once again down this path, repeatedly until we accidentally hit upon the root cause.

Informal root cause process provides no mechanism for distribution, neither does it ensure a repeatable or consistent outcome. This inconsistent outcome and lack of distribution means an informal process does not readily support effective learning.

3.7.1 Why Formalize Root Cause Analysis

There are many approaches to determining the root of our problems. In the automotive world, there are two typical approaches, the 8D or the 8 Discipline, or the A3 (named for the paper size). There are some benefits to a formalized root cause analysis. We can think of 6 reasons as listed below:

- Controls jumping to conclusions and just working on the symptom
- Repeatable
- Coordinates effort / focus
- Documents actions so we know what have tried and what is next
- Traceable for future events
- Provides a mechanism by which learning is shared

Formalized approaches can help control jumping to conclusions and just working on the symptom. A formalized approach to root cause analysis is such a way that will keep us from jumping to conclusions about the nature of the failure. We are a big fan of aircraft disasters. If you really want to understand what solving complex problems is really like, check out that show. It is seldom that the first thing we think is the problem is in fact the problem. There is also a significant chance that the root cause is not in fact a single thing, and very likely not the single thing we may immediately believe to be the problem often based upon our biases and experiences.

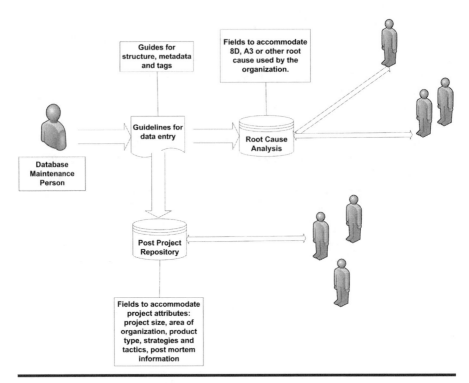

Figure 3.17 Root cause anslysis and post-project reviews are material from which to learn and distribute.

Formalized approaches, if we have done the work well enough, will generate notes, tests, and results and other documentation that would make it possible to recreate our exploration in as much as it could possibly be replicated. This gives us a sense of really understanding the nature of this problem. If we can replicate the problem, we are theoretically better able to solve the problem, or more importantly, we are able to see if we have solved the problem. The solution should prevent the problem from recurring.

Formalized approaches facilitate coordination of effort from the diverse perspectives, facilitating the nature of the problem and methods for us to explore these beliefs. With a team, we may get a multitude of ideas as to the root cause, and without some level of formalism, we may all charge off in many directions pursuing our own agenda or thoughts on the matter. Our goal is to quickly understand and solve the problem. With team members going off in many and unknown or uncoordinated directions, we are not efficiently making use of the organization's resources, time, and talent. A formalized approach helps keep the team connected to each other and to the objective and ensures the opportunity for team learning.

Formalized approaches document actions so we know what have tried and what is next. Without a formalized approach we would not know what things have been explored, what has been discovered, and what has been learned, nor be able to distribute that learning. We are able to build upon what has been tried and what has been learned. We can consider our next actions in the context of our past actions in the course of resolving this problem.

Formalized approaches provide a traceable foundation for future events. The formalized process will have some measure of recording the actions that are undertaken and the results of the exploration and the final solution. This information can be fodder or future work. We can capture this information in a searchable database that will make recovery of these activities possible rather than accidental by other people in the organization.

3.7.2 The 5 Whys

Another way for the team to understand how things are connected, including any anomalous performance exploration, is to use the 5 whys. This is exactly like it sounds, ask why and after every answer, ask why again. This ultimately leads us to the point where the root cause of the anomalous performance, stopping at the first why, leads to treating only the symptom and not the source of the problem. In fact, experience suggests often the true root of the problem is not addressed, but what amounts to a band aid rather than fixing the problem in a way that eliminates or

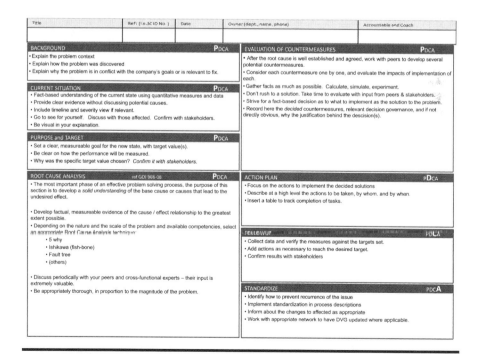

Figure 3.18 A3 is an approach to determining the root casue.

greatly reduces the probability of the event recurrence. In some cases, we may have to go even further than the five whys to really get to the source of the problem.

Don't play the blame game; you should be asking "why" five times, not "who." Don't stop the inquiries when you reach a "who" because this usually means somebody will get accused of causing the problem. Blaming does not help with psychological safety, and help with free communication, as well as facilitate experimentation, by eliminating the fear of reprisals,

Be mindful that there could be several valid reasons for a problem happening. Unfortunately, this method usually proceeds along just one path, which might not lead to one of these reasons. Even if it leads to a real cause of variation, this may not be a major cause, much less the largest one. In addition, the five-whys approach is not inclined to lead you to an unlikely or unknown cause, which is often the type responsible for a chronic quality problem. That's why this method is better suited for identifying the source of assignable variation where there is usually just one cause.*

3.7.3 A3

One form of root cause analysis is the A3, which is a graphical representation of the effort to determine the source of the anomalous or failing event. One of the benefits of the A3 approach, is that it encourages graphical representation of the problems and also the solutions and corrective actions. Visual representations of the problem as well as the solutions. A single page of information that describes the situation and the exploration and progress we are making in this regard.

1. Identify the problem
2. Visual representation of the problem
3. Set the new target
4. Determine the root cause
5. Develop countermeasures
6. Institute countermeasures
7. Measure performance – is this better?
8. Standardize, make this common practice

Each root cause the A3 is used to solve, represents some measure of learning by the team. Therefore each of the A3's are the repository for this learning, albeit not necessarily the best solution as a repository of the resulting work. This is not a searchable content but may end up in a book of all of the A3's similar to the lessons learned from project management that is sometimes included in a notebook. There are other was to store this information rather than a myriad of seperate documents that must be poured over to understand what may have been learned.

---

* Bothe, Davis, R. (2007). Reducing Process Variation, Using the DOT-STAR Problem Solving Strategy. ICedarburg, Wisconsin: Landmark Publishing Co. page 490

8D Summary Report

D0 WHO IS EFFECTED BY THE PROBLEM?		Tracking Number:	0
Customer:	0	1st Person to report problem:	0
Address:	0	Product Manager:	0
Date of Failure:	0	Value Stream Manager:	0
Time of Failure:	0	Description of use:	0
Part No.:	0	8D Report Number:	
Product Name:	0		

D1 TEAM MEMBERS		D2 PROBLEM DESCRIPTION
Champion:	0	0
Team Leader:	0	
Process Owner:	0	
Supplier:	0	
Customer:	0	
SME:	0	
QA:	0	
Other:	0	

PICTURE OR SKETCH OF FAILURE

D3 INTERIM CONTAINMENT ACTIONS
0

D4 ROOT CAUSE
LRC 1

LRC 2

LRC 3

D5 CORRECTIVE ACTION
CA 1

CA 2

CA 3

D6 CORRECTIVE ACTION IMPLEMENTATION & DATE	Date	Verified
1.		Yes
2.		Yes
3.		Yes

D7 ACTIONS TAKEN TO PREVENT RECURRENCE
0

D8 TEAM RECOGNITION
0

APPROVAL	Name	Signature	Date

Figure 3.19 The 8D is another method for exploring and discovering the root of the problem and corrective action.

3.7.3.1 8D

The 8D, also known as the 8 Disciplines, is another automotive approach to root cause analysis. It is called the 8D, which stands for 8 discipline consisting of 8 steps or phases. This sequence of events lead team through the discovery and experimentation work with just enough formality to provide the structure of steps. This includes the close out portion of the work where we thank and congratulate the team.

1. Plan
2. Team
3. Interim plan
4. Root cause
5. Choose and verify corrective action
6. Implement and validate corrective actions
7. Preventative measures
8. Congratulate the team

Like the A3, it is one thing to do the work, learn and solve the problems origins and corrective actions, it is another to put this information in a format that will be easy for those that are not part of this particular learning events, to at least become aware of the existence of these documents and learning.

3.8 Quantitate Analysis through Process Metrics

Where we have processes that are actually adhered, we are able to make some quantitative assessments of those processes. Control charts over time, are examples of this data collection. The sum of all of the specific process measurements provide us with information on a larger scale from which we can make decisions. This is especially true for strategic planning. Knowledge of the present performance via process statistics and understanding how these impacts the strategy

3.9 Unearthed! Finding Golden Nuggets of Knowledge within Performance Analytics

A review of these process metrics with a view of viewing how the performance and capabilities change over time in a dashboard type view, makes it possible to truly discover the strengths of the company upon which other things can be built. Understanding what works well or the strength of the company, are like discovering gold nuggets. These are the areas that can propel the organization to truly new heights. When we see what works, we can work to move these things that work in one location for consideration to other parts of the organization.

3.10 How to Discover Lessons Learned from Performance Analytics

Performance metrics at the micro and the macro level provide us with sources of understanding. Where our performance is lacking according to our objectives and strategies, we can determine ways to improve this area with focus being brought to the problem. For example, we can bring the organization's talent together to study and devise experiments from which we can learn and improve the performance. We devise plans for experiments using for example that Shewhart or Deming Cycles for the exploration, or some other structured approach.

Sometimes there are limits to being able to improve the performance. There may be one or more constraints within the organization that may limit the ability to internally achieve the objectives. In these cases, we need to think out of the box. When these constraints that are beyond what the organization is capable of adapting, we will need to consider other approaches:

■ outsource
■ joint venture
■ collaboration with schools or other organizations

Chapter 4

Change Management

4.1 Introduction to Change

In chapter 3 we discussed "Change" as being caused by the tension between the current state and the desired state and that learning is instrumental to change and the effectiveness of said change. While both terms, change and learning, have very different meanings they are inexplicably tied to one another. It is this very tie that has given traction to the learning organization and development movement. The change we discuss is not just within the organization, but with the social dynamic as well. Also, as we discussed in chapter 3 perspective of the individual, the group, the organization, and society as a whole affects the dynamics of change, the tension that promotes change.

Many people may consider change as something that occurs only when something happens to cause it or when a new plan or process is enacted. However, change is always occurring even when there is no visible cause (issue or accident) or even a plan for it. Even when an action is done the same way it has always been done a change can and often occurs with the individual conducting the activity: learning, or a motivation change. These types of change are rarely captured in any instruction or guidance, but they are occurring either way. As we discussed in chapter 1 (Leadership Equation) experience is a key driver to behavior and those experiences promote or can promote change within the individual and thus the team, and furthermore the organization as a whole.

4.1.1 Organization Development and Change

According to the book "Organization Development, A Process of Learning and Change" by W. Warner Burke and Debra A. Noumair the earlier thinking of planned change as it pertains to the change agent, Organization Developmental

(OD) consultant and/or change agent, was of data collector, data interpreter, feedback provider, and those such times or actions.* Current thought is that the OD consultant is more of a guide to help the organization with these processes.† While having an individual that is versed in the area of Organizational Development would be useful it should not be necessary as the organization itself should embody these processes. Since the role has evolved to that of facilitator for the OD consultant an individual that understands and adheres to the tenets of such thought processes as those of "The Fifth Discipline" by Peter Senge should be able to act as the OD consultant. This position would have to be properly monitored as an individual within the organization itself might bring their perspective biases to the situation. In these such instances an outside consultant should be used to negate any biases and aid in truth of reporting. Ideally, perhaps, this consultant role could be filled by the project manager. In fact, in an agile variant known as scrum, the role of scrum master serves as a consultant. Agile is a lean form of project management that is reviewed at length in later chapters. The scrum master and any project manager role can serve as the consultant. This may require adjustment, and that adjustment will either be reinforced or retarded by the organziation's culture and at the executive level.

It is important to recognize that the organization may have some measure of politics. This is not going to change, so it is important that the person underaking the work considers this in their approach. Whether the practioner is an internal employee or a contractor from outside of the organization, there are some key steps:‡

- identify key stakeholders that are instrumental in the change initiative
- find mentor from within the organization
- meet with the key players, especially from the political perspective
- follow up with each individual in writing with those items important to them according to your understanding
- map out all of the identified needs

4.1.2 Planned Change

Kurt Lewin developed a simple but effective three step model of change: unfreeze, change, freeze.§ In this section we will look at this model and some others and discuss how they might apply to a learning organization.

* Burke, W. W. (2015). *Organization Development: A process of learning and changing.* Place of publication not identified: Pearson.
† Burke, W. W. (2015). *Organization Development: A process of learning and changing.* Place of publication not identified: Pearson.
‡ Cheung-Judge, M. (2016). Organization development: A practitioners guide for OD and HR. Place of publication not identified: Kogan Page Stylus.
§ Cummings, T. G. (2018). Organization Development and Change. S.l.: Cengage Learning.

Figure 4.1 We take care in how we identify, alter, and integrate the change to the organization.

4.1.2.1 Unfreezing

As we alluded to in the section "What is Change" a repetitive action or task can either set the tone for change or create a pattern of habit(s) that serve little or no purpose except to stifle growth and development, i.e., change. Unfreezing in Lewin's change model prompts people to evaluate their perspective while seeking improvement. In a nutshell current processes must be reassessed in order for change to occur.[*] While Lewin's unfreezing portion of the planned change model has been the basis for several other planned change models and has withstood the test of time, we should look closer and from a learning organization perspective. Lewin used the word "reassess"; this suggests that there is a period between looking at or evaluating these processes. If an organization is truly a learning organization it is not a reassessment, but continual evaluation and when a change is implemented it would require check-points for determining if the initiative is progressing as desired and has not affected some other portion of the system unexpectedly.

---

[*] Morrison, M. (2015, September 13). Kurt Lewin change theory and three step model - Unfreeze-Change-Freeze. Retrieved January 10, 2019, from https://rapidbi.com/kurt-lewin-three-step-change-theory/

In the Action Research Model, the unfreezing section is comprised of perception of the problem: enter the consultant, data collection, and some feedback.* That is not to suggest that a consultant is required or desired in this process either; however wouldn't having someone who is familiar, the process owner or user, be more appropriate?

Another question for this model is regarding to data collection. What data collection would be done for an evaluation of change that is not already being done, and if that data is not already being collected, why not? Just about every organization collects data on their process, procedures, and project management activities. If this data is not based on determining improvements or changes, why bother collecting this data? It is true that there are times where being too close to a situation can lead to any of a number of biases; however, that does not necessarily preclude coaching from within the firm or the project. For example, we may see this bias originate due to a sense of ownership if an organization promotes development as seen in stage 3 and 4 Tribal leadership. If we understand the earlier material from the "Tribal Leadership: Leveraging natural groups to build a thriving organization,† this bias potential can be reduced or completely negated.

In the Positive Change Model, the unfreezing section is composed of initiate the inquiry, inquire into best practices (if such a thing may exists), and some discovery of themes.‡ This model differs for both Lewin's change model and the **action research** change model in that it is based more on positive aspects of a process§ while the other two look for shortcomings that want, or need, to be changed. This model is based primarily on positive psychology which put emphasis on creativity, optimism, and courage¶ instead of the previous psychology of determining the issue(s) that required action or correction. According to Kim Cameron's article in The Journal of Applied Behavioral Science titled Paradox in Positive Organizational Change this approach leads to effectiveness and change, but the negative emphasis has more impact.** This was centered on the thought that positive occurrences are evaluated more accurately and remembered longer than negative events or actions.††

---

* Burke, W. W. (2015). *Organization Development: A process of learning and changing.* Place of publication not identified: Pearson.
† Logan, D., King, J. P., & Fischer-Wright, H. (2011). *Tribal leadership: Leveraging natural groups to build a thriving organization.* New York: Harper Business.
‡ Cummings, T. G. (2018). Organization Development and Change. S.l.: Cengage Learning.
§ Cummings, T. G. (2018). Organization Development and Change. S.l.: Cengage Learning.
¶ Burke, W. W. (2015). *Organization Development: A process of learning and changing.* Place of publication not identified: Pearson.
** Cameron, K. S. (2008). Paradox in Positive Organizational Change. *The Journal of Applied Behavioral Science, 44*(1), 7-24. doi:10.1177/0021886308314703
†† Burke, W. W. (2015). *Organization Development: A process of learning and changing.* Place of publication not identified: Pearson.

Just as movement in a still room attracts attention, so negative (novel) events capture more attention than positive (normal) patterns. Furthermore, negative events often indicate maladaptation and a need to change, (and) one single negative thing can cause a system to fail, but one single positive thing cannot guarantee success.[*]

The positive change model parallels some of what we have been discussing about leadership and the facilitating of learning. This point is echoed by the study of highly effective teachers in K-12 public schools by Quinn, Heynoski, Thomas, and Spreitzer[†] when they found the use of a positive approach was helping the teachers and students learn. Their article actually only referred to the students learning, but it has been our experience that when the positive model is employed both parties, leader (teacher) and subordinate (student), gain some knowledge from the interaction.

While there are numerous beginning steps for change, many more than those discussed, the question arises what approach is best for your organization? That question can best be answered by matching the current status of the organization to the change model and determining if it will be effective. We could review the resulting change outcome. Is it as desired? Then perhaps the first change model fits the organization? We can think of it in this manner: when a new individual joins the team how do you bring them on board? What actions are taken to help them develop and how does this help change over time? Just because a shoe fits your foot in the morning does not mean it will feel good after working all day. This thinking is necessary for continual development. This continuous self-improvement and learning is the basis for a learning organization.

4.1.2.2 Movement/Change

The movement section of Lewin's change model is where the behavior of the organization, department, or individual changes.[‡] This change is due to intervention by the change agent promoting the change. While this makes it sound as if this action is caused by the consultant or a senior team member it can be promoted by the individual himself if the tension between the current perceived condition and desired condition is sufficient to cause actions. While this model seems simple in that it is only comprised of one step, it is actually quite complicated. It is complicated because of the nature of change itself. If a change is desired by one member of a

---

[*] Cameron, K. S. (2008). Paradox in Positive Organizational Change. *The Journal of Applied Behavioral Science, 44*(1), 7-24. doi:10.1177/0021886308314703

[†] Quinn, R. E., Heynoski, K., Thomas, M., & Spreitzer, G. (2014). Co-Creating the Classroom Experience to Transform Learning and Change Lives. *Research in Organizational Change and Development,* 25-54. doi:10.1108/s0897-3016_2014_0000022000

[‡] Cummings, T. G. (2018). Organization Development and Change. S.l.: Cengage Learning.

Figure 4.2 Before we make a move to the entire organization we should assess suitability.

group, but no others how does that one individual demonstrate the tension they see for change to the other members of the group? This has been the question many have asked and few know the answer to: enter the learning organization. If we look at the five portions of the learning organization: Personnel Mastery, Mental Models, Shared Vision, Team Learning, and Systems Thinking,* we can see how if one individual sees the need for a change the group would also see some need as well. However, this does not mean that the change desire would be agreed upon initially, but acknowledgement of a need is usually the hardest part of change.

In the Action Research Model, the movement/change phase described by Lewin consists of feedback to key client or group members, joint diagnosis of problem, joint action planning, action, and data gathering after action.† In this model the key difference is that there is a feedback loop called out after the action(s) or change has occurred back to the step of feedback to key clients or members. This addition to the change model puts it in alignment with organization development and the learning

---

* Kleiner, A., & Senge, P. M. (1994). The Fifth discipline fieldbook. London: Nicholas Brearley.
† Cummings, T. G. (2018). Organization Development and Change. S.l.: Cengage Learning.

organization in that a continual learning and developmental process is employed. Again, however, this model makes it seem if a consultant is required to execute the process and as we discussed in the beginning of this chapter that may or may not be the case based on the organization itself.

In the Positive Model, the movement/change phase consists of discovering themes, envisioning a preferred future, and designing and delivering ways to create the future.* This model also has a loop from the "Design and Deliver Ways to Create the Future" section back to the "Inquire into Best Practices" section, which is another example of loop learning like we saw in the action research model. While Lewin's change model and the action research model are both based on correction of some shortcoming the positive research model is based on positives. This approach to change has its basis in social constructionism. Social constructionism places more emphasis on interactions of people (experiences) to determine their view of reality.† As we have alluded to numerous times perception alters reality (socially) and our interactions (experiences) shape our perceptions. This is a subjective statement in that reality is what is real: *i.e, If everyone in a group calls a duck a chicken it does not change what the duck is, but does change its name so thus describing it to someone outside the group they would think it a chicken.* Using a theory like social constructionism for change promotes a sharing of experiences between people about their view of the organization to help develop a shared-vision, one of the tenents of a learning organization.‡ Also, if each individual shares their perspective of the organization it should bring the groups' perspective closer to what the organization actually is versus a jaded opinion of the organization. This clearer current understanding of the organizations' status will aid in determining the changes needed to obtain the desired results.

4.1.2.3 Freezing

The freezing or refreezing section of Lewin's change model is described as when the organization is at its new state (post-change) and employs a reinforcement strategy to maintain the new state.§ The reinforcement stategy for this new or desired state is ill-defined in Lewin's model. There are as many types of reinforcement strategies as there are change models, if not more. They are commonly broken into positive and negative reinforcements. A common error in reinforcement strategies

---

* Cummings, T. G. (2018). Organization Development and Change. S.l.: Cengage Learning.
† Andrews, T. (2012, June 01). What is Social Constructionism? Retrieved January 16, 2019, from http://groundedtheoryreview.com/2012/06/01/what-is-social-constructionism
‡ Kleiner, A., & Senge, P. M. (1994). The Fifth discipline fieldbook. London: Nicholas Brearley.
§ Cummings, T. G. (2018). Organization Development and Change. S.l.: Cengage Learning.

is the confusion between a reinforcement and a reward.* Reinforcement theory of motivation according to B.F. Skinner states that the individual's behavior is a function of its consequences (*law of effect*), i.e., positive reinforcement tends to reinforce behavior, but negative reinforcement reduces the likelihood of said behavior.† Reward is something provided by the individual or group desiring the specific behavior and may not be in alignment with what the recipient thinks appropriate or desired.‡ To put it bluntly reward is what the change agent thinks will work and reinforcement is what is proven to work (desired by the individual or group executing the change). Reinforcement is in alignment with Victor Vroom's Expectancy Theory of Motivation.

Lunenburg§ states that Vroom's expectancy differs from Maslow, Herzberg, and Aldefer because Vroom does not attempt to suggest what motivates but instead discusses the different cognitive processes of individuals that may produce motivational factors. The cognitive process evaluates the motivational factor (MF) of behavioral options based on the individual's perception of possible goal attainment. Therefore, the motivational force can be shown by the following: **MF = Expectancy x Instrumentality x $\sum$(Valence(s).¶** Expectancy is the individual's assessment of the relationship between effort and performances, i.e., will the effort applied produce the performance equal to or greater than itself?** Instrumentality is the performance to reward relationship, i.e., what is the probability that the performance will yield the desired reward?†† Valence is the value the individual places on the reward. Rewards that hold little to no value have a negative valence and are of no motivational

---

* Wright, Cook, & Morton. (n.d.). *Use of Reinforcement in Behavior Management Strategies* [Diagnostic Center, Southern California]. Diagnostic Center, Southern California, California. http://www.pent.ca.gov/pos/cl/str/useofreinforcement.pdf

† Juneja, P. (n.d.). MSG Management Study Guide. Retrieved January 16, 2019, from https://www.managementstudyguide.com/reinforcement-theory-motivation.htm

‡ Wright, Cook, & Morton. (n.d.). *Use of Reinforcement in Behavior Management Strategies* [Diagnostic Center, Southern California]. Diagnostic Center, Southern California, California.

§ Lenenburg, F. C. (2015). *Expectancy theory of motivation: Motivating by altering expectations.* International journal of Management, Business, and Administration, 15(1), 1-6, Sam Houston State University. http://nationalforum.com/Electronic journal volumes/Lunenburg, Fred C Expectancy Theory Altering Expectations IJMBA v15 NI 2011.PDF

¶ Lenenburg, F. C. (2015). *Expectancy theory of motivation: Motivating by altering expectations.* International journal of Management, Business, and Administration, 15(1), 1-6, Sam Houston State University. http://nationalforum.com/Electronic journal volumes/Lunenburg, Fred C Expectancy Theory Altering Expectations IJMBA v15 NI 2011.PDF

** Lenenburg, F. C. (2015). *Expectancy theory of motivation: Motivating by altering expectations.* International journal of Management, Business, and Administration, 15(1), 1-6, Sam Houston State University. http://nationalforum.com/Electronic journal volumes/Lunenburg, Fred C Expectancy Theory Altering Expectations IJMBA v15 NI 2011.PDF

†† Lenenburg, F. C. (2015). *Expectancy theory of motivation: Motivating by altering expectations.* International journal of Management, Business, and Administration, 15(1), 1-6, Sam Houston State University. http://nationalforum.com/Electronic journal volumes/Lunenburg, Fred C Expectancy Theory Altering Expectations IJMBA v15 NI 2011.PDF

value.* It is clear that this theory covers both physiological and psychological needs. However, it does not openly address either focusing on the mental process behind the assessment instead.

The freezing section of the Action Research Model is composed of "Data Gathering after Action" and if we are looking at it in the perpetual cycle (see the connection between "Data Gathering after Action" and "Feedback to Key Client or Group") it initiates another movement/change cycle. This is in alignment with what we discussed in the change section of the Action Research Model. This is the basic model most Organizational Developmental personnel prefer due to its cyclic construction. This cyclic nature can also be seen in the Positive Model for change; the only discernable difference between the Action Research Model and the Positive Model for this section is essentially where the loop connects back to as far as general change processes. The Positive Model loops back further into the "Unfreezing" section than the Action Research model.

4.1.2.4 Planned Change Summary

In the planned change section, we took a look at three basic change models by using Lewin's Planned Change model as a benchmark for comparison for the other two models. This was to show that while the philosophy behind change models has developed over time the basic structure remains similar to what was developed greater than fifty years ago. Change occurs when the tension between as is (perceived or real) and desired is enough to facilitate some form of action. This tension is affected by both the individuals within the organization and the environment of the organization. If the tension (need for change) is seen by the individuals, but organization is not perceptive then the change is less likely to occur. However, a change will occur in the personnel of the organization in this situation that will make any change desired later by the organization itself harder to facilitate. This concept is also conversely (Organization to Individual) true.

The philosophical change over time that has occurred has mainly been as a result of a deeper understanding of both social and individual psychology. This itself is a prime example of how learning and the collection of knowledge changes things at least as far as our understanding of those things. It may not actually affect the how or why, but once we understand more, our perception changes and thus changes what we think. This is evident by how social constructionism has become part of change models, something that initially was not even considered.

---

* Lenenburg, F. C. (2015). *Expectancy theory of motivation: Motivating by altering expectations.* International journal of Management, Business, and Administration, 15(1), 1-6, Sam Houston State University. http://nationalforum.com/Electronic journal volumes/Lunenburg, Fred C Expectancy Theory Altering Expectations IJMBA v15 NI 2011.PDF

Figure 4.3 It is important to explore when defects are found, that bring up change that may not be planned.

4.1.3 Unplanned Change

What is a unplanned change? While change is always occurring it happens whether it is planned or not planned. What we mean in this context is change in response to an accident or incident. This type of change usually is associated with a critique or team learning session and a cause map to facilitate a rapid response and return to the action that was interrupted by the issue or accident. This type of precipitous responses usually come without the checks and balances of a planned change and thus serves as little more than a bandage on a severe wound. Also, with an unplanned change there is usually little thought given to validating the change: quality points for verification, via follow on inspections or predetermined assessment points. This is not to say that all changes need to be planned; if the process for an effective root cause analysis is employed and follow up corrective actions are thoroughly reviewed and understood, this response can be as effective as a planned change. However, experience has shown that in most of these type cases, even when the changes are thoughtfully developed, little is implemented to ensure the changes last.

4.2 Social Dynamic of Change

Already discussed is how social networks within the organization can spread those things learned while doing the work. It is also true these same networks can help propagate and perpetuate the corporate change initiatives. Change itself is a process of social transformation for the organization and for the individual, and as such it is incumbent upon the organization to acknowledge and understand this impact. Experience suggests many change initiatives fail or take a very long time to take hold.

4.2.1 Social and Organizational Norms

Social and organizational norms are the behaviors that are most commonly accepted or considered appropriate.* This is not to infer that the action is deemed either acceptable or appropriate by the individuals that comprise the group but are by the group itself. It also does not infer the opposite either. This is to mean that while a group or organization may act in a particular manner it

Figure 4.4 The social structure of the organization has a big impact on spreading and perpetuating the change.

---

* Dannals, J. E., & Miller, D. T. (2017, November 10). Social Norms in Organizations. Retrieved February 4, 2019, from http://oxfordre.com/business/view/10.1093/ acrefore/9780190224851.001.0001/acrefore-9780190224851-e-139

may or may not reflect the norms of the individuals that comprise that group or organization. As an example, we have all seen people who act one way when in one setting and a different way when placed in another setting but doesn't agree with either (Descriptive and Prescriptive norms)*. This behavior would be in line with Argyris's espoused and action theory.† This dynamic has a major effect on how we must approach the act of changing or developing our organization. If a norm is what is considered to be accepted or appropriate, then we must look at who determines that to implement a change in this area. In this aspect of change the leadership is the primary change agent as that which is considered acceptable or appropriate is determined primarily by the leadership. That is not to say that there are not some societal influences on organizational norms, but that influence is not predominate.

I am sure that some of the managers who are reading this would be asking, "How do I change an established norm?" The first question is not how do you change the norm, but should be how was the norm established (see Bruce Tuckman)? This question will allow you to understand what actions to take to shift the norm. Did it become a norm because it was allowed to happen without any correction; was it the change of what was or is acceptable in the overall society now; or was it a shift in the organization itself?

The organization's social norms will influence the project norms, but not necessarily drive the project norms. We have been in projects that established their own norms, within some constraints, that are different from the overall organization.

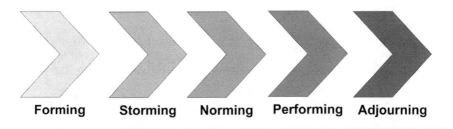

Forming   Storming   Norming   Performing   Adjourning

Figure 4.5 Team dynamic is not static as demonstrated via Bruce Tuckman's team development model

---

* Dannals, J. E., & Miller, D. T. (2017, November 10). Social Norms in Organizations. Retrieved February 4, 2019, from http://oxfordre.com/business/view/10.1093/acrefore/9780190224851.001.0001/acrefore-9780190224851-e-139
† Burke, W. W. (2015). *Organization Development: A process of learning and changing.* Place of publication not identified: Pearson.

4.2.1.1 Acceptance of Actions

If an action is done that is not in alignment with the current organization norms and no action is taken to provide some form of feedback as to its unacceptability, then that can be taken to mean that it is acceptable. This then and commonly is promulgated as the new norm for that activity or that individual at a minimum. The application of norms must also be equal; this means that for any group there should not be one norm for part of the group and another for a different section of the group. That would not make it a norm. This division of norms in and unto itself negates the norm for both groups and creates an atmosphere of animosity or ambiguity.

In our experience, projects can often develop a permutation of the organization's norms. The less bureaucratic level of formalism with the project management activities, the greater the possibility the project norms can deviate from the organization's norms. We are not suggesting that a project can have a radically different set of norms than the organization, only some local adaptation, subtle alteration to the orgranizational norms.

4.2.1.2 Societal Changes

As societal norms change so do the norms or at least the norms shown by businesses change. A good example would be that of sustainable resources. Society has become

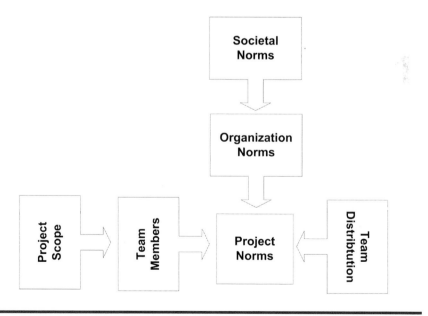

Figure 4.6 Societal cultural norms influence organization norms, and subsequently project norms.

more concerned with resource management and leveraged their consumer power to show companies of this concern. And thus, many companies have shifted to being centered around resource management, if not at least on the surface for the consumer to see. We must also address that not all the positions held by society, the group outside the company, are acted upon in such a manner as the example above. There are many cases where this group acts counter to its own words: another example of Argyris's espoused and action theory.* An example of this would be when the consumer disagrees with how a company does something, but due to price and availability they continue to buy the product of said company. At this point you are probably asking, "What does this have to do with organizational change?" and to answer that question we must look at the makeup of the organization and what their goal is.

The makeup of the organization is important because everyone brings their own norms in the beginning of their employment based upon those norms previously established in their lives. The norms that are brought may or may not enhance the organization; it is only through an open and honest dialog between the employer and employee(s) that this can be determined. This open and honest dialog is referred to as the mental model† or as I have referred to it in previous chapters, the open mental model. It neither accepts nor rejects the position (norm) of another but seeks to understand the basis for it to determine how it will aid in the growth of both the individual and the organization.

The goal of the organization comes into play in what type of organization it is, a learning organization or not. If the organization is not one that employs the learning organizational and developmental model, then the norms brought by the people who compromise the organization will have little to no meaning. This in most cases will promote worker dissatisfaction through lack of interaction.

4.2.1.3 Organizational Shifts

In line with societal changes upon an organization organizational shift in our context is a change that occurs due to a change in the management structure. We have all been a part of an organization that has had a change in the managers and thus a change in how the organization peruses its goals. While the overall goal of the organization may or may not change, the manner in which is taken to achieves the objective will adapt as learning and environmental factors require. This is predominately due to the new management's desire to align the organization with their perspectives. While as we stated this is commonly associated with new management it can also be related by new employees at lower levels. The norms they bring to the organization will have to be addressed in one way or another. These norms should not be dismissed without understanding if they would improve the organization or not. And the individual who brought those new norms should be provided some justification as to why or

---

* Burke, W. W. (2015). *Organization Development: A process of learning and changing.* Place of publication not identified: Pearson.
† Kleiner, A., & Senge, P. M. (1994). *The Fifth discipline fieldbook.* London: Nicholas Brearley.

why not they are accepted. This would be a motivational aspect of developing an individual and reinforcing the organizational norm, new or not.

4.2.1.4 Social Change and Trauma

It should be well understood that well engaged team members improve the probability of desired changes taking place and even taking hold. So what sort of things can get in the way of getting well engaged team members? In earlier chapters this has been discussed, but what has not been reviewed are the social portion of the change management that may make or break the change objective.

Change is generally not a rational process. Why do people change? Let me offer these statements as part of a change theory. People change because:

■ They become aware of some conditions, factors, or circumstances that make them less content.
■ They experience these conditions, factors, or circumstances as occurring outside their current ability to control.
■ They become aware that others, whom they respect, are experiencing this discontent and inability to control the events.
■ They also become aware that someone or some group whom they respect has proposed a way to deal with this shared experience of discontent and inability to control.
■ They become aware of a groundswell of support, especially among people whom they respect, for this new approach.
■ They join their respected peers in support of this new approach.*

The author goes on to conclude that for most people change is a collectively social and emotional transformation.

One way to assuage the emotional aspects of the change is to include the team members or employees in the change, that includes identifying what needs to be changed, and the planning for how to go about work of bringing the desired change to fruition. Afterall, the change will not take root or grow without the motivation and heavy involvement of those likely significantly impacted by the change, the employee or team member.

Organization change has been compared to the stages of death. It is possible that our team members may be going through some of these steps when it comes to changes in the organization. Changes do not impact singularly, but often some significant portions of the company.

■ Denial
■ Anger

---

* Scholtes, P. R. (1988). *The Leader's Handbook: Making things happen, getting things done.* New York: McGraw-Hill. page 221

- Bargaining
- Depression
- Acceptance

4.2.1.5 Social Change and Epidemics

We can learn considerably about the social component of change. The book *Tipping Point* by Malcolm Gladwell* explores the social reasons why some things seem to quickly establish and become a big sensation. These key players are identified as:

- Connectors: people with a special gift for bringing the world together. These people provide a social glue to the organization.
- Mavens: people who accumulate knowledge; these people are socially motivated to share knowledge and want to help others with decisions. Mavens are teachers
- Salesmen: are people with the skills to persuade us when we are unconvinced by what we hear.

It is also possible to look at the adopters to change similarly to how new technology products are introduced. In Information Week's article, *5 Social Business Adopter Types: Prepare Early* (the table below is derived from that article[†]), we can see that we have varying degrees of work depending on growth toward accepting and making the change we desire to see in the organization to take root.

Name	Description	Percentage
Innovators	Adopts because it is new, these are explorers.	2.5%
Early adopters	Opinion leaders, like innovators in quick to adopt but concerned about reputation and perception.	13.5%
Early Majority	Seeks productivity and practice benefits over reputation.	34%
Late Majority	Expects considerable help and support before they are willing to make the change.	34%
Laggards	Slow to adopt, resists change and forced to make the move and adopt the change.	16%

---

* Insert tipping point reference
† https://www.informationweek.com/software/social/5-social-business-adopter-types-prepare-early/d/d-id/898950 last accessed 1/28/ 2019

4.3 Change for the Sake of Change

There is an old joke, how many psychiatrists does it take to change a light bulb, only one, but the light bulb must really want to change. It is similar for organizations. Change can take great effort for an individual; an organization is a collection of connected individuals, which makes the change more complicated and difficult. Why, then, undertake change for the sake of change? If there is no specific goal or objective for the organization, some improvement, some benefit, why undertake the change? Why would a company spend time, talent, and resources to make the change? The answer, they would not. However, as we discussed in organizational shifts, we know that organizations do change for the sake of change or, better stated, so that someone can feel they have left their mark on the organization.

4.4 Change for Improvement

We have discussed change for the sake of change, change caused by organizational shifts, and change due to societal changes. We would be remiss if we did not at least discuss the real reason that a change should be implemented. Most organizations are in some sort of competitive environment, some companies more subjected to this than others. In response to this competitive pressure, the organization will adapt to the circumstances to ensure the company is truly a long-term endeavor. This may require constant adapting to forces external and internal to the organization, as well as the short- and long-term goals of that organization. It would be folly to believe that an organization will only need to change one thing and be done with the change. It is also folly to believe that simply saying "the organization needs to bring products to market faster" works.

4.5 Know your Gear Pattern

There are many things that impact the way our company works and therefore the best way to introduce changes to the company will require considering these other attributes that influence the way the organization works, navigating those that help and those obstacles that hinder our change initiatives.

- ■ Organization structure – the structure of the organization influences and can easily hinder our change objectives. Consider the functional organization, often referred to as a silo or stove pipe organizational structure. Communication between the departments is often difficult; competing priorities between those team's present challenges as well. The problems that arise from this competitive environment may have been solved via compromise or another approach which may have led to a sub-optimized solution.

- Management philosophy – the company's approach to management will have implications on the way we approach the change. For example, a command and control approach would require an approach that differs from an organization that has long established roots in employee empowerment.
- Market demands – also can be the pressures of delivery on our organization and can distract or corrupt our change management initiatives. Unless we connect the daily work with the change we want to have happen in our organization, we can expect to see some resistance. The more stressed our people are by the demand of the job, for example throughput demands, the less available they may be for the change.
- Legal constraints – if our company produces products that are subject to legal constraints, the uncertainty of these uncertainties likely do us no favors when it comes to the change.
- Pre-existing policies and procedures – our company has some associated inertia in part comes from the processes and procedures used to perform the work. A company may work diligently to ingrain the present way of working, and to move from one way of doing the work to another can take time and changing of habits the company once thought to be beneficial.
- Geographic distribution – organizational change must also consider the geographic distribution of the company, which would include things such as specific language and social norms for the region. If the work of the company requires these various geographic regions to work together rather than being separate and unique entities, we have further communications and logistical complications to our organization change.
- Socioeconomic construct – an organization may be the proverbial big fish in the town when it comes to employment. In these cases, the company may have considerable leverage or ability to push the desired change onto the employees. If the company is the best employer in the town, and people do not wish to leave that town, the employee is, so to say, captive.

4.5.1 Selecting the Right Change Management Strategy

Like any endeavor the best chance for success is matching a strategy to the strengths and away from any weaknesses. Weighted and unweighted decision tools such as Pugh matrix can help in the decision-making process, as well as decision trees, Strength, Weakness, Opportunity and Threat analysis, and other decision critiquing methods.

Selecting the best strategy may not be so easily determined even using these tools. There may be times when these tools provide no solace or help at arriving at the best solution. No matter the approach taken, it is necessary to take measurements of key variables. Those variables depend entirely upon the objectives and goals of the organization. It is not possible to provide a prescription without understanding the attributes of the company as well as the objectives of that company. No matter

**Self Directed
Work Team**

Figure 4.7 There has been a movement toward self-directed work teams.

the objective, the strategy, or the associated risks, measurements will inform the status of the work, and this can be compared to the end objective where alteration of strategy or tactics is taken.

There are limits to these tools and techniques. The outcome is only as good as the critical thinking and effort put into the assessment. Not matter how the strategy is derived, identifying specific measurements that are associated with the desired improvement area will be prudent. In this way, it is possible to assess the efforts put forth against the objective, providing some feedback regarding the suitability of the efforts undertaken to meet the objective.

4.6 Unintended Consequences of Change

It should be clear after the previous chapters that things happen in which we could have never conceived or envisioned the consequences. Therefore, our explorations should be incremental, testing out those things we think we know, without exposing the entire organization to the risk of change that is not well considered. It is true that it is not possible to predict the total range of unintended things that can happen in the course of our doing the work. That is the reason we run these exploratory testings; we consider those results before we set about inculcating this change to the organization at large.

Of course, there are times when the unintended consequence is favorable or represents an opportunity upon which we can build or extend the improvement. In these cases, we can work to understand the nature of the opportunity (positive unintended consequences) and determine if this discovery is something accidental or perhaps in fact serendipity due to the exploration we have undertaken. If it is serendipity, it may be that this is not really an opportunity but some random event that coincides with the effort of improvement we have undertaken.

4.7 Management Effect on Change

Management likely means different things to different people. There are probably as many definitions of management as there are people, and equally as many opinions or perspectives about what constitutes good management. To be sure what was considered effective management 30 years ago would be considered by and large ineffective by today's standards.

To be sure, management must be behind the change and plays a significant part in the change. However, there is a line between helpful, and overbearing. There are many management styles, some of which will aid learning, facilitate experimentation and learning, and other styles will squash exploration, experimentation, and learning. The range of management expression that can be employed organizations have a variety of structures and there has been movement toward empowerment via self-directed work teams. These teams do not have a single person sanctioned as a leader from the organization. Rather, the leadership is more nebulous and depending upon the situation or circumstances rather than a person defined by the organization as the lead.

4.7.1 Laissez-Faire Management

Management must take a hand when it comes to ensuring the organization, individuals, and the systems have a focus that is convergent or congruent. There may be times when management should take a more hands-off approach, this is called Laissez-Faire (an policy of letting things take their own course - non-interference). However, management has responsibilities to the organization, employees and shareholders. Should it be possible that management can have this approach?

4.7.2 Intrusive Management

Intrusive management is sometimes colloquially referred to as seagull management. It is the name of the management philosophy that refers to the manager that flies in, squawks and craps on everything and then flies off. Intrusive management can

Leadership Style	Description	Style Leadership	
		Task Behavior	Relationship Behavior
Autocratic Leadership	This style of leadership is based upon the leader and their control and authority over their personel. This type of leader makes the descisions without consultation from subordinates and informs them what they should do and expects timely and efficient response from them.	Y	
Democratic Leadership	This style of leadership is based upon communication and the subordinates providing imput to help make the decisions. While the leeader retains the responsibility they have remited their authority.		Y
Transformational Leadership	This style of leadership is all about change and challenge. These leaders promote challenging goals for all involved and assist personnel to obtain these goals through empowerment.	Y	Y
Team Leadership	This style of leadership uses a vision of a future state (application of mission, vision, and values statements) to capture the desire of the person or group to achieve that future state, in visioned.	Y	Y
Facilitative Leadership	This style of leadership bases its' actions on measures and results from the group. More affective yeilds less managerial involvement, less affective yeilds more managerial involvement.	Y	
Laissez-faire Leadership	This leadership style takes the Democratic leadership style to the next level in that it remits authority to subordinates and they are emabled to proceed as they determine necessary with little to no managerial involvement.	Y	
Transactional Leadership	This leadership style is based primarily on quid pro quoe: subordinates obtain immediate and tangable rewards to comply with leaderships direction. This style can provide guidance on the how meet expectations and what rewards will be received contingent upon results.	Y	Y
Visionary Leadership	This style of leadership is employed by those leaders that understand that all objectives are obtained from and with employee assistance. This leader shares and nurtures their vision within the employee to make it become a group vision and then all parties work toward that end.	Y	Y
Coaching Leadership	This style of leadership is operationally centered and subordinates are assisted in improving their performance, knowledge, and skills.	Y	Y

Figure 4.8 Management style has impacts on the work and the relationships.

interfere with team learning as the manager directs and defines the actions the team is to take. This sometimes missing and sometimes heavily directing are not consistent and not helpful for team development.

4.7.3 Authoritarian Management

Authoritarian management is sometimes required, but when it comes to experiments and learning by doing the work, this is not the management style. Authoritarian management, if ever, is for times when the organization is exposed to serious risks, damage to customers and employees, or exposure to costly legal actions and then it may require authoritarian approaches. Experience suggests that authoritarian management style does not allow room for team learning, that much of this style consists of command and control and directed work. This command and control approach has an advantage for acutely time sensitive actions, but it is not a helpful approach when it comes to experimentation and learning This managemnet style prizes objective and immediacy over learning and experimentation.

4.7.4 Consultative Management (Democratic)

Consultative management is an approach wherein the management does not take a unilateral decision on how to proceed without the team members. Consultative management approach will be one that empowers the employees to contribute their ideas; in fact, it is not just desired but it is expected. This is exactly the opposite of the authoritarian approach to management. The manager does not set instructions; there may be organization process assets to which the tean must comport, but there may be times when either this process documentation does not exist, or cannot be exactly executed according to the process standard, thus allowing space for learning and creation.

When it comes to continuous improvement effort, consultative management also is part of any organization improvement. For example, root cause analysis is not the sort of thing that comes from a management structure but from those closely tied to the work. Prudent management approaches will try to get as many varied inputs to organization improvement as possible, and then use some mechanism to evaluation for benfit and probablity of success.

4.7.4.1 Coach

Coaching management approach considers the talent and competencies of the team members, and works to develop these. This style of leadership is like the coach of a sports team, they help the individual team members increase and inprove their respective competencies and capabilities. and the capabilities of the department or company. The coach works to evoke identify organization objectives and goals from the team member as well as uncover actions to take to achieve those goals. In this way, the coach is helping the team member achieve their objectives by ensuring the individual gets project work that helps the individual to grow and develop those skills to be able to achieve their goals as well as that of the organization.

4.7.4.2 Visionary

Visionary leaders inspire and tap into the emotional component of the work and the objectives of the work that is presently underway. The visionary connects the individual to the work creating a bond with the individual and the goals and objectives. As the name indicates, the visionary works to create and establish a vision of the organization. The vision is not very helpful if the vision remains in the head of the manager. It is therefore important the vision be articulated sufficiently to engage the team members. There are limits to this leadership style, for example, this vision focus is on a long time horizon, and is not good for the short term or immediate activities or effort.

4.7.4.3 Servant

There is arguably a new approach to the work at some companies collectively referred to as agile. In agile (a variant of which is a scrum), the team is empowered and as close to self-organizing as an organization can get. There is a responsibility within that agile within this approach known as scrum master. The scrum master helps the team to organize the work and help to solve problems. The role of the scrum master is a servant leadership role. This approach, when executed well, can go a long way to building team morale, along with helping the team members find work within the project that more closely matches the desires and motivating work for that individual.

> A leader is best when people barely know he exists, when his work is done, his aim fulfilled, they will say: we did it ourselves. ~ Lao Tzu

4.7.5 Pacesetter

This style of leadership is employed when quick progress is required. We need fast results. These leaders are focused on performance, specifically output and throughput. This leadership approach requires a team that is well established and more to the point well trained in their respective craft. This is not a style that is conducive to learning on the job, as what is prized is the speed of execution and fast results. Learning requires time to explore and assimilate what is observed.

4.7.6 Transformational

Transformational and coaching styles are similar, both require constant and clear communication with a focus on identification and achievement of goals. Like the pacesetter, an emphasis is placed on maintaining morale; however, unlike the pacesetter and the focus on the goals of the individual, the focus is on the organization's objectives. Transformational leaders, because of their focus on the organization objectives, will need significant delegation of areas of responsiblity. Therefore, this type of leadership requires that the level of capability of each team member match that of the delegated responsibility. This can be a great opportunity for team learning, as the team members will need to be empowered to accomplish the objectives, and since the focus is on the objectives and the end results, the methods may not be dictated. The exception may be in the case of mandatory processes and adherence.

4.7.7 Transactional

Transactional leaders will focus on the performance and provide incentives for that performance. The leader or manager will establish the rewards for specific performance, usually monetary. The reward system can have negative implications, driving behavior contrary to the organization's objectives and goals.

4.7.8 Bureaucratic

Bureaucratic leaders focus on the procedures and policies of the company. This makes the style a bit comparable to autocratic style. Bureaucratic styles focus more on doing things by process and procedures and autocratic styles are more driven from command and control of the leader. There will be a formalized area of responsibility that goes along with the process and proecedures. In this way, any learning by an individual will likely be in their area of responsiblity and by dint of execution in the form of the processes. This can dampen cross functional learning.

Chapter 5

Following Up to
Ensure Success

No matter the objective, strategy, or tactics taken, it is necessary to understand the present position of the company as it compares to the desired result of that organization. Like a pilot measuring the route to the desired destination, they must navigate bad weather, account for wind impact to course, and a myriad of other factors to ensure safe arrival at the destination. It is similar for steering the organization, only more complicated since for an organization to change requires more than one person (pilot) or a small collection of people (the flight deck and air traffic control) to be involved. Unlike the pilot scenario, it is important to keep all relevant staff engaged in the change process. Besides the extra sets of eyes on the effort to ensure we are actually making progress this constant review promotes inclusion and engagement and help effectively navigate risks to success.

Following up, it seems, is is no easy task, experience suggests this to be a common failure mode in projects and organization improvement. It is not as simple as measure things, and follow up on what is witnessed; those things are just the mechanics. The method in which the measurements are acquired matter, as this may tell us something of the validity of the measurements or whether the measurement adequately represents the true situation. This requires measuring the appropriate variable and measuring appropriately as to not bring any bias or error into the measurement. To be able to take effective action requires learning about the situation or process.

In quantum physics, there is a principle known as the observer effect. The observer effect states that the act of observing a phenomenon changes that phenomenon. Attaching measuring instruments such as oscilloscope probes, for example, alters the characteristics of the electrical signal under exploration. There

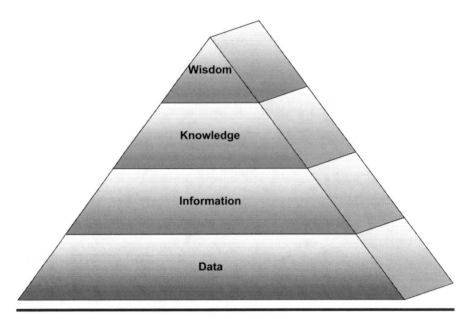

Figure 5.1 There is a hierarchy of knowledge.

is a similar principle for psychology by the same name and is sometimes referred to as the Hawthorne effect that originated from a study of the Hawthorne plant of Western Electric Company by Elton Mayo and Fritz Roethlisberger in the 1920's. This study started as an exploration of the effect of work environment (for example lighting) on employee performance. The result of the study was quite interesting.

At the lowest level, clumps of data are throughout the company. Collecting these clumps, and manipulation (not corruption) from raw numbers to something understandable from which we could learn requires careful actions This means data manipulation without bias. The results, of this manipulation is information from which we can take actions to promote greater understanding. For example, projects produce data not matter the method of project management employed. In this way, measurements are fodder for understanding what to change, and provide clues as to how to change, ultimately to see the impact of those changes and ensure the company moving in the desired direction.

5.1 Hawthorne Study

There are times when we set out to understand how things work, with some notion of what matters. Our experiments will often reflect this bias. For example, if we believe light to be a particle, then we will set up an experiment to see if we are correct, which will include looking at light from the particle perspective. The perspective or theory selected will influence the parameters of the experiment. However, it is possible (and in this case is also true) that light has wave properties and particle properties. An experiment focused on proving or disproving particle theory will not discover this wave element and will lead us to the conclusion that light is a particle.

> It is usually agreed that, historically, the merger of industry and the behavioral sciences in their current form becan with the research conducted by Elton Mayo and his colleagues in the Hawthorn plant of Western Electric Company.*

The original objective of the Hawthorne study was to understand how workplace illumination affect worker productivity.[†] The study discovered that as illumination goes up, so to did productivity. That is not odd. However, as illumination decreased, the productivity also increased, including as low a level as moonlight. This resulted in the abandonment the illumination studies, changing to areas such as rest periods, work week, incentive plans, free lunch and supervisory styles. Eventually the team brought in Elton Mayo who brough a *"psychology of the total situation"*. He concluded

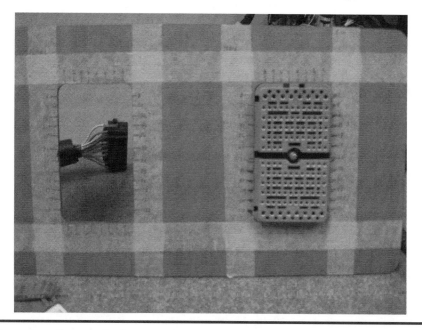

Figure 5.2 Changes forthe organization of for the product are simiar, check and then change.

---

* Luthans, F. (1972). Contemporary readings in organizational behavior. New York: McGraw-Hill.
† Hopp, W. J., & Spearman, M. L. (2012). Factory Physics. Milano: McGraw Hill. page 36

that the results were "*primarily due to a remarkable change of mental attitude in the group*". The simplistic distillation of this over the years has resulted in the moniker the Hawthorne Effect, which suggests the increase in productivity is due to the attention given to the workers under study. Mayo thought this overly simplistic was more attributed to the groups sense of belonging in connection with the work.

5.2 Measure Twice, Change Once

It may sound easy but measuring comes with many challenges. Measurements will often provide the rationale as well as the direction for the organization to change. Understanding what to change, and how to go about doing so, will require some understanding of where the company is presently and where it wants to go in the future.

When it comes to measurements, we must consider all the variation that comes with variables and measurements. There is variation in the process (σ_p) variation due to our sampling routine (σ_s) and variation due to measuring (σ_m).

$$\sigma_t^2 = \sigma_p^2 + \sigma_s^2 + \sigma_m^2$$

The measurement variation is determined by identifying the variation due to the scale or physical measurement system and that of the human interpretation of that scale. To understand this, we perform Gauge Repeatability and Reproducibility (Gauge R&R).

$$\sigma_m^2 = \sigma_r^2 + \sigma_h^2$$

The Gauge R&R is part of the Measurement Systems Analysis (MSA) book published by the Automotive Industry Action Group (AIAG) and is part of the Advanced Product Quality Planning process typically employed in automotive product development and manufacturing. To understand the details of this process, consult that book. However, the objective is to understand the variation in the measurement system due to the tools used in the measurement system along with the impact of the people using those tools on the resulting measurement. Each of these impacts the final reported or recorded result.

> Repeatability reflects the variation in measurements made by an operator using one gage to repeatedly measure the same feature of the same part. Reproducibility reveals how closely one operator can duplicate the measurements of a second operator for the identical characteristics of a part using the same gage.*

---

* Bothe, D. R. (2002). *Reducing process variation: Using the DOT*STAR problem-solving strategy.* Cedarburg, WI: Landmark Publishing. Page 166

No matter the measuring system approach, time should be allocated to analyze the system to understand the veracity of the system or the system's ability to adequately inform the true circumstances.

5.2.1 What Should Be Measured?

In some cases, the organization is likely already taking a variety of measurements that inform performance, cost, and allow for some predictions. Organizations that have a high degree of processes often have data from those processes that can facilitate understanding, provided the appropriate things are measured appropriately. If this information is at hand, then the chore is distilled down this data, that is, turn it into some sort of interpretable information from which decisions can be made. However, it could be prudent to review how the data was collected and question whether this data is representative of the process from which the data theoretically originates. Experience suggests it is possible the measurement is taken from a process although few, if anybody, are following the process. Neglecting to consider this will provide a distorted view of the situation and therefore the experiments performed to learn how to improve will also be impaired.

5.2.2 How Should We Measure?

As good as modern camera equipment and control systems are, it is possible that the sample size could be all products and the measurements and calculations could be automated also, thus removing as much as possible the human factors in the data acquisition, at least beyond the equipment set up.

The *Leaders Handbook* provides 8 simple steps as hints for getting started.* Below is a short synopsis of what should be thought through before we charge off measuring.

1. Define the purpose of the data gathering systems.
2. Pick a priority measurement target.
3. Identify the purpose of the process to be measured.
4. Identify the measurement and the purpose of the measurement.
5. How will this measure fit into a larger system of measures?
6. Develop operational definitions.
7. Plan and prepare for the data collection.
8. Gather the data.

While these 8 steps are a good start they neglect to address the gaming of data due to misunderstanding. By that we mean that if data is collected by a group, and they assume the data is collected for other than process improvement reasons,

---

* Scholtes, P. R. (1988). *The leaders handbook: Making things happen, getting things done.* New York: McGraw-Hill. Page 242

possibly manpower reduction, they might manipulate the data such that they feel safe. According to Burke's interpretation of Lewin's model for change the data collected to facilitate change is the individual's reaction to the collection of that data.* To this end, we say that communication of the purpose of the data collection must be effective and minimize the adverse reaction to the collect of said data.

5.2.3 Who Should Measure?

The measuring is as much about involvement of the team as the review of the results of the measurement are, or at least it should be. The goal is not to run as quickly as possible, but to move as much of the team toward this understanding of the present process or situation, as well as deriving methods for improvement. To do this requires involvement in the objective in such a way to facilitate team learning. This does not happen from reading a book or searching a database for something the team member may know nothing about. How do you search for something that you do not know exists?

In many cases measurements are automated when the process has a simple such as an assembly line or other simple process. In fact, we have seen this automation of data collection come with some downside, as the team members no longer are concerned about the process data since it is automated and on display for all to see. Perrhaps this is an overconfidence in the automated system, that creates a gap in the team members attention and knowledge.

While these throughput numbers can point to and organization or product functionality issues[†] they rarely provide a revelation or connection to true process improvement. When you couple this with the flaws inherent to individual data collection it would seem there is no real answer to who, what, when, where, and

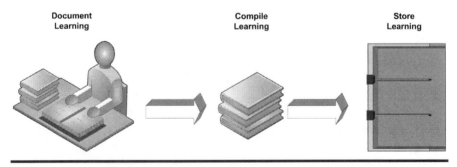

Figure 5.3 After taking the measurements we need to find ways to store so we can turn into information.

---

* Burke, W. W. (2015). *Organizaton Development: A process of learning and changing.* Place of publication not identified: Pearson.

† Cummings, T. G. (2018). *Organizaton Development* and Change. S.l.: Cengage Learning.

how data for change should be collected. So, how do we proceed? Let us think first of the system and how it is comprised. To answer the "who" question we need only determine the purpose of the data collection. When we understand who will be affected by the changes facilitated by the data and how that relates to the system as a whole we will understand those groups and teams that should be collecting and analyzing it. The key here is systems thinking in that it provides us an understanding of the ties between processes and thus facilitates a more effective change because it is aligned with the larger parts of the organization*

5.2.4 How Do We Turn Data into Information?

The approach we take to analyzing this raw information will be influenced by what it is that is *desired to be learned*. In an earlier chapter, there was a review of common Total Quality Management (TQM) tools that help to turn data into information from which learning and subsequent action can be taken. These tools can facilitate understanding and it is beneficial for many if not all of our team members to be

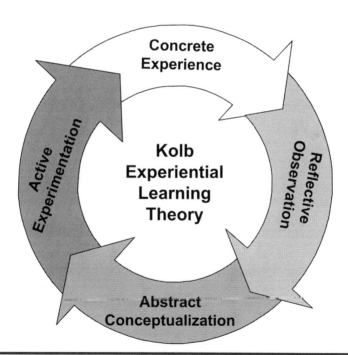

Figure 5.4 The importance of experience on learning is demonstrated in Kolb experiental learning theory.

---

* Kleiner, A., & Senge, P. M. (1994). *The Fifth discipline fieldbook.* London: Nicholas Brearley.

skilled in these techniques. If we approach the data that has been collected with a specific item to be learned then that is all we shall find, and we may not find data that helps in understanding that specific item. Care should be employed not to miss the hemorrhaging part of a process because we are looking for a splinter. The Pareto analysis is a good TQM tool to help us prioritize.

If we look at Kolb's experiential learning cycle, we see four stages of learning. You are probably asking, "Why are we talking about learning in the section of turning data into information?" Turning data into information and then using that information to facilitate a depending action is the very definition of the learning process. Kolb's model consists of four sections: Concrete Experience, Reflective Observation, Abstract Conceptualization, and Active Experimentation, with each stage both being supported and supported by its predecessor and successor.[*] We are discussing this because to change the raw data into information we need experience with how the system operates or should operate and an open mental model about how the system can and should be affected by external forces.

5.2.5 How Do We Display?

It is important to remember that this exercise in measuring and understanding is not just for the person making the measurements, that specific department, or just for management. It is for all our team members. A part of the goal is to propagate all the learning in the company, through the many experiments that are underway at any given time within in the organization. As the saying goes, "it is okay to make

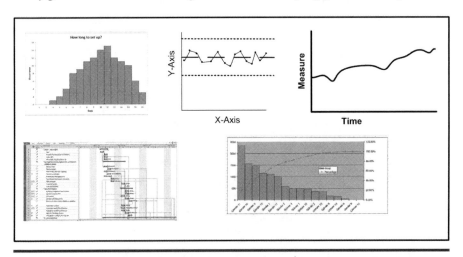

Figure 5.5 Project dashboards display the state of the project for all to see.

* Mcleod, S. (2017, February 05). *Kolb's Learning Styles and Experiential Learning Cycle*. Retrieved February 19, 2019, from https://www.simplypsychology.org/learning-kolb.html

mistakes" but the appendage to that saying can often be "but can't we make different mistakes for a change."

There are several ways in which displaying the measurement results. For example, manufacturing organizations may have electronic signs around the facility that presents the latest state of the key performance information (KPI) for the various departments as well as the company at large. The data may be presented in graphical form as a dashboard of performance of the collection of key metrics of the company. In fact, it is quicker for the mind to assimilate a collection of ideas. Reading and understanding takes time, graphical representations can be more quickly understood. The problem is when the graphical representation becomes so remedial that actual imparting specific information, is impossible - think the green smiley face graphic, everything is going well. By what measure?

Projects require measurements the same as operations of the organization. In fact, organizations with mature project management practices, will often have project dashboards that keep key elements of the project easily visible. In agile or lean approaches, this dashboard may be stripped down, but the dashboard still exists. In these instances we may use a Kanban approach to the work flow and measures, a quick Trello example is provided (we use the product but have no business connections to the product).

The data gathered and the objective will have some bearing on how the data is displayed. An executive may not always need to see the minute division of the data where project managers and team members will need more specific information as their understanding of the system is more detailed and they are responsible for taking action or overall interacting with the system.

It is beneficial to make these data display systems as prominent as possible within the organization or the department. Displays that figure prominently in the organization make it possible for other departments to see the state of their work and connecting work. A constant focus on the things the company believes important helps instill focus and can help reinforce the cultural connection to the measurements.

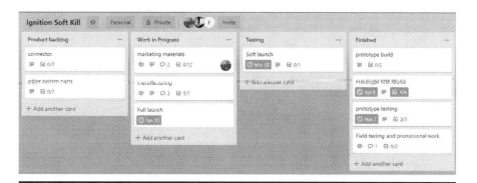

Figure 5.6 Kanban boards can be used for project management as well, this one is an online version called Trello.

5.2.6 Design Process Performance Metrics which Drive Improvement

The first step of designing process performance metrics for improvement is understanding what to measure and the why behind that measurement. This should be approached in a twofold manner: one for the issues which impede the growth or change and another for nature of the change itself. This is that change and/or development has two distinct parts: those actions or items which make it grow and sustain it, and those actions or items which naturally inhibit or slow its development. In the book "The Dance of Change" by Peter Senge this topic is related to biological growth. For an organism to grow it must have certain things it requires, and this and other factors naturally inhibit this growth.*

While it would seem that these topics belong in the preceding chapter they are more integral to developing a useful metric through process understanding than they are in developing the ideas for a change.

5.2.6.1 Inhibitors to Change

If we use the model of biological growth like Senge does in *The Dance of Change*, we can see that anything that promotes growth or development can also be an inhibitor. This can result in a demonstration of the theory of constraints. The process is developed, puts demand upon resources, this demand it takes more resources which begins to reduce the rate of growth. At some point could and probably will actually diminish throughput and growth. Looking for these types of links, System Thinking,[†] between the change and its resources we can identify resource indicators that becomer metrics that will key us into these constraints before they occur. Another point in the resource are is, "How many other areas rely on that resource and what is their rate of development or growth in that resource?"

Some of these types of inhibitors may require more of a non-quantifiable way of measuring due to being more of a cultural dynamic of the organization itself. There may be no tangible quantifiable measurements to gage progress or limits. There may be a qualifiable metric or event that can help us to glean some perspective. According to Burke in his book Organization Development, A Process of Learning and Change is best done by identifying the critical values and incorporating them within the organization's behavior, thus promoting the cultural change.[‡] Qualitative data may not be possible, then develop qualitative measurements to ascertain some connection or correlation between the efforts undertaken and the desired impact

---

* Senge, P. (1999). *The dance of change*. News York: Doubleday.
† Kleiner, A., & Senge, P. M. (1994). *The Fifth Discipline Fieldbook*. London: Nicholas Brearley.
‡ Burke, W. W. (2015). *Organization Development: A process of learning and changing*. Place of publication not identified: Pearson.

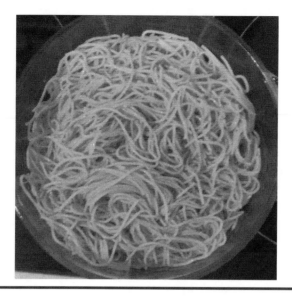

Figure 5.7 Sorting out how to approach organization change is like untangling a tangled up mess.

on the behavior and culture of the organization. It should be acknowledged that the qualitative mechanism may be more difficult to identify and assess, but these are still useful. A behavioral change or cultural change could be assessed with quantifiable data, but this attribute might take more time to develop into something measurable.

5.2.6.2 Necessary Change Items

We have reviewed numerous items that are required for change, but not addressed how to determine a link between a growth enhancing item and the change itself. Since we have discussed growth items previously, we will be using this section to discuss how to determine change items. One may think this is an easy process, but in truth it is one if not the primary reason most changes fail after the' initial surge. This topic is also important when determining how and what to look at for the analysis of a change. Let's continue the example of a plant. When we think of what a plant needs to grow we think of water, sunlight, and soil. This is true for the initial growth of the plant, but when we delve further into the development or growth of the plant we see things like space for the roots, restrictions on the available sunlight due to other plants, seasonal dynamics, compatibility with plants in the same area, and we could keep going with the list, but the point has been made. When we look at a change in the long term we can apply these types of dynamics, and when we do, we also see that even a small or seemingly small change can have further reaching dynamics than we first thought. This type of thinking or analysis is a combination

of both Peter Senge's "The Fifth Discipline"* and his book "The Dance of Change"†
and W. Warner Burke's book "Organization Development, A Process of Learning
and Change,"‡ just for starters.

Applying the principles of growth (change) analysis previously discussed, will
help in sustaining development and potentially change. There are also other items
or issues that will need to be addressed to take the potential for actual change and
development. One other such item or issue would be the nature of a habit. While
we did not address "*habits*" in the previous section specifically we pointed to other
inhibitors to change and we address it here because it is key to making a change
stick instead of allowing the situation to revert back to a previous condition and then
thinking the change was ineffective. Habits, good or bad, are or have become part
of our subconscious mind and any change to that habit requires effort and energy,
which is naturally resisted unless the gain perceived or reality is greater than the
effort or energy expended for the change.§ When we apply this line of reasoning to
our change and subsequently its analysis, we look for patterns: habit, reinforcement
to sustain the desired change.

5.2.6.3 Associated Growth Metrics

In the previous two sections we have discussed inhibitors to change and necessary
items for change and how they relate to the system as a whole, the group, and the
individual through our example of the growth cycle of plants. When we apply these
type of analytics to our change during its development we can better understand
how to see the indications of a change throughout an organization. It would seem
that we may have gotten in front of ourselves by saying "analytics". However,
this is not actually the case. When we are first designing or creating a change we
should think of the possible outcomes and how they would manifest themselves as
information or signs within our organization. This perspective also pushes those
developing the change to view the system as a whole for that change and not just
focus on a selective portion of or process associated within the organization, which
is another reason for change failure as we have discussed previously and is a prime
example of stage three tribal leadership or rice bowl mentality that plagues many
managers and organizations.

Under the aforementioned: the change to any one section of an organization or
department should be developed with at least the portion of the organization that
would naturally precede and follow the group. This review of the change through

* Kleiner, A., & Senge, P. M. (1994). The Fifth discipline fieldbook. London: Nicholas Brearley.
† Senge, P. (1999). *The dance of change*. News York: Doubleday.
‡ Burke, W. W. (2015). *Organization Development: A process of learning and changing*. Place of
publication not identified: Pearson.
§ Parvez, H. (2018). PsychMechanics. Retrieved February 26, 2019, from
https://www.psychmechanics.com/2014/12/why-habits-get-formed-nature-and.html

the work pipeline can assure the change has no adverse impact. I like to coin this as supplier-user-customer organizational dependency, though this dependency is all within the organization and may actually consist of more than the three groups depicted due to there being more than one of each section: supplier, user, or customer.

5.3 Change Management

5.3.1 Excessive Change

There are Dilbert cartoons that present organizational change in very unflattering ways. This is probably because organization change is often done poorly. Excessive change can provide the appearance to the staff of instability in company focus or objectives. Organizations are a collection of sub-systems and systems, various departments, various organization hierarchy and structure as well. Changes left uncoordinated can result in changes that cut cross purpose, that is, ineffective at best and damaging at worst. Changes ad hoc in the various systems can result in a system that worked but could be improved into a system that no longer works. Unless there is some competent coordination and configuration management, the result can be a destruction of what marginally worked and inability to easily go back to the incarnation of the system that sort of worked.

5.3.2 Minimalistic Change

Not all changes have to be earth shattering, in fact, a continuous stream of small increments are often better ways to change, as this allows for learning and adapting. As a matter of fact, any change comes with a degree of uncertainty and risk. Knowing this if we approach change as a group of small increments or only as truly needed we can reduce the resistance to the change and possible negative outcome. However, this approach also comes with a downside. The downside being that in an attempt to minimize the organizational effect of a dynamic change an opportunity for substantial growth and development could be missed. Determining when the minimalistic approach should be employed is a difficult task at best, as with any type of change. To provide more information of the minimalistic movement let us look at an article by Ross Smith on the Management Innovation Exchange. In this article Mr. Smith discusses the dynamics of minimalist management. He discusses the natural tendency of a manager to just jump in and offer advice and assistance thinking it is adding value and justifying their existence when in all actuality it could be undermining the motivation of their subordinates and stifling their innovation.* This same principle could be applied to the minimalistic change

---

* Smith, R. (2011, June 06). Minimalist Management -- When Less is More. Retrieved February 19, 2019, from https://www.managementexchange.com/blog/minimalist-management-when-less-more

model in which management and leadership step back and reduce the restraints of their personnel in the form of less processes, metrics, status reports, and unnecessary feedback.* We are not stating that these items should be eliminated, but their effect on the production personnel should be reduced to its bare essential level.

5.3.3 Effective Change

What would be the criteria for an effective change? This seems like an easy question to answer, but as we delve into it you may not think that way. On the surface an effective change would seem to be one that produces the desired results: an increase in production, a decrease in errors, and even an increased profit margin. It would probably also have to be a lasting change, as if resorting back to the previous state could negate any gain received by the change and possibly produce a false indication for a change to the change that was first implemented. If we take just a few seconds to look up "Effective Change" and "Effective Change Management" on the internet we would find countless articles on 8, 6, or 4 critical and/or essential steps to effective change and change management. While they all have validity and each model could apply to a different situation the sheer number of options can cause confusion. Therefore, rather than promote one over another we will look into the basic ways to determine the headway made by a change effort as discussed in Burke's book Organizational Development, A Process of Learning and Change.

5.3.3.1 Quantity of Problems

While the number of problems may increase or remain constant the nature of the problems changing is a prime indicator that the change has had some effect on the issue it was designed to resolve.[†] However the new issues could be related to the change, but to determine this some form of evaluation of the new issue and the change must be conducted. Understanding of the various parameters that can impact the area of interest is part the learning process.

5.3.3.2 Level of Frustration

While this would seem to be the opposite of how it should be, when people express frustration about the progress regarding change that is a clear sign of progress itself.[‡] This position is supported by both Maslow's and Herzberg's work in the areas of

---

* Smith, R. (2011, June 06). Minimalist Management -- When Less is More. Retrieved February 19, 2019, from https://www.managementexchange.com/blog/minimalist-management-when-less-more
† Burke, W. W. (2015). *Organization Development: A process of learning and changing.* Place of publication not identified: Pearson.
‡ Burke, W. W. (2015). *Organization Development: A process of learning and changing.* Place of publication not identified: Pearson.

grumbles (hygiene) and meta-grumbles (Motivation). When we look at these works collectively, we can see that these "Meta-grumbles (Motivation)* are an indication the people doing them are doing so because they have a desire for a change and this is an opportunity that can be used to help facilitate a change.

5.3.3.3 Reporting

When an issue becomes more important people tend to bring it up in as many venues as possible to attempt to ensure that the item or issue gets the attention they feel it deserves. Using this line of reasoning when change efforts and the status of those efforts becomes an active part of the regular reporting or reports it is a positive sign that the change is taking hold.†

5.3.3.4 Progress Assessments

Progress assessment falls along the line of reporting in that when assessments, reevaluations, and key events associated with change progress are acknowledged in or on their own shows the importance of the change. This is also a prime motivator in that these type events or reviews can be used to praise the accomplishments of individuals and the team.‡

Assessing progress may be a little bit like evaluation of the organization's talent. Using a single point of reference only provides a single point of view, a single point of view that would be subjected to those biases discussed earlier. The approach to evaluation should include more perspectives to ensure that the progress being reviewed is assessed from as many angles as possible to come to a conclusion that is consistent with the facts.

5.3.4 Changing the Change

When most people or an organization think about change they do not necessarily think about changing the change in the actual process of the change. Thoughts are like we should finish the change to determine how it works when fully employed, or if we are going to change the change we should revert back to our previous starting point so we know where we are starting from to analyze the new change. While these are options and might actually be the answer they should not just be jumped to, as with anything in a change. If there was or is a good plan associated with the initial change then the current status (position), of the organization or team should

---

* Maslow, A. H. (1954). *Motivation and personality.* New York: Harper & Row
† Burke, W. W. (2015). *Organization Development: A process of learning and changing.* Place of publication not identified: Pearson.
‡ Burke, W. W. (2015). *Organization Development: A process of learning and changing.* Place of publication not identified: Pearson.

be known. Having said that, the team should determine if sufficient information is available to enact a new change from the current position. It is a rare occurrence that the first attempt at any change does not evolve into a different change by maturity or even several different changes. This would be the "Developmental" portion or organizational development.

5.3.5 Summation of Change

Through this chapter and other chapters, we have alluded to change needing a measure of effectiveness. And that these measures should be measures should be embedded into the change itself as benchmarks to determine if a course correction is required or desired. However, in the one subsection we give an example of things that cannot actually be measured or analyzed as an indication of the progress of a change. It is important to acknowledge that one will not always have some numerical data, quantitative or qualitative, that will help. It is also possible that the best data we have is minimal or vague at best. We should seek to understand the meaning of the indicators, whatever those are. What measurement or visible symptom would we see that infroms we are on the correct path? I liken it to having a book with all the answers to our questions, but, not being able to read, what purpose would it serve?

5.4 Total Recall!

Past experiences suggest that the larger the organization, the less likely the learning is to get spread. We have worked in organizations where managers have been heard to say, "it is okay to make mistakes, but can't we make different mistakes?" This is the result of any learning being localized, if even that. What actions can we take to ensure that what is learned moves beyond those initially learning it?

5.4.1 How to Remember What You've Learned

"It is okay to make mistakes, but can't we make some different ones for a change?" This was a lament of a manager that kept watching the same decisions lead to the same outcome. Experience suggests this happens much more frequently than a person would think. It is important to learn from these events, not just those individuals or team members that have been initiated, influenced, or been impacted by the events. To be sure each situation is different, so a chain of events in one set of circumstances may not exactly apply to a slightly different set of circumstances. In large organizations, there may be many experiments or other sources of learning going on at any time, each of which are context informing. That is, without the background context, there may be no real ability to reuse this or claim it as learning. Each time something happens that is a teaching event or teaching moment for the team, it is something that should be considered available to the rest of the team, and posterity.

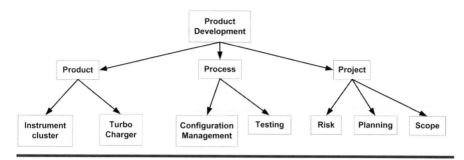

Figure 5.8 An example of the structure of the database for a product development organization.

5.4.2 Lessons Learned Storage and Handling

Not that formalized documentation is the be-all-end-all for how to both capture the learning and perpetuate the learning throughout the organization from now until the future. However, when considering the limitations of communications as the sole mechanism for storing, it should be clear that success requires more than communication between individuals and teams. Part of the work must include ways to record beyond those that have experienced that specific set of events and subsequent learning. Perhaps, modern databases that metadata tags to be associated with the data.

5.4.2.1 Database Storage

In some instances, capturing what is learned can be put into a database. Modern databases with metadata tags make it possible to capture things a team learns in a way that can be recovered by others in the organization. An organization with which we have worked used a tool from Wjj Software.*©™ A tool like this can help record those things learned in such a way to be useful. The old method of recording things the team has learned in a book, which collects more dust than eyes from other team members, will not likely produce the results desired.

Tools *can* help, but there are more fundamental things required to maximize the results from using the tool. For example, there will be a need to segment the database, that is, develop the hierarchy of the tool to meet the needs of the organization and, more specifically, to make the database a suitable repository for the things the team learns. For example, one company that employed the use of a database in product development structured the system to support the constituent products for the vehicle. Each of the constituent parts had a field for the part name. There were assorted fields under this part, associated with subassemblies and specific

---

* http://www.wjjsoft.com/innokb.html

things learned over time when it came to that part and subassemblies. Field failures, and root causes as well as corrective actions of those failures, are also recorded in this database. Other structure alternatives may look like:

- Organization's Departments
- Discipline (example: engineering, configuration management, purchasing, quality)
- Products (systems, subsystems components)
- Processes (product development or manufacturing)
- Process maturity
- Self-directed work teams

The development of the database requires considering the extensibility, that is, more than the immediate use but how the database system can be extended as more things are learned. In the modern interconnected world, the database can make it possible for those things discovered at various sites around the world to be recorded. The many experiments regarding productivity, quality, or products can be easily put into a system that any other person in the company that has access can see the results.

Databases are part of the organizations knowledge infrastructure. This represents not only an investment in this infrastructure, but an ongoing investment. The system consists largely of storage, data transportation, and data transformation.*

As repositories of information for the business careful consideration of the security issues related to the information is important. This requires walking a balance between ease of access while thwarting would be attackers trying to acquire or disrupt the use of the information. The storage space allocated must be enough for the present amount of material recorded on the server with plans for upgrading that are congruent with the rate of growth of data stored. Experience suggests the reliability and speed of access will play a factor in the use of the system. Modern organizations have wired and wireless internet connectivity, and this facilitates ease of access. In addition to ease of access from the organization facilities, it is also possible for team members to view off site and perhaps even on their smart phones.

Introducing a tool to the company without any support is a recipe for failure. In fact, ideally those that will be using the system should have been included in the development of the system specifications and logistical needs as well as specific function content.

5.4.3 Communities of Practice

Communities of practice can sometime get a bad reputation. In some cases, this becomes a euphemism for outsourcing key portions of the organization to another

---

* Cash, J. L., Jr., Eccles, R. G., Nohria, N., and Nolan, R.L., 1994. *Building the Information Age Organization: Structure, Control, and Information Technologies.* Irwin

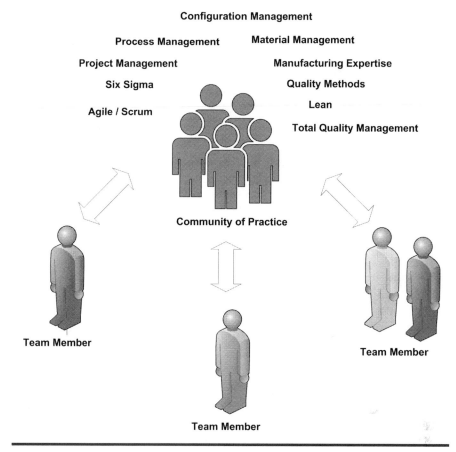

Configuration Management

Process Management   Material Management

Project Management   Manufacturing Expertise

Six Sigma   Quality Methods

Agile / Scrum   Lean

Total Quality Management

Community of Practice

Team Member

Team Member

Team Member

Figure 5.9 Communities of practice can provide resources to the other parts of the organization in a specific domain.

part of the organization, or even to a supplier. This displacement of the work, can have an impact on employees if the portion of the work the employee finds enjoyable is relegated to these communities of practice. This is not what communities of practice are intended to be; however, rather, it is an aberration. It might be in the organization's best interest to not couch or guise intentions through this use of this phrase.

Communities of practice are where individuals with interest in the topic gather together to develop the organization's relationship to that topic. Those that are part of this team are not solely those that have decades of experience in the topic, but also those that have expressed an affinity or aptitude as well. The intent is to develop this community in such a way as to have this community help the various parts of the organization understand the subject matter better, how best to apply it specifically in the context of the organization's work, as well as provide future guidance on the subject matter allowing the organization to prepare for these external changes so as not to be such a shock when these future events happen.

It is possible the topic upon which the community of practice ruminates means different things to different parts of the organization. Therefore, it is good for the team members of this community of practice to have the range of experience that matches that of the organization. This is especially true for groups or teams that are globally distributed or where sites each have a different set of advantages. For example, some sites may have a human capital advantage; another may have a technological or automation advantage. The way each of these interpret the application from the community of practice may differ by necessity. In this way, besides a variety of progress on the level of skill in the topic of the community of practice, it is essential to include a variety of functional areas in which the topic is applied. For example, configuration management community of practice in a product development and manufacturing concern could include talent representations from the following:

- Purchasing
- Hardware engineering
- Software engineering
- Product testing
- Manufacturing

5.4.4 Change Your Oil Every 3,000 Lessons Learned

This is not really about oil changes; however, like anything else, benefits form a constant or recurring review. Over time and experiments needed additional features or quicker performance of the system may be discovered or required. It is a good habit to make this system an integral part of the continuing improvement philosophy of the company, with a constant review. In an earlier section we discussed the importance of "Habits" as a necessary part of any change if it is to be sustained.

5.4.4.1 Maintaining the Lessons Learned Process and Tools

No matter the solution used for collecting and storing, there will need to be some guidance on how the system works, and the rules for applications. Errant input into the system will lead to building upon this errant information, the garbage in, garbage out rule. The organization may decide to supply some guidance on how to post those learnings. For example, perhaps there is a review of the lessons learned by the team impacted, or perhaps, and more appropriately, the team should be part of developing the lessons learned. There must be some true root cause analysis competencies within the group, thus ensuring a true account of the situation and that action is taken to improve. The value of the lessons learned database reduces when suppositions and conjectures are the content.

5.5 Lowering the Water Level

When it appears that your organization is drowning with issues that never go away there are two options, learn to swim or drain the water level such that you can just stand and not drown. Learning to swim is a metaphor for the workaround that people have developed to keep the process moving. And draining the water is a metaphor for reducing the issues impeding the team from obtaining their goal.

5.5.1 Learning to Swim

While it would seem on the surface to be a good thing that the team can develop ways to keep the process moving, it is if used only as a temporary solution to an issue while the long term plan is developed. However, as we all know this is rarely the case as evident by such comments by individuals as, "If we are going to make mistakes can't we at least make new ones?" or "The process says do it this way, but we do it like this to make it work." It is these very type of issues that make change difficult because the starting point may not actually be known due to workarounds and the motivation of the people is diminished by constantly seeing the same mistakes and having to deal with it. When issues such as these go unchecked then the poor experience portion of the leadership equation (see the leadership equation section) increases and motivation declines, thus making change even more tenuous.

Figure 5.10 Tools help us do the work, but tools are not the be all end all.

In situations of repeat problems and workarounds there are commonly key indicators of their existence, the first of which is twofold: personnel could either withdraw from or become more boisterous about the issues that are of a reoccurring nature. The aforementioned condition or symptom as the case may be is the worse of the two. This is because at that point they have ascertained that no action on their part will facilitate a change so they have reconciled themselves to not providing any input. The second shows there is still some hope within the individual as described by Maslow's discussion on levels of frustration (Meta-grumbles)[23].

5.5.2 Drain the Water

As we discussed in the beginning of this section another option would be to drain the water level; remove some of the issues that are necessitating the need to learn how to swim. There is no such thing as an organization that does not have some water in the pool. There is always room and need for improvement, especially in today's ever evolving and fast moving world. The key is to choose the bucket that will remove the most amount of water or produce the greater motivational shift to support further change. Which approach is better would be determined by the initial starting point of the organization, the initial water level, and the willingness of its people to carry a bucket, motivational aspect. If the motivational aspect of the organization is high

Figure 5.11 Drain the demontivating parts of the change, change tempo if needed.

then a larger bucket, a change plan, might be acceptable, whereas if the motivational aspect is low several smaller buckets, rapid change items, might be the key. Either way these type of change dynamics requires that the person or, better yet, the group structuring the change knows about the people who are going to be affected by the change in a motivational manner. What is meant by a motivational manner is how they will respond to a change initiative based on their current mental outlook of the organization and its treatment of them. An example would be if someone has been provided only negative experiences as a part of the leadership equation; then they are less likely to accept the change proposal or support it without additional justification or reasoning.

The irony of experience is that we must work to gain experience and it is the nature of experience, good or bad, from work that tailors our response to improve the very process that decreases our motivation to do so. If we were to develop a curve of the worker life cycle we would see that most of those people with the greatest experience, those who know most of the issues needing change, are the least likely to either embrace a change or sponsor one.

5.5.3 How not Learning to Swim Can Help with Motivation

As we have referenced to numerous times up to here experience of our people, teams, and organization is the primary component of change dynamics in that experience directly affects every one of these places. While we have emphasized change planning, measures of effectiveness of change, and follow up to changes we would be remiss if we did not emphasize the motivational aspects of the change and its planning. They are directly related in that key points can be structured into a change plan to provide positive feedback and experiences. If this is done effectively it may not even matter if the change that was sought is obtained and there would be an increase in the motivation, through positive experiences, which could facilitate a better, more consistent change.

Chapter 6

Mechanizing Knowledge

It is likely not necessary for the entire organization to learn from the same experiments or exploration. It is more likely that each area has its own strengths, challenges, and constraints. In this way, some lessons uniquely apply to a specific part or parts of the organization. Recall the lament from the manager, "it is okay to make mistakes, but can't we make different ones." This requires some sort of perpetuation of what is learned, moving past the immediate to future events.

> Progress, far from consisting in change, depends on retentiveness. When change is absolute there remains no being to improve and no direction is set for possible improvement: and when experience is not retained, as among savages, infancy is perpetual. Those who cannot remember the past are condemned to repeat it.
>
> **George Santayana**
> *Life of Reason Volume 1*

In addition to mechanizing the learnings so other parts of the organization can take some action, it is necessary to act upon what has been learned at some future date. It is not enough to go to training; it is only beneficial if that training is applied. This is just as true for on the job training or learning by doing the work. With a physical incarnation of the lessons our present team has learned, we have a way to demonstrate to any new team member how we have gotten where we are presently. This material can be used as part of the organization's onboarding process. For those unfamiliar, the onboarding is the formal introduction of the new hire to the organization and its values and history.

In process driven organizations the things learned in these experiments should be used to adjust the process flow and process instructions. This is one way of moving

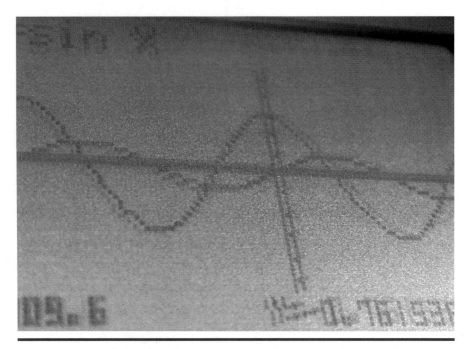

Figure 6.1 Learning, unlearning, amounts to spinning wheels not much progress.

what was learned and recorded in the database into actual practice. Updating processes and process documentation should not be taken lightly. In truly process driven organizations the work can have a level of formalism and that can be driven by legal, cost, or another environmental factor. In these instances, changes to the process must be well understood and that includes variation in inputs, process, and outputs.

It is similar for the communities of practice, what is known by these people, needs a clear and short route to the rest of the organization. The community of practice may issue guidance documentation or updates to the database based upon questions that are asked, building a frequently asked questions (FAQ) section of the database. Recording this expertise in process documentation is another way to ensure this knowledge from the community of practice.

In any of these cases or scenarios, it is important to enact what has been learned. Databases will not work if these are not used. If these are used, as in read but not applied, that too is a failure. The goal must be to create a habit out of both exploration and learning, as well as applying that learning. That is what is meant by mechanizing knowledge.

6.1 Prevent Unlearning Through Holistic Change

There is a term, backsliding, that is used at least here in the south, and it means to descend back into a previous, bad way of behaving or acting. It could just as easily apply to the change management initiatives of the organization and more specifically any learning. After all the work to get better or do better, it is possible that the organization will go back to performing and behaving as before the change. That prior way of behaving and acting was understood to be wrong, in error, or just plain bad. The goal of change is not to dither around some central point like some sign wave where the net effect is zero, but to make progress in such a way that the sum of these incremental progresses over time produce some great amount of progress and capability for the organization.

To prevent unlearning requires making a habit of this new way of doing the work. This sounds obvious, but experience suggests this to be not so easily achieved. The individual team members can help drive this behavior. It is not well for the individual nor the organization to spread inaccurate learning. A part of this change management initiative may be to develop the organization's learning and distribution capacity. In this way meeting specific objectives via learning may not be the end. In fact, it should be our governing philosophy to be continuously learning.

6.1.1 How to Implement Lasting Performance Improvements through Aligned Contextual Changes

We have seen how important spreading the learning is to a team, department, and an organization. Spreading this learning throughout the organization is a non-trivial task. So what sorts of things can we do to help propagate what is learned throughout the organization? There are opportunities to use technology, structure the organization, and many other perhaps not so obvious mechanisms to move the organization toward the desired state.

This is a good time to discuss variables when it comes to experiments. There are two types of variables, independent and dependent. The independent variable is the variable that is controlled; any change to these variables is performed under strict controls, to test the impact on the depending variable. The despendent variable is that being tested and measured for impact.

6.1.2 Technological

Technology can help our organization to record and spread what is learned. Database updates can be used to send notifications to smart phones and email addresses of those interested in the topic area where the new information or learning is attached. For example, with configuration management, perhaps there is some interesting learning based upon some other part of the organization, some experiment that has been run, and some learning that originates from that. The teams or team members can post the things they learn from the experiments they attempt in the course of doing the work.

When it comes to product development, technology that helps us quickly build a version of the product from which we can explore is very helpful indeed. Long lead

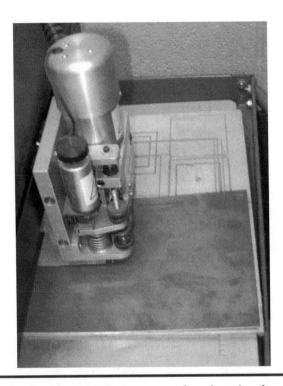

Figure 6.2   Technology can help in many ways from learning the work gets done, to learning about the product.

times mean long learning cycles and that runs contrary to a company that desires to get the product accurately to the market as quickly as possible. Interaction and experimentation by the project team and customers with the product will help drive the product to the desired result. In addition to interation with the product, interactions within the team. There are opportunities for technical learning in idea generation, exploration of alternative approaches, adaptations, and improvements can be great opportunites for exploration. These are opportunities for individual and team learning in product development.

6.1.3 Organizational

The organization has an interest in creating an environment in which the team members grow. This may require investment in a formal education system, as well as but equally informal systems like coaching, mentoring, and other consultation types or exchanges. The level of organizational formalism will have implications on learning and distribution of that learning. In this regard, mechanizing the knowledge via organizational structures, or lack of strucutre, can be of service.

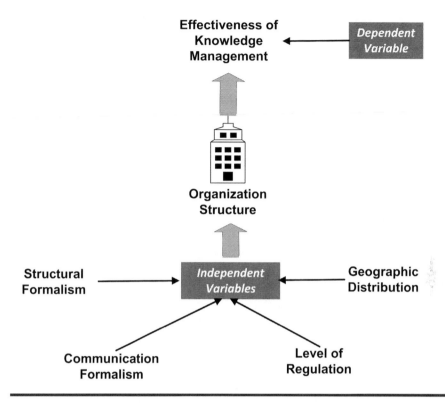

Figure 6.3 The organization structures that get in the way of mechanizing learning.

The educational system of an organization should make training and technical assistance available to work teams for any aspects of the work in which members are not already sufficiently knowledgeable or skilled. Well structured teams have a good mix of task and interpersonal skills – a pool of talent that members can further expand by sharing their special expertise with one another and by learning together from team successes and failure. Even so, teamwork commonly requires members to handle work-related issues for which their existing knowledge and skill are insufficient. Outside help and expertise can help a team transcend the limits of members' present expertise.

There is learning that happens in the everyday work. This type of learning does not require the organization to do much more than to provide an environment that is suitable for self-learning and team learning.

The organization creates an environment in which the members of the team can thrive. This begins when the organization hires the individuals and is advanced when the organization pours the collection of hired individuals into a group and casts them as a "team." The biggest contribution to the employees learning is creating an environment in which the individuals want to learn, and more importantly want to learn from each other, and teach each other.

6.1.4 Cultural

Creating a culture around continuous exploration, experimentation, and learning will help propel the organization down this continuous improvement road. The impact of culture on the way things are learned can be demonstrated from an excerpt from, *What makes your brain happy and why you should do the opposite*, mindful of sharks.*

> In October of 1997, observers from the Point Reyes bird observatory witnessed a killer whale clashing with a great white shark near Farallon Island, twenty-six miles off the coast of San Francisco. The site made for salacious nature news. Speculation about what would happen if the apex predators met has always piqued curiosity.
>
> Turns out, it was not much of a fight. The orca had little trouble dispatching her menacing opponent, and then proceeded to dine on its liver, leaving the carcass for seagulls to pick clean. This outcome may have disappointed many who expected a bloody, jaw to jaw battle between these titans of the deep, but it tickled the fancy of academia to the point of giddiness.
>
> To understand why, we have to take a step back to examine how killer whales learn their namesake trade. Like humans, orcas have culture. But unlike most human cultures, orca cultures revolve around one thing: hunting behavior. Some orcas hunt herring, others seals, others stingrays and others – sharks. The observers on the ship had witnessed an orca conducting the business of its shark-hunting culture.
>
> The next discovery was how the orca so handily defeated the shark. In every orca culture, a hunting technique is learned through demonstration and imitation. That's a big part of what makes orcas such efficient predators – they learn the best, tried-and-true hunting techniques from each other. When one orca tries a killing method that works well, others take notice and copy it.
>
> Scientists speculate that at some point an orca discovered that if it rammed a shark hard enough from the side, the shark would flip over and become motionless, unable to defend itself and inflict injury. In effect, that pioneering orca induced "tonic immobility" in its adversary – a temporary state of paralysis many species of sharks fall

---

* DiSalvo, D. (2018). *What Makes Your Brain Happy and Why You Should do the Opposite.* Amherst, NY: Prometheus Books page 29–30.

into when turned on their backs. Human discovery of tonic immobility in sharks is relatively recent, making the orca's behavior all the more remarkable.

The point to this is in killer whales, the culture drives the learning of the pod and the individuals, and that learning came from within the pod. Additionally, "experiments" that lead to a dead end are not continued. Specifically, if the first orca that tried to kill a shark in that way had failed, that behavior would not have propagated through the pod and ultimately to members of the future pod. Only successful hunting experiences will move through to the future. Orcas do not pass on errant hunting techniques; however, this is not true for humans.

No matter the effort, people will be the way things are successfully accomplished. We have all heard organizations profess, accurately, that people are the greatest asset of the corporation. This is true especially for creating an organization that has an effective learning system. The people will either support or take the effort, or they

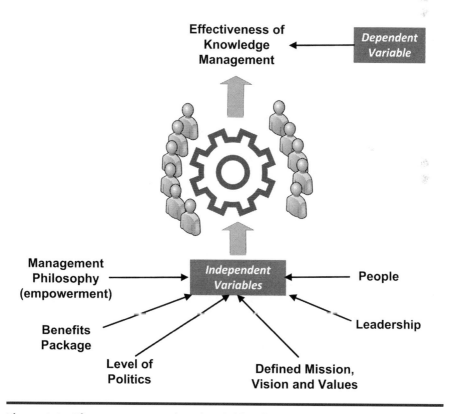

Figure 6.4   There are many cultural variables that will impact the success of our knowledge management effort.

will not, and this is a part of mechanizing the work or creating a habit. One of the problems is when the organization hierarchy says these things are important but then pushes action to countermand this original direction we do not have time for doing it this way. Rather than explain why and that this course of action is an exception to our rules, the leadership rushes this exception. From experience, there are an abundance of examples of change initiatives that fail because of the organizational hierarchy saying one thing is important, followed hard with actions that run contrary to the original language about what is important.

Humans pass on information and methods that may not work; our brains are set up to see patterns, even when pattern may not be there. Couple this with the fact that our natures and our learned biases lead us to believe we are right whether or not we really are.* Neuroscience research on the human brain shows that people are not just uncomfortable with uncertainty, but our brains crave certainty. Our need to be right is actually a need to feel right, leading neurologist Robert Burton to coin the term "certainty bias" to describe this feeling and how it skews our thinking.†

Given this need to be right so we can feel right, it is a wonder that anything goes right! This is a fundamental reason for ensuring there are multiple eyes on the subject matter at hand, along with open mental models and voicing assumptions to make it possible to have those assumptions actively critiqued for veracity.

It may be easy to see how organizations may find it difficult to improve or grow into a learning organization. It is important for an organization to learn and spread that learning, but it is important that what was learned is understood, and not some supposed to be learning as the earlier quote from Mark Twain about the cat on the stove (though the cat on the stove sounds like a problem no matter the reason or if the stove is hot). Perpetuating something as knowledge means that something should have value and be, in fact, knowledge. Spreading other than knowledge is spreading supposition or wishes. There is a difference between known things, and guesses.

6.1.5 Better Tools Make Better Products

Tools can help, but only under certain circumstances. From experience, a common mistake is to expect the tools to save the project, the department, or the company. The issue is a tool or collection of discrete tools that are not connected to the entirety of the work, do not help, and in some cases hinder the organization's progress or capabilities. Tools should not be the goal. The objective and goals of the organization are what is important, not the tools. From experience we have seen companies that

---

* DiSalvo, D. (2018). *What Makes Your Brain Happy and Why You Should do the Opposite.* Amherst, NY: Prometheus Books page 31
† Daniel Kahneman and Amos Tversky, "On the Reality of Cognitive Illusions," 103 (July 1996): 582-591

rather than take a cohesive approach to tools, they take a discordant, discontinuous approach to how tools are used in the company.

6.1.5.1 How to Implement Technology Related Corrective Actions

Anecdotally, technology related corrective actions, or technical related corrective actions, are generally easier than social or cultural. Often the technical changes are easier to quantify the change needed as well as derive metrics that inform the progress toward implementing the changes. For example, consider a process change or a tool change in the organization. It is possible to set up metrics of the use of this tool. A specific example could be that of the bug reporting software tool that we are working on to get all projects to use. We can compare the projects that require testing, and see how many of those projects are putting the defects or fault reports into this new system. The same can be for other technical or process corrective actions.

Consider a process, wherein after monitoring output, and finding areas for improvement, we then want to distribute this proposed change to the process, or the resulting learning from this series of events, so others may either use or adopt a similar process. This may even apply to a company that may use less processes, as in formalized, and rely more upon the individual teams to understand the situation and determine the best way to meet the demands of that set of circumstances.

6.1.6 Better Teams Make Better Tools

Tools are not the savior of the organization, it is the talent. It takes more than gathering up the talent and putting them in a room and yea verily a team. A team can arise from this collection of individuals, but requires the environment be suitable. Have you ever worked at a place that had the tools to be used to do the work clearly defined, perhaps compartmentalized? Tools that are not interconnected with the rest of the organization reduce visibility of the work by dependent groups. Anybody experienced in projects will recognize one of the risks to project success is dependent or how the parts interconnect especially with regard to communication. Tools such as these only reinforce the a disparate approach to the work. Sometimes these disparate tools can be overcome by altering the organization's strucure, or identifying communication improvements. The depenencies remain, however, these can become more clearly visible by the co-located team or group of people seeing the same information, and certainly a common set of tools.

Teams that learn together and across disciplines, for example software development, configuration management and software testing, are all inter-related or conected. There are product development life cycle tools that help soften the boundaries between departments.

6.1.7 Better Understanding Makes Better Teams

Teams are not formulaic; there are things that can happen to either drive the individuals apart or bring the individuals together. An environment of employee empowerment helps move things in the right direction, if the collection of individuals is converted to a team. Have you ever worked in an organization in which the tools are mandated from the executive or management arm of the company? How did this work out? Experience suggests there are at least two failure modes that happen. One is disparate unconnected tools; each department or competency area has their own tools. This lack of view into the work flow causes difficulty; for example, the test group reports defects in a tool that all developers cannot accesss or even project managers. The second is closely related to the previous, when the tools are selected by politics or organization competing interests rather than taking a system level approach, which often leads to communication challenges.

While not denying the inevitability of rough spots in the life of any group, I nonetheless do not count as effective any team for which the impact of a group experience on members' learning and well-being is more negative than positive. If a group prevents members from doing what they want and need to do, if it compromises their personal learning, or if members' main reactions to having been in the group are frustration and disillusionment, then the costs of generating the group product were too high.*

6.1.7.1 How to Implement Cultural Related Corrective Actions

Unfortunately, there is no script for achieving changes to the culture that arise out of corrective actions. In fact, cultural changes are largely emergent and attaching a specific set of actions to any culture change is nigh impossible at best. We can never know the range of variables and the magnitude nor combinations that produce a specific and desired cultural change. Does this mean all hope is lost? Not necessarily, there are some things we can do to influence the culture.

Those things that are valued, the things we believe are necessary to improve, should be experimented upon, and tested to see if what we believe to be good is in fact something desirable. Some things may be more obvious, for example, saying our people are empowered, while taking action that runs contrary to our beliefs. This is especially true for the mission, vision, values, and principle documentation. No matter the mechanism, to say one thing is important and act contrary creates confusion at best and at worst erodes levels of engagement.

---

* Hackman, J. R. (2006). *Leading Teams: Setting the Stage for Great Performances*. Boston, Mass: Harvard Business School Press.

Chapter 7

Training and Development

7.1 Tools and Techniques

In this chapter there is a review of the many things we can do to help ensure the development of our organization. There are tools and techniques that can help the teams to grow and therefore the organization to grow. In fact these tools and techniques could be as simple as how we set about doing the work.

No matter what we choose to do, we need to ensure an environment of active learning.* Active learning is not a defined process, but varying ways of teaching with the goal of actively engaging the individual in their learning. There are many more things than what we typically think of when we think of how we teach or train:

- games
- contests
- role playing
- role modeling
- discussions and debates
- demonstration videos
- walk-throughs
- guided practice
- solo practice

Active learning puts the onus on learning directly where it belongs, on the student. To get to this point will require more than just a script that goes along

---

* Jackson, T. (2003). More activities that teach. Cedar City, Utah?: Red Rock Pub.

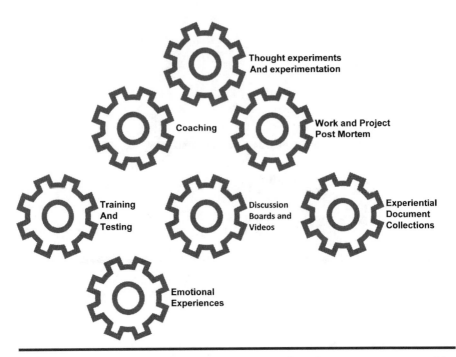

Figure 7.1   There are many ways to help encourage learning or create opportunities for learning.

with a slide deckd to training. An active learning environment encourages practice during the training in a place that allows for experimentation. This participative environment has no resemblance with a type of presentation. Lecturing to people is not the best way to encourage learning. This applies to anything from technical parts of project management and product development to what is often referred to, incorrectly, as the soft skills, those associated with people, motivation, and organization development.

7.2 Training

There are a number of ways in which we can train our team members. Our organization may decide it is better to train internally, or externally. We may use direct or distance learning or some hybrid approach that includes elements of both. For events where a more formalized training is deemed required, the focus of the training should be very specific, with questions. No matter the approach we take to training, good on the job training will consist of:

- demonstration of the method or behavior in pieces
- guided practice with student and trainer
- solo practice the student with review by trainer and post analysis

Figure 7.2 Training can take place in a conference room; the content and what happens in the room is much more important.

A good way to fail when applying training to improve an organization's capabilities is to not have a solid grip on what is important to know. Objectives from any training should be specific and readily demonstratable at the end of the training, that is, the person undergoing the training has new behavior or new skills that they are able to apply. To ensure this, we must ensure that the individual leaves the class with these skills (more on that later).

7.2.1 Direct and Online

When we say direct, we are referring to training that occurs within a classroom or in the environment in which the subject of the training would typically take place. There is a subject matter expert, and there are students in one physical location. Direct has advantages: the instructor can see the faces and gage engagement of those in the training. Direct also has an advantage when there are mechanical or manipulation parts of the training, as in instruction on how things are assembled, with demonstration, guided practice, and then a review of solo practice. Sometimes direct is the only reasonable choice though it may be seen as more costly. There are times, however, where the direct training can be reinforced with online material for post-training review, or when online training could also work.

With the lower cost and sometimes no cost shareware version of learning management systems such as Moodle,* it is not necessarily an expensive proposition to have any internal or external training augmented with distance learning or supplemental material. Our organization may be dispersed and perhaps distance learning approaches are part of developing the competencies of our organization. Whether the material is developed in house or in the classroom, online material can help move what is known within the company to other parts of the company.

7.2.2 Internal Training

It is possible, and perhaps desirable, to bring the training of the organization into the company. The organization may have an internal department that is responsible for the training. In this way the training has a measure of repeatability, and who knows better than our team members, on what our organization needs to know. Every organization is different, the opportunities and risks to which the organization is exposed are different, even when the industries are common. Teaching and training are skills unto themselves, so our organization may wish to develop internal training to meet these needs. Internally developed training makes it possible for the organization to develop training that specifically meets the organization's specific operations and operating environment.

Internally developed training will require not only expertise on the topic at hand, but also on the topic of what it takes to teach or train. We can solve some of this dilemma perhaps by make the use of any communities of practice that we have in our organization. Coupling this group with that part of our organization that has expertise in teaching and training could be fruitful.

However we proceed, the person training will be important to accomplishing the training. Some guidance is provided by George M. Piskurich:[†]

- Has-in-depth knowlege of content
- Exhibits confidence in self and the process being taught
- Is credible
- Follows the trainer guide
- Explains well
- Understands the basics of how adults learn
- Develops rapport with the trainee
- Involves the trainee in the training
- Can read body knowledge
- Exhibits proper body language

---

* https://moodle.org/ last accessed 5/20/2019
† Piskurich, G. M. (2009). Rapid training development: Developing training courses fast and right. San Francisco: Pfeiffer.

- Makes good eye contact
- Listens well
- Is receptive to trainee's ideas
- Checks for understanding with questions and by repeating trainee comments
- Asks good questons and waits for answers
- Is patient
- Is flexible
- Has no annoying verbal or non-verbal habits
- Smile

7.2.3 Rapid Training Development (Team Members Train Team Members)

For in house rapid training development, it is appropriate to have some templated form to ensure the suitability of the training to meet the objectives of the organization. One such example of internal on the job training (OJT) can be found below:*

- Materials
- Objectives
- Prepare trainee
  - Purpose of session
  - How sessions will be conducted
  - Problems others have had
  - Evaluation
  - Any Questions
- Key learning points
- Expected results
- Work standards
- Sequence of activities
- Demonstration
- Observation of trainee performance
- Evaluation

Our interest is to quickly produce sufficient material to impart what is known to people that do not know. The training material need not be highly polished presentation material, in fact, this training can often happen without presentation material, depending upon circumstances.

---

* Piskurich, G. M. (2009). Rapid training development: Developing training courses fast and right. San Francisco: Pfeiffer.

7.2.4 External Training

Having taught businesses through technical schools in the United States, for example Rowan Cabarrus Community College, I have seen that this is a very cost effective solution for some training for the organization. There are times when the local government offers some subsidies for this training as part of the continuous development of the local or state workforce.

A company will be in need of some training for their employees and staff at-large and the community college, in conjunction with local subject matter experts on the topic, will work with the community college to understand the true need of the client, and then set about building training objectives and material to make that happen.

7.3 Agile Approaches

This is not a book about agile, but these approaches to the work have gained momentum over the years, having started out as the method of software development, but that is not the only place this approach applies. Agile focuses on the work rather than processes and seeks to set an environment that is conducive to turning the collection of individuals into, not only a team, but a self-directed, self-organizing team. The agile manifesto describes the priorities below:*

- Individuals and interaction over processes and tools
- Working software (product) over comprehensive documentation
- Customer collaboration over contract negotiation
- Responding to change over following a plan:

Agile has a different approach to management as well. Rather than top down control of the work, the organization conducts business in ways to facilitate learning as well as the development of the team into a self-directed work unit.

In agile there is significant focus on team developing and learning along the way; there is recognition that the team does not know everything, and there needs to be time for team learning along the way. There will be time allocated along the way for improving the way the group works as well.

Not sharing failures means those failures will come back to haunt other team members, as they must learn about this failure by actually failing again. An agile saying is ***fail fast and fail often***. This agile saying is used to encourage reacting to failure in a different way. Specifically, there should be no fear of failure, do not cover up the failure, but broadcast the failure so all can learn. However, taken to the extreme we may have a negative impact on the corporate culture.

* https://agilemanifesto.org/ last accessed 4/1/2019

Fail fast in the context of agile and from experience is to devise experiments in the work from which we can learn. These experiments should be of short duration so we can quickly learn and adjust. For example we have an idea for a specific design approach that we are not certain will work, we devise a quick experiment and identify specific measurements that will allow prediction of the success or failure of the approach.

The **fail often** portion of the saying is that we should be constantly learning, pushing the envelope and as such we run the risk of a string of failures, as we fail often and learn. To be clear, the goal is not to fail for the sake of failure. The work environment should be such that it is okay for failure to exsit and that fear of failure should not stop us from trying new things and learning. All of these require an environment wherein failure is not a disaster for the person's work and career, and the team members are constantly exploring to find better ways to accomplish the work. However, a more cavalier interpretation of the saying may lead to some unintended consequences.

> When leaders do not fully understand or appreciate a term, the result can have the opposite effect of what they wish to achieve. Worse, when we muddy the waters with language such as "fail fast, fail often" with what we intend, it can cause irreparable damage, particularly to organizational culture.*

7.3.1 Daily Stand Up

Those familiar with the agile or scrum approach to working know that in these approaches the team comes together every day to discuss the objectives and actions to be accomplished or believed to be accomplished that day. However, this strategy need not be limited to project management work. In fact, I know of a manager of a large department that employed agile techniques in the context of the line organization. This manager saw a significant improvement in throughput as well as improvement in morale. Agile standup brings the team together every day to talk about those things upon which the team members are working. In these meetings progress on work objectives are constantly discussed, as well as those things that are impediments to their respective work objectives

1. What did you get done yesterday?
2. What are you doing today?
3. What are your impediments?

---

* https://www.forbes.com/sites/danpontefract/2018/09/15/the-foolishness-of-fail-fast-fail-often/#5cdf874459d9 last accessed 5/20/2019

Figure 7.3   We share information and perspectives in the daily stand up scrum meeting.

These discussions reveal the problems or things not going according to the plan to the entirety of the team members. This allows the other team members to ask questions about the difficulty in the attempt to better understand the nature of this difficulty. Understanding the nature of the difficulty can raise ideas of how to meet the challenges from the rest of the team. There may be other team members that have the knowledge of the domain or specific problem attributes or possible solutions that can help, and this open discussion with the team encourages this exchange, mental model proposals, as well as uncovering underlying assumptions that may be exacerbating or inhibiting resolution.

7.3.2 Pairwise Learning (Spike)

Also, with scrum comes the approach to learning about things that the team does not know, both technically and functionally. This approach is called the spike. There are times when the work is beyond what the team may know. This is especially true when it comes to product development work. This lack of knowledge can take on a variety of causes; the difficult part is to recognize what is not known, and then find ways to understand and learn about what is not known. The starting point is to recognize that we do not know what is necessary to know to proceed. Thus, the first hurdle is to not delude ourselves regarding what we know or do not know.

Sometimes the reason for that disparity of what we know and what we need to know is because the team is missing some domain experience or knowledge, for example, some technology or process that up until this point upon which we have little or no experience. When this happens, we need not put at risk all the depending work or activities or objectives by attempting to proceed without learning. The next step is to identify specifically what should be learned. What is it we need to know, and to what degree? It is recognized that it is not possible to articulate this perfectly, because we do not know much about this, but there should be some guidance to those that will do the exploration. This framework for the exploration should be developed by the team members. This multiple perspective will help ensure that the exploration is successful, that is, bring back to the rest of the team answers to questions that have been raised.

The spike can be focused on technical uncertainty, or on the product from a feature or functional content of the product that the team has questions. Therefore, the talent that will be required to explore and understand the solution will vary. The decision on the scope of the exploration as well as who will be part of the exploration will originate from the team.

7.3.3 Retrospective

A defined objective or set of work results are accomplished at the end of the sprint. After this work has been completed, if this is a product, there will be a demonstration of the product to the customer. This provides an opportunity to learn about the customer's needs for the product. Thus, this only applies to product development work. The retrospective is just like it sounds: we consider what we have just done to see if there is something better we can do. Is there a process change? Is there a team arrangement alteration? The team looks over their shoulder at the work that has just been completed to see how things can be made better, and what is discussed, or the focus is not dictated from a manager or an executive, but within the team.

7.4 Coaching

Coaching does not apply only to agile teams; however, coaching is integral to the work in agile approaches, especially in the version of agile known as scrum. In scrum, there is a position called a scrum master. This person is not a project manager as in scrum or agile approaches there is usually no position of a project manager. The scrum master is more like a coach. This coach will guide the team through any processes the team believes is required to be able to achieve the objectives of the team. Since these objectives are connected to the organization, the method is to be consistent to meet the organization's objectives as well. In addition to ensure the processes work for the team, the coach is also responsible for ensuring the work that comes into the team is understood well enough by the organization to warrant the team getting involved. This requires exchanges between the customer and the team, and the scrum master will work to ensure these events and the input work list are clear enough for the team to work. Additionally, the agile coach is responsible to help clear away impediments or obstacles for the team. This will require understanding the nature of the obstacle from the team's perspective and working with the team members as well as the organization to find a suitable solution.

Coaching is not telling, as much as it is guiding. The coach adopts an eastern philosophy or style of leadership notably from Lao Tzu, *"A leader is best when people barely know he exists, when his work is done, his aim fulfilled, they will say we did it ourselves."* In this regard the coach really helps the team do what they believe is required. It is important for the team to drive the work, to set a pace for the work that is maintainable, and commit to specific deliveries and deliverables.

While coaching is core to agile approaches to project work, this should not an exclusive place for the practice. Access to coaches should be posible not only for the technical aspects of the work, but for the team building, learning and capturing and disseminating that learning throughout the organization, or at least to areas that may benefit.

7.5 Experiential Collection

In some of our other books with Taylor & Francis, we have included stories that describe situations and events. Stories are used to articulate an event and perhaps provide fodder upon which to ruminate, comparing the story to real life circumstances in which an individual or team may find themselves. These approaches are like thought experiments, only these represent true events, approaches. Thinking about these past situations may be similar or even exactly like those with which we are presently confronting, but it can help to think of alternative approaches to the situations we encounter, and what type of actions can generate what types of results. Of course there are limits; often cause and effects are not absolutely known unless the team has gone through root cause analysis as part of the effort. Stories are often an interesting way of exploring events and can be helpful as part of on the job training efforts. Each of the approaches below provides some structure for telling stories of experiences and exploring, at least from an anecdotal perspective. However, gathering these as case studies within the organization may be of benefit in uncovering the myriad of parameters and interactions that result in the situation under exploration.

1. SOARA
    a. Situation
    b. Objective

      c. Action
      d. Results
      e. After action
2. STAR
      a. Situation
      b. Task
      c. Action
      d. Result
3. SCQ
      a. Situation
      b. Complication
      c. Questions
4. WWHS
      a. When
      b. What
      c. How
      d. Share

In fact, it may be interesting to use a format such as one of these, if the company sets up a database with metadata search tags. These stories and experiences can be recorded along with those other lessons learned approaches into those databases discussed earlier in the book.

7.6 Lessons Learned Post-Project

Many organization's have post-project lessons learned that are recorded in some way. In our experience, these lessons learned work have many limitations. The first of which is when these lessons learned are undertaken. For example, consider a project that takes two years to accomplish and the first time we ask about lessons learned are at the end of the project. How accurate do you think the results will be handling lessons learned?

In addition to the problem of lessons learned at the end of the project, in our experience, we also see a selective interview of the project team members. Project managers may want to show the good side, the positive learnings of the organization rather than inteviewing all team members. This is likely at least in part, due to the space in time, for the project lessons learned. The cognitive biases discussed in the appendix can also cloud the approach; for example consider the impact of optimism bias or confirmation bias on these lessons learned activities.

There is some good news, however; if your organization has a stage gate approach to project governance, we need not wait until the end of the project. Each of these gates has specific, associated objectives. For example, in automotive projects we can have a series of gates that look like:

- Voice of customer
- Product development
- Process development
- Product and process validation
- Launch

A stage gated project makes natural points for dwelling on what was learned within that phase and perhaps should be part of the gate targets. Specifically, there can be learning expected to accomplish during that phase and not just the project objectives for that phase. Identifying this learning at the start of each phase, actually within the objectives of that phase, will help in integrating the expected learning in that phase. The project should plan for this learning, including this in any estimate for the project.

7.7 NATO's Lessons Learned Process

Lessons learned are so important for improvement and growth, and being able to compete in an increasingly complex subject and marketplace. There are few things more complicated than working in coordinated multiple governmental

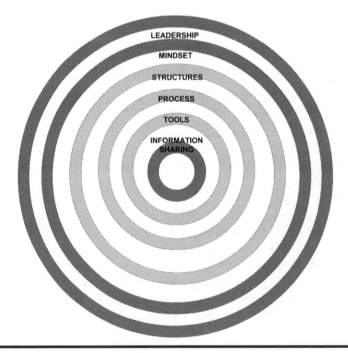

Figure 7.4 NATO has a prescribed approach to lessons learned.

organizations. North Atlantic Treaty Association (NATO) lessons learned are built upon three pillars:*

- Structure—organization structure with dedicated personnel
- Process—develop processes to handle and share lessons learned
- Tool—for collecting, storing, and assisting with staffing selection and support

To support this work will require:

- Mindset—learn from others, and integrate where applicable and share your learning with others
- Leadership—timely effective decision making throughout the process

7.8 Temporary Assignments

Temporary assignments can help transfer learning about one department or multiple departments into other areas of the company. Temporary assignments are opportunities to grow the individual's competencies and to spread what the individual has learned in their past position. Besides learning more about the company, the individual will learn more about this other part of the company. If these two areas have interactions within the organization, for example there is a supplier customer relationship between them, this provides an opportunity to understand the challenges of that part of the organization and for the temporary assignee to help coach and educate on how the work of this supplying group is used in the depending group.

Upon completion of the assignment, if the assigned individual is sent back to his group, they are in a better position of understanding about this chain of the work. They can now influence the customer side of the relationship to make alterations that can improve throughput or quality of outcome or output based upon the learning during the stint with this other group.

It is also possible to have a temporary assignment based upon a broader objective. For example, perhaps there is a department initiative to thoroughly document the ideal way the work should flow through the organization, and produce process documentation that represents this idealized way of working. This actually happened at a company at which I worked. At the end of a very large project, the lead engineer, who had managed the technical portion of the project, was then employed to work with the various department managers and their respective teams to elicit and document the needs for each department along with scripting the optimum way for the work to wind its way through the organization. The result was a collection of

---

* http://www.jallc.nato.int/products/docs/Lessons_Learned_Handbook_3rd_Edition.pdf last accessed 5/23/2019

documents, but, more importantly, an agreement between the various departments was made regarding not just the flow of the work, but also the preferred attributes of those artifacts and exchanges.

7.9 Job Rotations

Job rotations are not like temporary assignments, but a continuation of the employment, from one part of the company to the other. Sometimes this is due to the employees; they desire to see and work at other parts of the organization. For example, a global company may afford an employee the opportunity to move to another part of the company in another part of the world. This sort of opportunity can provide a great morale boost for the employee. This is not the only benefit, or better said, job rotations can provide this and other benefits even if the job rotation is within the organization.

For some company's job rotations are used as a method to cultivate key talent that will one day be the executive class of the organization. One of us has worked at a company that would create a path for key talent to work 6 months to a year at one place, then move to another part of the company to learn about each part that constitutes the whole of the organization. To be sure this did not solve problems, but it exposes these people to the problems of the various parts of the organization, which gave them perhaps a unique perspective to be able to solve these problems or at least understand the limitations of the organization.

7.10 Failure Resume

Falure has a bad name, generally discussing these events are resisted, we work hard to avoid failure and subsequent discussions. Avoiding talking about or sharing these failures is not benefical for the individual, the department or the company. A company that has a culture that encourages hiding these less than stellar performances or spinning the results, obfuscating any learning. It is important to refer to these events as what they are; if it is a failure, we should not delude ourselves into believing the results are something they are not.

Not sharing failures means those failures will come back to haunt other team members (or even the same team members), as they must learn about this failure by actually failing again. There is an agile saying: ***fail fast and fail often***. This agile saying is used to encourage reacting to failure in a different way. Specifically, there should be no fear of failure; do not cover up the failure, but broadcast the failure so all can learn. However, taken to the extreme we may have a negative impact on the corporate culture.

Perhaps given the potential negative impact on the organization's culture, a different approach is required. An approach that recognizes failing is not likely terminal, and certainly not the sort of thing of which we should be ashamed. Rather than focus on failing in the form of a saying that can infer our goal is to fail and fail often, we can drive the culture to look at failure as one of the steps toward learning.

> A Smith College initiative called Failing Well is one of a crop of university programs that aims to help high achievers cope with the inevitable setbacks. Smith students were asked to create a "failure resume" – something any of us could do by jotting down a few setbacks, and any lessons learned – and then sharing it with others who have done the same thing.*

Analyzing past failures is not an academic exercise. Recognize that failures can have a negative impact on future work undertaken, including motivation. This initiative brings the failures into the light of day. We are compelled to talk about failures and thus reduce and perhaps remove any stigma that may be associated with failure. To paraphrase the old motorcyclist saying: there are two kinds of people, those that have failed, and those that will fail. Bringing these potential failures (and not be afraid to explore) to the surface this part of the work helps people and the organization grow.

7.11 Pre-mortem

Pre-mortems may sound like a peculiar way of thinking or approaching learning. We are perhaps familiar with the post-mortem. This is what happens after a death event. Post-mortems are used to ascertain the cause or causes of the death. The pre-mortem is used at the beginning of the project in an effort to draw the experiencs of the team to consider what will fail and how it can fail. To be successful, the team members need to be able to speak freely, to voice those things to which our project and organization may be subjected. How can our project fail? What will be the precipitating factors that will push the project into this failure mode? Thinking about this is thinking about the future and exploring what may happen in advance. The team will need to know the scope and the direction in which the project intends to take to achieve the project objectives. A diversity of thought is required to get a multiplicity of perspectives. At the end of this work, the team will have created a list of things that can go wrong within the project and perhaps rank the failures in terms of severity and probability of occurrence.

The pre-mortem brings these possible future failures to the entire team into discussion, learning each other's perspective those things that may go wrong. The results of which can help drive the actions to explore the probability of failure and

---

* Napper, P. & Rao, A. (2019). The power of agency: The 7 principles to conquer obstacles, make effective decisions, and create a life on your own terms. New York: St. Martin's Press. page 13.7

perhaps alternative approaches or solutions to these areas of potential failure. Where there may be uncertainty regarding the risks or failure modes, for example, the input may be opinion or perspective related and not necessarily experiential, the team may devise experiments to determine the validity. Some of these risks can be avoided by altering the scope, strategies, and tactics that the project intends to undertake to achieve the project objectives.

7.12 Thought Experiments

You may have heard about thought experiments. These were made famous by Albert Einstein, and his exploration on relativity and the properties of light. He used thought experiments to explore the nature of things like time and light. These experiments provide input for further exploration to draw more substantial conclusions. This may manifest as process and product experimentation.

7.13 Discussion Boards

Discussion boards are a very inexpensive method for sharing what is known, and these are generally well understood. If you are into racing or automotive parts, you will see many discussion boards or forums on vehicle configurations to improve the speed or performance. The discussion boards are maintained perhaps by those communites of practice, where those who are having difficulty with some specific issue can post questions to the experts, connecting specific application needs with individuals who have greater experience in that area. For example, perhaps we want to know what level of configuration management should be applied to a project that is much different than our past work. We can pose questions to this group, and get their input on the best manner to proceed. Sure, we could easily walk up to the

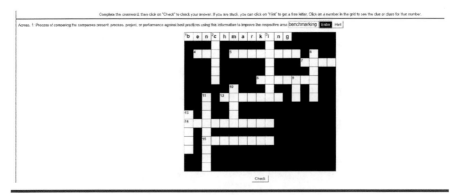

Figure 7.5   Tools like Hot Potatoes can help with developing games to encourage learning and even assess what the student has learned.

group and ask the question, but then this becomes a one on one event. That is not necessarily bad, but posting the question and responses via the discussion board now has made this experience known to anybody who would go to the discussion board seeking answers to this particular condition.

7.14 Gamification of Learning

Learning happens in many ways, and gamification is one of those things that is used to encourage the investment in time by the individual. We have used games in teaching classes, both in classrooms as well as in virtual class settings. The graphic above was made with Hot Potatoes. The tool can be found at ***https://hotpot.uvic. ca***, though this is not the only tool available (by the way we are not connected with the tool or the developing organization). Another tool we have explored is Quandry2, which is a decision based tool found at ***http://www.halfbakedsoftware. com/quandary.php***. This tool allows the student to explore sequences of events. The generator identifies the ideal sequence of events that are based upon some principles articulated to the student. The student then applies these principles to unlock the ideal sequence of events. This can go for multiple rounds. This site contains some examples: ***http://www.halfbakedsoftware.com/quandary/version_2/examples/***

We have connections in business and at universities, and we have noticed that there are many organizations applying gamification to learning within the organization, to the point of developing specialized games on specific topics that the organization assesses to be instrumental for the success of the company. This is different than using tools produced by a third party. Gaming learning taps into the playing side of the individual which is different than the work or learning in the historical studying of a subject. This can also foster a healthy competition between team members.

One of us, during our undergraduate degree, had experience with a group of people that studied together, worked hard together, and shared what each other knew. However, this collaboration had limits. Each person worked to get better grades, finish the test quicker than the others, have better project outputs, and the like. This did not change the collaboration. It is possible to have friendly and constructive competition. We know this runs contrary to many beliefs.

7.15 Testing

Testing people is often maligned. It is thought of to rank the team members in some sort of hierarchy or show the individual just how much they do not know. That should not be the objective of testing and testing certainly should not lead people to thinking that is why testing is performed. We do not know what we do not know in many cases. Continuous learning, like continuous improvement, requires finding out what we know (not guess we know) and do not know, as well as learning what we need to know. Testing has a place, but not how it is perceived to be used.

The first part is to evaluate what a person knows in a very defined context. This does not mean the use of statements like "knowledge of configuration management." This means nothing, and there is no way to evaluate this effectively. What does this mean in tangible and measurable attributes? A good way to think about what is needed is to consider Blooms taxonomy for how to structure the learning objectives.

Blooms taxonomy is a hierarchy that helps to establish the way to articulate the level of competency. There are degrees of knowledge when it comes to the topic under consideration. For example, simply being able to recall the steps in a process is one level of understanding. This level of understanding may be transferred from one person to another in several ways and perhaps in a relatively short amount of time. Recall is not truly understanding. The level a person is required to know on a topic likely depends upon the nature of the work. For example, an engineer may need to understand configuration management, but not be required to understand or create the configuration management system of the organization or for the project.

1. Recall
2. Understand
3. Apply
4. Analyze
5. Evaluate
6. Create

The objectives of the learning will be written based upon the level of understanding the team member or team needs to know. Writing learning objectives is like writing product specifications. It is important to write the objectives in such a way that confirmation of achieving the objective is well understood. That allows for creating a training event or teaching opportunity to be well scripted and planned. At the end of any formalized training event, there is a comparison of the objectives of the training and the results to ascertain the actual accomplishment via some demonstrable contrivance.

- ■ **Poor objective**: acquire knowledge of earned value management
- ■ **Good objective**: able to calculate Cost Performance Index, Schedule Performance Index, Schedule Variance, and Cost Variance.

7.15.1 Formative Assessment

Formative testing is used to ascertain what a person knows now at the begining of the training event. Where is the individual on this specific knowledge curve? This input will be used to move the person from what they presently know to the desired state of what we wish them to know. This exploration will happen in advance of the training or at the very least at the beginning of the training. This question approach works for more than contrived training events, but also for on the job training.

7.15.2 Summative Assessment

Summative assessments are those that happen at the conclusion of the training activities. The summative evaluation is used to ascertain how much of the training was actually absorbed by the student. Summative assessments let those providing the training know what portion of the training did not translate well and was not understood by the student. The point of the test is not to humiliate or to be used to brow beat the student, but to understand what portion of the training needs to be revisited with the student. Conversely, if the student understands the material well, the summative assessment will provide some clues to that end. When the summative assessment is handled well by the student, there is confidence that the student may be armed sufficiently to take on the challenge. That is the point of the training after all, to arm the student with knowledge to be able to meet the challenges of the workplace. This includes on the job training.

Chapter 8

Learning and Leadership

8.1 Organization Application

In this section we will be discussing the application of critical and creative thinking, our understanding of perspectives, and system's thinking to help us develop a learning organization. We have touched on many different topics in the preceding chapters, but have given no direction to do one thing or another. As a matter of point we have at several times stated that only the organization can truly teach themselves to become a learning organization. While an organization might need an outside activity or individual to aid in developing some of the critical thinking processes specific to organizational development they should not be required for situation diagnosis (i.e., what are the inhibitors to ... or our issues are...). If an organization feels that they need outside assistance to understand an issue internal to itself, they should probably be asking the following questions:

- What is stopping us from identifying our own issues?
- Have we identified the issues, but not acted upon them?
- Do we have workarounds to our processes and if so why?
- Who knows about those workarounds and have they been brought to the attention of senior personnel?
- Does information flow, where does it flow to, and what is done with said information and why?
- What is the difference between teaching a process and developing creative thinking?
- How, if at all, does critical and creative thinking apply to a learning organization and organizational development?

These are just a few of the questions we should be asking ourselves to determine what actions need to be taken and by whom. As we will discuss in the following sections each level of the organization needs different information and will take different information based upon that information. However, the information is generated from another section, usually the preceding group (proceeding process), and the group developing the information needs to be familiar with what the information is used for in the long run.

8.1.1 Management

Management is defined as: Interlocking functions of creating effective policy and organizing, planning, controlling, and directing an organization's resources in order to achieve specific objectives.*

Management has been around since the beginning of civilization yet we have just recently begun to develop theories related to management.† While management has been around for centuries its focus was not business as we know it today. This was primarily due to there being no business of a size to warrant or to be considered to warrant management except politics and the expanse and maintenance of the empire.‡ It was not until the 19th century that theories of management were starting to develop. Some examples of management theories are classical management, scientific management, bureaucracy, human relations, contingency, and system theories.§ It was not until around the 1900's that Frederick Winslow Taylor started developing management as a science that management was given any real thought.

According to Frederick Winslow Taylor in The Principles of Scientific Management 1910 the initiative of the workmen (i.e., their hard labor, honesty, and the resourcefulness) is obtained with more consistency using the scientific approach to management, but this approach places new responsibilities on the management personnel.¶ These new responsibilities would fall into four different areas:

First: Replace the tribal knowledge of the work with a scientific method.
Second: Develop the worker through teaching, training, and proper selection (job-fit).

---

* Good one to know! (n.d.). Retrieved April 8, 2019, from http://www.businessdictionary.com/definition/management.html
† Edunote.info@gmail.com. (2018, August 14). How Modern Management Theories were Developed. Retrieved April 8, 2019, from https://iedunote.com/modern-management-theories
‡ Edunote.info@gmail.com. (2018, August 14). How Modern Management Theories were Developed. Retrieved April 8, 2019, from https://iedunote.com/modern-management-theories
§ What Are the Six Theories of Management? (n.d.). Retrieved April 8, 2019, from https://www.reference.com/business-finance/six-theories-management-414ed1cc88eb1ecc
¶ Taylor, F. W. (1998). *The principles of scientific management*. Originally published in 1911. Norcross, GA: Engineering & Management Press.

Third: Honestly collaborate with the workers to employ the scientific principles used to develop the tasks.

Fourth: Equal division of labor and responsibility for both management and worker, each doing what they are best suited.*

During the last 100 years there have been numerous theories on leadership styles, leadership approaches, and actions of leaders (Style Leadership Theory[†]). Before we proceed with our discussion on managers and supervisors we must look at some of these areas in the leadership area to better understand how they would apply and when a shifting of the style or theory might be necessary or occur.

In the book Multiplier by Liz Wiseman, she points out that there are two different leadership approaches that she refers to as Diminishers and Multipliers. Both of these require very intelligent people, but use their intelligence in different ways. Diminishers approach the people with perspective that the team members will never figure what is going on and the appropriate action to take without the leader. Multipliers, on the other hand, see their people as intelligent and able to figure things out on their own and would rather guide or help the team to do just that.

From her book below are the five disciplines of each category:[‡]

■ Multipliers – believe that people are smart and can figure things out
   - Talent Magnet
   - Liberator
   - Challenger
   - Debater
   - Investor
■ Diminishers – believe people will not figure it out without the leader
   - Empire builder
   - Tyrant
   - Know-it-all
   - Decision maker
   - Micromanager

Both can get results, but the larger magnitude and more sustainable approach is accomplished by the multipliers. The multipliers create an environment where those on the team are continuously learning and exploring opportunities. It is an environment to which talent will flock as team members will be expected to demonstrate what

---

* Taylor, F. W. (1998). *The principles of scientific management.* Originally published in 1911. Norcross, GA: Engineering & Management Press.

[†] Oakleaf, L. (n.d.). Organization and Administration in Recreation, Sport and Leisure Management. Retrieved May.

[‡] Wiseman, L. (2017). Multipliers: How the best leaders make everyone smarter. New York: Harper Business.

they know and can accomplish together. The leader is a challenger – setting stretch goals to help the team develop their skills and competencies while doing the work. They are good at discussing and debating decisions and alternatives, which provide opportunities for learning. These leaders free the people to make decisions and act on what they know and provide opportunities for learning in doing so.

Contrast that with the Diminsher, where all the decisions will be made by this leader. The Diminisher will hire smart, talented people, but then by dint of making all the decisions will erode the team member's confidence and remove opportunities for learning.

If we look at the leadership table, we can determine which leadership style relates to the Multiplier and the Diminisher and how all of this directly relates to the Style Leadership Theory. Doing this will allow us to complete the manager and supervisor puzzle in our following discussion. However, we must keep in mind that no one leadership style or theory can pertain to every situation or individual and as managers and supervisors we balance the goals of the organization, the group/department, and the individual to produce effective results.

There are some modern organizations that have reduced the management levels. For example, the software gaming company Valve provides a unique approach to the organization structure. The employee handbook is an interesting read that describes a truly unique approach to the work.* From the very first paragraph on how to use the book, it is clear this is not the typical welcome to the organization, human resources book.

> This book isn't about fringe benefits or how to set up your workstation or where to find source code. Valve works in ways that might seem counterintuitive at first. This handbook is about the choices you're going to be making and how to think about them. Mainly, it's about how not to freak out now that you're here.

This manual is professed to be written by the team member's using these team members' experiences with onboarding in the organization. In addition, there is explanation to those new acquisitions, of the reasons for the lack of hierarchical structure, and it is worded in such a way to clearly demonstrate the reasons for this structure while also pointing to the expectation upon the new hire.

> Hierarchy is great for maintaining predictability and repeatability. It simplifies planning and makes it easier to control a large group of people from the top down, which is why military organizations rely on it so heavily. But when you're an entertainment company that's spent the last decade going out of its way to recruit the most intelligent, innovative,

---

* https://steamcdn-a.akamaihd.net/apps/valve/Valve_NewEmployeeHandbook.pdf last accessed 5/14/2019.

talented people on Earth, telling them to sit at a desk and do what they're told obliterates 99 percent of their value. We want innovators, and that means maintaining an environment where they'll flourish.

The new employee book goes on to explain that the company is the newly hired employees to steer toward opportunities and away from risks. The work further describes how the employee selects the project, not the typical associations where the employee is assigned a project with the associated objectives and work products. Essentially, an individual has the choice of what needs to be done and whether any specific individual wants to do it or can accomplish the objective. Essentially the team member finds out what they work on by free association with the other team members learning about their respective areas of interest. Even when it comes to deciding what work poses the best business impact, the new hire is able to have influence. This includes commentary on group think; just because another team member says it is not good to work on a certain project or set of work, critical thinking on the topic from the new employee is expected.

We were so taken by this atypical handbook that we made several attempts to have a discussion with members of this organization but were unable to do so. We encourage any readers of this work to check out their employee handbook; it will likely give you some ideas for how to change your organization.

8.1.2 Learning

The project work itself, no matter the method, is an opportunity for the individuals and the group to learn. This can be a form of personnel training. There are more learning opportunities than some off-site event. One thing we did not cover is that there is a difference between learning something and developing a true understanding of that thing or applying critical and creative thinking to the processes, procedures, and the project. For example, a person can learn to push a button given a specific event or indicator lamp, that does not mean they know what has happened or what the switch activation does to abate the situation. There are many theories about learning styles, both pro and con, and the application of what is learned in a critical or creative manner. At this point you are probably asking, "what does this have to do with management?"

We started our discussion with Introduction Learning and Thought, Importance to the Organization and in that section, we worked into the Mission and Vision statements. The Mission and Vision statements are set by the management and should be used to create a culture to promote growth of the organization in a particular way by providing its people with direction consistent with the aspirational objective of the organization. When people have a question on "How should we proceed" the vision statement should be their guiding light, not the management team, and the mission statement should be the map to the guiding light. Last, but not least, there is the values statement. If the vision statement is the goal, and the mission statement is the road map, then the values statement is the rules of the road. This will seem to be a circle in that if management sets the mission, vision, and values statements they should be the guidance, right? No, even if management does create these three statements they must be followed or enforced at all levels of the organization and be the guide of everyone's attitudes and actions. Management that behaves contrary to these documents, will nullify these documents to the point of the team members not behaving according to these expectations.

What would your mission statements be that would support developing a learning organization? Could you then develop a value statement to support that mission statement? One of the first questions from management when approached with a question from the team should be, "What does our mission, vision, and values statements tell us to do?" This approach helps reinforce the importance of the mission, vision, and values statements and guides the individual to creatively think of how they apply to the organization. This approach is in line with the empower management approach where people are prompted to come to their own conclusions, thus providing the team with an opportunity to create and buy in to the outcome. Matching our words to our deeds promotes the mission, vision, and values statements through active application.

8.1.3 Management and Change Management

How does management play a role in change management? Change does not always require a manager, that is change is coming whether you like it or not. We manage change to encourage a change that moves in the desired direction, that is the reason for management. The change happens, and often is emergent. Emergent in that it happens in small steps, not bursting into view all at once. This requires paying attention to these subtle clues. This is like starting a fire, we set kindling and early starting material, and when the fire appears to be taking hold, we take more actions to encourage the growth. We do this following the rules of fire making, for example placing the additional material in such a manner that allows air circulation and a higher level of combustion. Like building a fire, developing a corporation's culture requires attention to the dynamics and a response that supports those emerging symptoms that support the objective, as well as a response for emerging events that run contrary to the organization's objective. Inattention to these emergent events by management or project managers results in culture changes that are not desired. By that we mean those changes that promote workarounds, sub-optimization of the entire processes of the organization, or restricts dissemination of knowledge. These are not good results from change, as they are not captured formally and are commonly employed by those who are in phase three of Tribal leadership: I am great you are not,* which is counter to a healthy organization. It is important to re relate

---

* Logan, D., King, J. P., & Fischer-Wright, H. (2011). *Tribal leadership: Leveraging natural groups to build a thriving organization.* New York: Harper Business.

change management to our mission, vision, and values statements. Actions that allowed to diverge from these core statements can easily happen, and if we do not address this discrepancy will result in culture that has nothing to do with our desire. This discrepancy will result in morale issues and confusion of the team members.

How does management play a role in change management? Change does not always require a manager, that is change is coming whether you like it or not. We manage change to encourage a change that moves in the desired direction, that is the reason for management. The change happens, and often is emergent. Emergent in that it happens in small steps, not bursting into view all at once. This requires paying attention to these subtle clues. This is like starting a fire, we set kindling and early starting material, and when the fire appears to be taking hold, we take more actions to encourage the growth. We do this following the rules of fire making, for example placing the additional material in such a manner that allows air circulation and a higher level of combustion. Like building a fire, developing a corporation's culture requires attention to the dynamics and a response that supports those emerging symptoms that support the objective, as well as a response for emerging events that run contrary to the organization's objective. Inattention to these emergent events by management or project managers results in culture changes that are not desired. By that we mean those changes that promote workarounds, sub-optimization of the entire processes of the organization, or restricts dissemination of knowledge. These are not good results from change, as they are not captured formally and are commonly employed by those who are in phase three of Tribal leadership: I am great you are not, which is counter to a healthy organization. It is important to re relate change management to our mission, vision, and values statements. Actions that allowed to diverge from these core statements can easily happen, and if we do not address this discrepancy will result in culture that has nothing to do with our objective. This discrepancy, left unaddressed, will result in morale issues and confusion of the team members, or at least will demonstrate that the company vision, mission and values statements are just words and mean nothing.

8.1.4 Information and Reporting

Think about a manager or project manager. What reports do they receive and how many of those reports contain data that either represents the current status or provides useful information? Progress and status reports are something that managers and project managers often request and are needed for their jobs. However, experience suggests many of these reports contain information that is either tainted by the perspective of the provider or burdened with irrelevant information. Tainted data can happen accidental in the gathering, or a function of self-preservation, that is consciously manipulated to lead the person viewing the information to a desired conclusion, often favorable. Both failure types benefit from team perspective and a safe environment, no fear of reprisals for saying or reporting the facts. Another failure mode is information that has little or nothing to do with the objective or goals. In fact, a mass of data can make understanding a situation difficult, it diffuses focus, clouds the issues and prevents crisp movement toward learning and moving toward our goals. Using the minimalistic management* and change models you as a manager should be asking several questions:

- What information do I need to understand what is happening?
- How much of that information do I need reported that I cannot obtain on my own through observation and attention to detail?
- Do the people providing the information understand its purpose and what do they see as required information?

These are just a few of the type of questions that a manager or project manager might want to ask themselves to determine if they are receiving useful information or bogging down a system with unnecessary and irrelevant data collection. The manager should provide rationale for the information and will aid those providing information to help in developing useful metrics and frequency of tracking. In fact, a manager should not unilaterally define the measure or how the measurements are

Figure 8.1 There are limits to documentation, at the extreme, the paper can divide the people.

---

* Smith, R. (2011, June 06). Minimalist Management -- When Less is More. Retrieved February 19, 2019, from https://www.managementexchange.com/blog/minimalist-management-when-less-more

obtained or the tools (for example, like those discussed in the TQM section) should be used to analyze and present the data. This involves the team, engages the team and exercises their skills in measurement while being coached by the manager or project manager.

As with most things going too far in any extreme does not solve anything, so care must be employed to strike a balance between needed and useful, to avoid unproductive and burdensome. The balance of this information can be achieved but may require the assistance of the owners of the processes, procedures, and projects being monitored or managed. These discussions and subsequent measurements can clarify system performance and identify constraints or bottlenecks. Trend data can help us understand to natural variation in the system that truly helps in understanding the system as well as being a precursor for system improvements via change.

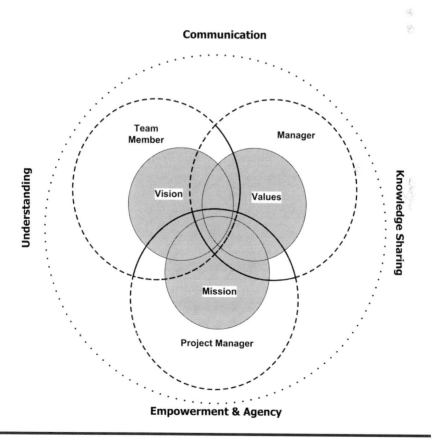

Figure 8.2   Mission, vision, and value statements have impact on the system and personnel.

8.1.5 *Inculcating*

Inculcating has several different meanings: Teaching, Instructing, Coaching, Training, Indoctrinating, Instilling, and Impress upon. At least part of the point in the vision, mission and value statement is to encourage some types of values over others, focused on achieving the mission, and directed toward some vision that the entire team can support, hopefully enthusiastically. While inculcating is most associated with changing someone or something through persistent instruction may sound like nagging (some say project managers must know how to nag), if the lesson is important to the organization's success consistency is our only hope of achieving the change we desire. The same is true for our communication, if we want open and safe communication, we must reinforce the organization's value for communication and demonstrate or model this behavior. Words will not matter of the actions run contrary. The same is true of the actions only match when it is convenient or when the actions come with some consequence. The true test of leadership and perhaps character, is behaving in accord with our values even when it comes at a cost. There are many inhibitors to communication and words that promote a defensive, aggressive or a strong positional authority. This approach to communication run contrary to helping inculcate the desired behaviors (hard to imagine the vision statement that matches). There may be times when it is strong language or exercising positional authority are required, however, this should be done with explanation You should ask, "How do you not use your positional authority and yet maintain it for times when it is required?" All of this must balance being responsible to the people whom we are leading and for the efforts we are managing.

One of the interesting definitions of inculcating must be teaching. This teaching should focus on things like the mission, vision, and values statements of the organization with a slant towards critical and creative thinking associated with processes and procedures of the organization. Teaching also applies to any continuous improvement efforts the organization has underway, perhaps more so. In that we mean that we should promote our people and our organization to always be seeking to make the next thing: people, job, procedure, process, and project, better. This constant improvement based upon the mission, vision, and values statements of an organization is the exact meaning of a learning organization and the quintessential part of organizational development that lasts. Patience and communications are required for teaching, it should clear that commanding is not teaching.

We intentionally develop the organization's culture to create an environment in which there is a high degree of repeatability, and to ensure the organization is successful. The organization sets the behavior expected from the employee and the values the organization believes are conducive to good stewardship of the organization while ensuring the learning and individual growth. To be sure, the organization is not static, but will require adaptations over time. The principles the organization attempts to instill in the employee does not mean check the brain at the door.

8.1.6 *Knowledge Sharing*

Let us not delude ourselves. We all know that knowledge sharing is important to the health and growth of teams and organization development. All we must do to verify this is conduct a search on the computer about "Knowledge Sharing" and we will see hundreds if not thousands of articles. We can also look at the more effective organizations and see that they share knowledge in a more productive manner. Then why do we not share knowledge freely if we know it can only help our organization? I am sure we have all heard the adage that "Knowledge is Power." It is this very reason why it does not commonly flow as it should. In the book "Tribal Leadership" they refer to this as phase 3: I'm great you are not.[*] This zone is about personal accomplishment and feeling let down, high personal goals and/or standards but feel others do not have these same standards or goals.[†] This either comes from a lack of goal sharing or knowledge sharing sponsored from a sense that they can only rely on themselves;[‡] therefore they control information in a manner that sustains this model. The irony of this is that without the sharing of knowledge these individuals will obtain a plateau based on time and can progress no further.[§] It is when those people realize that sharing this knowledge and allowing others to develop, they themselves and the organization will develop more and be able to facilitate higher objectives.

Highly performing people, like those commonly selected for or are in management positions, are very susceptible to the pitfalls of assuming they are the hardest workers, and few can perform at their level. They think they must control information (Knowledge) as to not overload others. There is also a darker side of this where some control this information to secure their position of power. This could be from a sense of insecurity in their position as well. Either way this position is self-defeating in that it is seen by others as office politics and creates negative experiences for everyone involved. And as we discussed using the leadership equation these negative experiences demotivate personnel and create the next generation of stage three leaders. The question is how do we not promote or how do we get past this stage three? The answer to this is as varied as the people who go through it, but there are some key areas we could concentrate on, such as a strong values statement that promotes development of self and others to a higher level and a lack of concern of position or power, both of which are key to stage three. The higher level of development we speak of is in the form of collaborative and creative thinking. This model plays against the standard training model in that it is not the conformist or

---

[*] Logan, D., King, J. P., & Fischer-Wright, H. (2011). *Tribal leadership: Leveraging natural groups to build a thriving organization.* New York: Harper Business.

[†] Logan, D., King, J. P., & Fischer-Wright, H. (2011). *Tribal leadership: Leveraging natural groups to build a thriving organization.* New York: Harper Business.

[‡] Logan, D., King, J. P., & Fischer-Wright, H. (2011). *Tribal leadership: Leveraging natural groups to build a thriving organization.* New York: Harper Business.

[§] Logan, D., King, J. P., & Fischer-Wright, H. (2011). *Tribal leadership: Leveraging natural groups to build a thriving organization.* New York: Harper Business.

those that adhere to the standard outline and consistently yield the desired answer, but those who are able to develop their own answer commonly working as part of a team for overall improvement for the tasks at hand.*

8.1.7 Management Changes over Time

Everything changes with time including what is considered good or effective management. According to a paper written by Ellen Van Velsor and Joel Wright for the Center for Creative Leadership the five most important competencies over the last 20 years have changed in a rather dynamic manner.† Whereas 20 years ago technical mastery, self-motivation and discipline, confidence, effective communication, and resourcefulness were the top five, now the top five are self-motivation and discipline, effective communication, learning agility, self-awareness, and adaptability and versatility.‡ As you can see the dynamic has shifted in such a manner as to appear to desire a motivated individual with good communication skills who can learn about numerous topics quickly versus an individual who is technically savvy, self-motivated, and confident with less communication skills. This shift should not be surprising in that we have seen a shift in society toward the group dynamic and away from single point source. This can be considered good or bad, but either way it is what we have to work with and will assuredly change again in the next 20 years. The point that we as managers need to draw from this is we must stay in tune with these changes as they develop because they will affect how we are to manage our people and even more so how we will help their development and that of our organization. Also, as the people who are aligned to this current model become supervisors and managers the information, they will need to assess the overall health of projects and the organization will change.

Habits are something that we all contend with both good and bad. As we discuss the changes in management and how we manage, one of the items we must address is "Habits." While by the definition of a habit it is a constant item, it would not seem to fit within the arena of changes if we look further into how habits play into an organization we would see that habits are the cause of the majority of cyclic change. When we determine an item or action that needs a change we are in all actuality addressing a habit that has been developed by either our people or our processes themselves. As we all know and have had to deal with for both our own habits and those of our organization it is easy to fall into allowing a habit to return after we have facilitated a change to said habit. This is a natural function of how our brain is designed to make space for new information and decrease response time to items it has defined as routine (Habits). However, that is exactly why we must work harder

---

* Logan, D., King, J. P., & Fischer-Wright, H. (2011). *Tribal leadership: Leveraging natural groups to build a thriving organization.* New York: Harper Business.
† Van Velsor, E., & Wright, J. (2012, October). *Expanding the Leadership Equation Developing Next-Generation Leaders* [WHITE PAPER, Center for Creative Leadership].
‡ Van Velsor, E., & Wright, J. (2012, October). *Expanding the Leadership Equation Developing Next-Generation Leaders* [WHITE PAPER, Center for Creative Leadership].

to change and maintain changed those items that have become habits. Another word for habit is routine and while most organizations view routines as a cost savings and an asset they, as with most things, come at a cost. And that cost would be a natural resistance to being changed.

8.1.8 Summation

Things are often connected in ways that are not apparent. It is often a lack of considering these connections that produce unintended consequences. Unintended, because there was little or no critique of the strategy or review of the subsequent actions, or way these actions discovered and discussed. The goal of this was to show some possible interrelations with the discussions we have had up to this point and relate it to management and project management positions. Since organization's are techno-social systems, a prescriptive approach is not viable. Though the technical portions may be something quantifiable to some degree, the social part depends on the organization's industry, objective, and talent.

8.1.9 Project Manager

What is the difference between a manager and a project manager? While there are times when they seem similar, there are times when they seem worlds apart, and then there are even times when there is no difference because the role is satisfied by someone acting as both and yet neither. In the previous section we defined a manager and discussed their role within the organization. In this section we will do the same for project managers and contrast those against management. When you look up project manager online you will get numerous definitions, and the truth is the role of the project manager will depend upon the organization, industry, and a good many other factors.

8.1.9.1 Learning

In the management section we discussed the mission, vision, and values statements and how management should embed learning into these three foundations of the organization. Now we are going to discuss supervisors and how they are going to employ these three corner stones to aid it getting things done. While it is challenging for management to develop these three statements they do not have to attempt to make them work through the effort of others. Let's look at the mission statement. It gives us a goal: we are going to do "X" or become "Y," and every goal brings about change by the nature of the goal itself. Therefore, a supervisor must be an agent for change. Now you are probably asking, "Why is this in the learning section? It seems more connected to change rather than learning." To learn something is to change in the most fundamental way. And if a supervisor desires changes, to meet the mission of the organization, they must promote learning and a learning environment to meet that objective.

Most supervisors came from the workforce and have, hopefully, developed some knowledge of the processes. They have also seen firsthand the effect the environment established in the organization and its effects on obtaining the goal of the mission statement. They must use these experiences to produce both a better environment for further learning and positive experiences to maintain positive motivation. When a supervisor or work leader promotes a positive environment for learning, has an open mental model, those personnel being supervised should no longer feel they are being supervised. They should feel that their input is valued and they are a member of the team. This feeling of belonging will promote or can promote those individuals to better understand the processes (learn) to provide even more to the team.

I saw this on social media, and could not help but capture it. This is exactly what we do not want to happen.

Example:

Worker: I have an idea; we could do this task better if we do …....

Supervisor: That is interesting. How would doing that affect the remainder of the team, process, or overall system?

Or

That's why you're a worker. You don't understand the process.

Worker: I have not thought about that.

Or

Feels their suggestion for a possible improvement is being dismissed and will not make further suggestions about anything. Even issues that require adjustment. Prime example of how negative experiences produce disengaged workers.

At this point the conversation would more than likely end.

Supervisor: Let's break it down to see if we can determine how it would, but first should we involve anyone else in this discussion if we're going to determine how it would affect these things?

This is the start of positive re-enforcement. It will still require follow on actions by both parties: supervisor and worker(s). If no follow on occurs then it will appear as placation to the worker and will actually produce a greater negative response than being dismissed.

 Allen Holub
@allenholub

 Following ∨

Learned helplessness is what happens when a company stops crushing the motivation out of people & they still feel crushed. However, the term is usually used by managers at companies that are still doing active crushing, often accompanied by an eye roll. That's real helplessness.

3:00 AM - 14 May 2019

Another option would be if the worker has thought about the effects on the other portions of the organization. The supervisor could ask the worker to support their assessment and if they had discussed it with other members of the team.

While this is not direct learning, it is application of understanding: critical and creative thinking, it is much better. Learning is important, but applying that learning in ways the improve the team and the organization is where real progress is made. The use of the model above serves many purposes: to foster people to look past the surface level of a change (systems thinking),* building a sense of commitment within the group (shared vision),† building collective thinking skills through transforming conversations into functional actions (Team Learning),‡ and helping the worker to desire to develop their understanding of the processes to provide better contribution toward the desire goals (Personal Mastery).§ This is four of the five disciplines discussed by Peter Senge in his book "The Fifth Discipline Fieldbook". The only remaining one is Mental Model and it too is covered in the example above, but we thought it should be addressed separately due to its many sides.

Mental Model or, as we like to refer to it Open Mental Model, is not only a learning tool, but a motivational tool as well. It is a learning tool in that it requires reflection, clarification, and constant improvement of our perspective of our environment.⁋ It is a motivational tool in that with an open mental model we are not using cognitive biases to shut down the opinions of others, but rather asking about how they were developed to increase our own understanding. This leads not only to our increased understanding, but their feeling of a sense of belonging to the team. Point of truth, as a supervisor there will be times when this approach is not able to be employed, but when those times occur a follow-on with that or those individuals needs to occur to ensure they understand the why behind that action. For the most part I attempt to follow the model that Mr. Anthony Jared employed: a leader or supervisor is a servant to their people in that you are to help them achieve both their goals and that of the organization and the best way to achieve this is through positive learning on the part of all parties.

8.1.9.2 Project Manager and Change (Habits)

The project manager is in a position to facilitate the cultivation of good habits. Habits are our brains way of reducing the clutter of things it must actively work on or worry about. When an item becomes a habit the brain files it away to use as an automatic response to a set group of criteria. While this helps us to have

* Kleiner, A. & Senge, P. M. (1994). *The Fifth Discipline Fieldbook.* London: Nicholas Brearley.
† Kleiner, A. & Senge, P. M. (1994). *The Fifth Discipline Fieldbook.* London: Nicholas Brearley.
‡ Kleiner, A. & Senge, P. M. (1994). *The Fifth Discipline Fieldbook.* London: Nicholas Brearley.
§ Kleiner, A. & Senge, P. M. (1994). *The Fifth Discipline Fieldbook.* London: Nicholas Brearley.
⁋ Kleiner, A. & Senge, P. M. (1994). *The Fifth Discipline Fieldbook.* London: Nicholas Brearley.

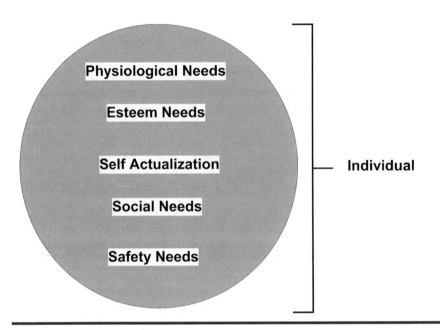

Figure 8.3 While we all have needs that must be fulfilled, the order is as varied as the individual who has them, for example Maslow uses the "Starving Artist."

more mental power to develop different ideas it comes at a cost. Habits, either good or bad, are harder to overcome (change) than something that has not been established as a habit/routine. Thinking this through, we can see why the mission, vision, and values statements can be such a valuable tool in organizational growth and development; they can make growth and development a habit. However, this is only if these statements, mission, vision, and values, are structured usefully and actually supported. As I am sure, you all have worked for an organization that has had a great mission, vision, and values statement, but that is where it ended, with the paper it was written on.

You are probably asking, "What does this have to do with the project managers, they do not write these statements?" And that would be correct, they do not. However, each project or group of people working together will need to have a connection to these statement. They also need the support of managers to inforce them. So, it would seem this is more like a managerial issue. However, the majority of an organization's environment is set at the mid-level: supervisors, who are attempting to create an environment that upholds the organization's statements. There can be a disconnect between managers that are looking for results on the current hot item and most supervisors are looking at so many more items such as development of workers, processes inmprovements, and keeping the organization's work flowing. This is one reason that some organizations have moved away from having managers and are embracing team supervisors or just

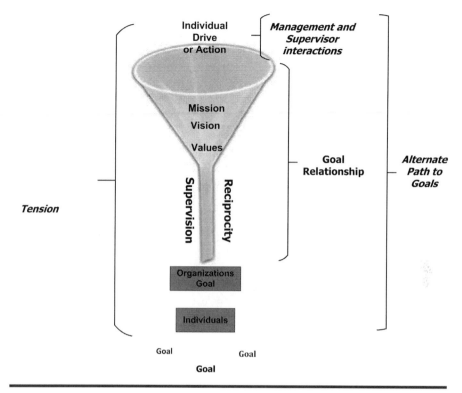

Figure 8.4 The system of organization improvement is complex.

the team concept: no positional supervisor or manager. This model fully embraces their mission, vision, and values statements and all employees are held to them through organizational norms. We have written much about organizational norms throughout several previous chapters, but at this point we need to discuss them further.

According to Oxford Research Encyclopedia social norms: are a powerful force in organizations.* They go on further to discuss two components to social norms: regularity among a population or group and personnel within the group are aware of the norms and the regularity of said behavior.† Also, according to an article from "psychology and society" organizational values present what the organization believes is important or acceptable and provide norms for the people employed

* Dannals, J. E., & Miller, D. T. (2017, November 10). Social Norms in Organizations. Retrieved April 26, 2019, from http://oxfordre.com/business/view/10.1093/acrefore/9780190224851.001.0001/acrefore-9780190224851-e-139
† Dannals, J. E., & Miller, D. T. (2017, November 10). Social Norms in Organizations. Retrieved April 26, 2019, from http://oxfordre.com/business/view/10.1093/acrefore/9780190224851.001.0001/acrefore-9780190224851-e-139

there.* This article links the values statement an organization has to what its people have or view as their norms. Like social norms, organizational norms assert pressure or influence on people to follow without the hierarchy of the organization needing to take an action through the individual's desire to belong or be an accepted member of the group. This takes us full circle: from the individual's basic psychological needs to being a member of an organization.†

8.1.9.3 Motivational Cycles

In the beginning of this book we discussed Maslow's Hierarchy of needs and how these needs provide motivation for that individual to conduct or perform some action to obtain said need. Now we are going to look at this from the supervisor's perspective. There are four basic motivational drivers: Need, Drive, Incentive, and Goal or Reward.‡ This article goes on further to state how each of these basic motivators are codependent. It states that a "Need" is a physical condition that promotes tension within the individual, but does not necessary produce motivation.§ This tension may give rise to some form of action from the individual until it is met. This action can be considered "Drive." However, drive does not ensure a specific behavior. For a specific behavior to occur we must introduce an incentive. This directed or specific behavior yields the goal or reward that was promoted by the need.¶ The reason it is called a motivational cycle is because it continuously repeats itself when a new goal or need, or a revision to a previous goal or need, is introduced. How does this relate to supervision? It relates to supervision in that: "Incentive", the directing the behavior in a specific manner. Knowing an individual's goal or need and showing them how (incentive) can help them achieve (Drive) their goal (Reward) goes a long way in establishing trust. While some people feel this is manipulation helping someone see a way to achieve "THEIR" goal through completing an alternate task should be viewed as reciprocation as long as the individual sees both as having a related value. This is where the societal, group, and organizational norms play back into motivation and since these norms are or can be enhanced through the mission, vision, and values statement, mainly the values statement, it just reaffirms the importance of both these statements and their enforcement.

---

* (n.d.). Retrieved April 26, 2019, from http://www.psychologyandsociety.com/organizationalculture.html

† Maslow's Hierarchy of Needs. (n.d.). Retrieved August 6, 2018, from https://simplypsychology.org/maslow.html

‡ Smirti. (2019, February 15). Motivation Cycle - Fundamentals of Psychology. Retrieved April 26, 2019, from https://www.managementnote.com/motivation-cycle/

§ Smirti. (2019, February 15). Motivation Cycle - Fundamentals of Psychology. Retrieved April 26, 2019, from https://www.managementnote.com/motivation-cycle/

¶ Smirti. (2019, February 15). Motivation Cycle - Fundamentals of Psychology. Retrieved April 26, 2019, from https://www.managementnote.com/motivation-cycle/

We can now look at the Rule of Reciprocity since we have begun discussing "incentive" as part of motivation and how this plays into motivation. According to Sociologist Alvin Gouldner there is no group on earth that doesn't follow the Rule of Reciprocity and cultural anthropologist Lionel Tiger and Robin Fox go on to state that it is central to the human experience and responsible for how society is organized into interdependent groups.* When I think of more than one person trying to achieve one goal by himself, I think of Zig Ziglar and his book "The Secret of Closing a Sale." When I was at the Recruiter School for the Navy, they used this book to teach us about reciprocity and individual goal obtainment. The school, using this book, told us that if we showed the individual how the Navy could help them achieve their goal then they would be more likely to join. The key was to determine the individual's real goal, not just what they would say, and being truthful in how this goal or goals could be achieved. This is no different than in any organization, department, division, or team. While in most cases we as managers and supervisors do not think of these type of issues because the individuals who are working with us are receiving a paycheck, and that should be their reciprocity, this stance does not provide any motivation for true engagement of the work force. This mentality might suffice for young people just starting out who have only the goal of a check, but it will come at a cost of a disengaged worker later in their career when higher aspirations are more prevalent. If we employ this thought pattern and couple it with the Leadership Equation, we can see how an organization has a dramatic effect on their people from the very start. And they should periodically reinforce how the project (organizational goal) will help the individual achieve their goal and the supervisor of said individual should also know if the goal of the individual has changed and how this new goal is supported by the organization's goal.

In summing up motivational cycles as it pertains to the supervisor, we need to remember that nothing happens without tension between an existing state and a desired state, and that when this tension does exist it needs goal relation to the organization's goal to become useful to the organization. We must also note that the reason this applies to the supervisor and not the manager is the supervisor has more interaction with a larger number of people who make up the organization. This obviously shifts as the structure or the organization shifts and should be accounted for as such.

8.1.9.4 Knowledge Sharing

In several sections of this book we discuss knowledge sharing in the form of passing lessons learned from one group to another. However, this is just a small portion of what and how knowledge sharing should be employed. We also discuss knowledge sharing as a part of office politics. This is more in line with lack of knowledge sharing

---

* Rieck, D. (1997). Influence and Persuasion: The Rule of Reciprocity. Retrieved April 29, 2019, from http://www.directcreative.com/influence-and-persuasion-the-rule-of-reciprocity.html

and is likened to the brokering of knowledge to retain or achieve some position of power or perceived power over another individual or group of individuals. I have added to the old adage that knowledge is power to the point of saying that knowledge is like a brick: it weighs the individual down when held close and only when shared can it be used to build something great. As a supervisor the sharing of knowledge is of the utmost importance because it has many more facets than the knowledge sharing of management personnel and/or employees. At the supervisor position the information, knowledge in its raw form, must be filtered to its intended recipient in both directions and in such a manner as to not become entangled in the political arena. This makes the task for knowledge sharing more difficult because each audience has a different use for the information and more than likely a different use for it as well.

If we look at the basic question, How, What, When, Where, and Why, we can easily ascertain the difference in discussions that would be held for the same knowledge sharing between a supervisor and employee, that of a supervisor to manager, and that of supervisor to supervisor. As an exercise think of something you will or have shared with an employee and then think of how you would present that to a manager and supervisor. Then perform that activity in the reverse direction. When completed with both of these actions ask yourself, "Why was the information presented differently?" The presentation of knowledge is most commonly tailored to the expected use of the individual or group it is being provided to with the intent of producing some action or help in achieving some goal (providing incentive) that is desired by either one or all parties involved in the exchange. This tailoring of information can be both good and bad as the manipulation of information can either overload or poorly direct the recipient. This is where the term office politics comes into play, manipulation through minimal information, and where negation through overload comes into view as well: too much information serves little to no use. As with minimalistic information to gain an advantage, so can information overload be another form of an advantage game that appears more as information (Knowledge) sharing than the minimalistic approach, but is probably more destructive than the other. This excessive information also can make its recipient feel inadequate and is an example of several cognitive biases. It is the very nature of this triple bladed sword that renders useful knowledge sharing problematic.

8.1.10 Worker

While there are numerous sources that put the onus on supervision and management to maintain worker morale and to provide a work environment that is conducive to growth and development that is not the case with this book. For any activity to be successful all parts of it must function well and together and that includes the workers. I would actually have to say that the worker has a greater part to play in their own destiny now than in previous years as the corporate culture and social dynamics has developed more toward a happy, productive, and well informed worker. Whereas in the past it was more geared toward the company and their goals with little thought to the worker taking the organization there, we can actually see this change in the research and development of workplace (social) psychology, organization development, and occupational health and safety, just to mention a few areas of change. We can thank the information age for these changes and we can expect more as we learn more and that information is shared throughout society and thus all levels of every organization.

8.1.10.1 Empowerment and Agency

In the parlance of the business world, empowerment is the authority given by the company to the employees to do what is required to get the job done. There are certain things that must be in place within the organization to make empowerment work. It is not as easy as waving of the hands and yea verily thou art empowered. Words alone will not work, but the words and actions must be congruent. The actions of the company and the management must be consistent to ensure empowerment.

As can be seen over the course of many years, in the Gallup study, employees are not often fully engaged. This brings up the concept of agency. Agency is about being active, not passive. It is the ability and desire of people to take active measures to meet challenges and opportunities as these are presented. Executives are working to create an environment that ensures the best performance from all members of the team. This requires the team members to have agency. Agency is that feeling of being in control of your life. Agency provides an impetus for an individual to act, both in their personal life as well as their work life. Empowerment is giving the authority to the employee or worker, and agency is that within the worker that will ensure actions take place as needed.

A good example of the prerequisites for empowerment can be found on the leadership freak blog:*

1. Confident leaders who elevate others. The people at the top have the most power to make people feel safe. Fearful workers reflect controlling leaders.
2. Frequent feedback given in small doses.
3. Clear boundaries. Transparency regarding nonnegotiable policies, for example.
4. Predictable responses to failure.
5. Structures that protect against catastrophic failure.
6. Reluctant intervention from leadership.
7. Team members who know and leverage their strengths and weaknesses.
8. Shared values. Strongly aligned values are the foundation of trustworthy empowerment. Never give power to those who don't share your values.
9. Clear vision. Empowerment is chaos apart from clear vision.

* https://leadershipfreak.blog/2014/04/27/12-requirements-for-powerful-empowerment/ last accessed 5/2/2019

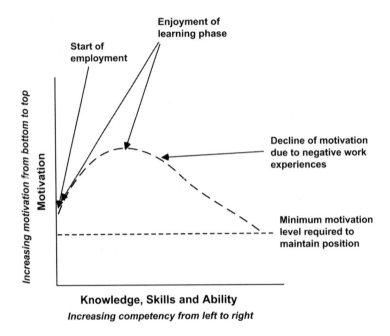

See leadership equation.

Figure 8.5 Poor experiences over time will likely impact the motivation of the team members.

10. Short-term goals that provide daily direction.
11. Shared and agreed upon accountability.
12. Taking responsibility as well as authority. Empowered people own and fix their own screwups. Running to mommy-leader to make everything OK reinforces helplessness.

An organization that is inconsistent in the application of these principles will find developing an empowered organization difficult, and in fact this empowerment philosophy is a prerequisite for the follow on part of agency.

In their book, *The Power of Agency*, the authors Paul Napper and Anthony Rao describe the seven principles for building agency:*

1. Control Stimuli – cut back on distractions, consciously choose the focus of attention and effort.
2. Associate Selectively – suitable support network that helps maintain motivation and well-being.

---

* Napper, P. & Rao, A. (2019). *The power of agency: The 7 principles to conquer obstacles, make effective decisions, and create a life on your own terms.* New York: St. Martin's Press.

3. Move – the body is just as important as the mind, balance work with life and physical activity, develop and maintain strength and stamina.
4. Constant Learner – actively question, listen and constantly work to know more, integrate learning as part of the daily routine.
5. Manage Emotions - control strong feelings and beliefs that may impede or derail, working with people and building agency requires a safe space for exploration and learn, strong emotional outbursts may not help.
6. Check Intuition – sometimes intuition is helpful, and sometimes it is more like jumping to conclusions use intution wisely and not impulsively.
7. Deliberate then act – think first, uncover alternatives, and rationally and systematically weigh the options, before deciding or taking a clear and decisive position.

There has been much written on psychological safety in the workplace. Empowerment and agency are contingent upon the level of psychological safety. Exploration can mean failure at times, and the organization's response to that failure (item 4 predictable response) will set the tone for amount of exploration, and how much agency the employee will have, or believe they have. Where empowerment is an external environmental attribute, agency is internal. However, if the environment is poor, there is likely no internal agency, or a strong sense of agency.

8.1.10.2 Learning

When an organization obtains a new member of the team that individual most commonly comes with a high level, or higher, of motivation than a more seasoned member and less experience with the processes of the organization than the longer term member. As this new member gains a better understanding about the organization and their position over time through experiences and training, both of which are learning, their level of knowledge will increase and their motivation will commonly decrease. This effect of this declination of motivation is most commonly due to the negative experiences experienced by that individual as we discussed in chapter one as the leadership equation and the effect of experiences. The relationship between learning and motivation is very direct, in that we mean that as an individual or group of people become more informed, learn, their motivational requirements and motivation change as well. Organizations need to view learning as active and passive. Active learning can be considered that which is learned through training specifically designed for a task or position, whereas passive learning is that which is learned through the environment which someone works in.

Training has become very institutionalized for the sake of ease of delivery, rapid deployment of training, training for the sake of training, or training to make something work. We use the word learning rather than training because learning something requires a greater understanding be developed then that provided by superficial training. Even though we have previously discussed different styles of learning and tailoring the training, hopefully learning based, to those styles, we do not promote that any one style is effective or that you can truly determine, if one even exists, what style best fits an individual and even if you could the cost of restructuring the training for every individual would be neither effective nor logistically feasible. The two things we are promoting are that the training provided should facilitate learning and when delivered to individuals it should be in such a manner to cause understanding of the process or procedure in a manner that allows both the teacher and recipient to improve both self and the process or procedure. This would be an example of all the five disciplines discussed in The Fifth Discipline.

In the previous section we discussed what we are calling active learning: structured and presented training that is designed to facilitate learning a specific topic. This section we will discuss passive learning: learning that occurs through observation by the individual and interaction with other people at all levels. We could look at passive learning as environmental learning. In that, we mean the climate and culture established by management, supervision, and other workers through the organization's mission, vision, and values statements and how those statements are actually employed. The key is how they are actually employed because if these statements are not in fact followed they create a negative passive learning environment. Passive learning, like active learning, is a two-way street in that all the parties involved in the interaction take something away from the interaction or lack thereof.

How is active and passive learning something the worker is responsible for? To answer that question, we need look no further than the book The Fifth Discipline and read about personal mastery. Personal Mastery as described by Peter Senge is learning to improve one's self and promote an environment that excites others to do the same.* We must remember that learning and being taught something are two different things. If we are just taught how to tie our shoes that is all we can do with that information, but if we are challenged, by ourselves or others, to develop an understanding of tying our shoes we can apply that or those principles to numerous other endeavors. This deeper understanding can also be used to develop our systems thinking.†

8.1.10.3 The Worker and Change Management

Workers don't manage change do they? This is a rhetorical question. Of course workers don't "Manage" change, but they play a large role in both the effectiveness of and implementation or lack thereof in change management and the changes themselves. To provide an analogy it is like driving a car. The car does not determine where you drive it per se but does determine numerous facets of how you get there: stops for gas, max speed, ease of directing or lack thereof, responsiveness to corrections in direction or speed, and even if you will make it to your destination at

---

* Kleiner, A. & Senge, P. M. (1994). *The Fifth Discipline Fieldbook*. London: Nicholas Brearley.
† Kleiner, A. & Senge, P. M. (1994). *The Fifth Discipline Fieldbook*. London: Nicholas Brearley.

all (breakdown). In this example there are several variables, but these variables can be controlled to some extent (i.e., the gas mileage will vary based upon the manner in which the vehicle is driven). The same would be true to the manner in which the worker is treated and allowed to develop or is developed.

Let us think about the message we provide our personnel, both through our mission, vision, and values statements and through our actual actions and interactions with said personnel; do we maintain a consistent message and do we provide an explanation for when we do not maintain these constant? There are times when a change is implemented that management and supervision must employ different styles of leadership to different individuals and this change of style could produce negative reactions from the worker(s). This reaction could then be seen as a negative change result by management and supervision and an otherwise needed or affective change could be cancelled. Worker reaction to a change should be discussed and understood. And this can only be done through open and active discussion and exchange of information and ideas.

So to extend our analogy used in the beginning, we should maintain our vehicle (motivation and develop our personnel), we should not drive in an unsafe manner (do not unnecessarily cycle our personnel), and we should keep their tank full (always be sharing and developing our personnel).

8.1.10.4 Inculcating

In the management section we discussed inculcating and we said that this word has many meanings, both evoking positive and negative connotations. We also went on to discuss that inculcating has the meaning of teaching and that this teaching should be based on the mission, vision, and values of the organization. This would be primarily because these are the things that will set the culture of an organization. So why would we discuss this in the management section and in the worker section? We discussed how management can set the stage for an organization's culture and/or environment, but those in management are not the actors on the stage. As we have alluded to throughout this book no one part of an organization can make a learning organization, but any one part can stop it from becoming one. The one part of an organization that is most commonly the largest and with the most dynamics is its workforce. The good news is that the workforce sets cultural norms within itself; thus with the right reinforcement or incentive it will direct itself. However, this establishment of organizational norms could also hold negative values if not properly established and nurtured. It also has external forces acting upon it in the form of societal and group norms which each individual who works within the organization brings with them every day to one extent or another. This, like with most things we have discussed, is both positive and negative depending on how it is employed within the organization, department, and team/group.

So how do we apply this in a manner that will promote a learning organization? While there is no one size fits all answer there are some key tenets such as promoting an environment that is open and embraces the differences within the group. This is not to say that lively discussions should not occur, but they should be done in a manner that allows the development of a better understanding between all concerned versus using cognitive biases and other such techniques to stifle one or more of the parties involved in the discussion or activity. This would be an example of what we have coined as an open mental model, which is likened after one of the fifth disciplines, mental model,* but taken to its logical next step.

8.1.10.5 Knowledge Sharing

Knowledge sharing for the worker is different than knowledge sharing for other members of an organization. As we discussed throughout this book and asked questions about in the supervisor section called knowledge sharing, the messenger and recipient of knowledge (initially information) determine the manner of delivery and actions from that information. This tailoring of information (from now on we refer to as knowledge) by the parties involved in the exchange is based on the perceived understanding of the use and need from said knowledge. This would make it seem that as one developed a better understanding, systems thinking,† the amount of work accomplished and the delivery quality would change as well, resulting in continued improvement. As a member of the team develops their knowledge sharing can become more refined, more detailed and continuously reviewed by the other team members for veracity. So, let's take that one step further into rate of change. Where do we suspect the greatest rate of change in a member's knowledge level occurs? Logically it would be the new member or the member with the least experience in some specific area. This relatively larger rate of change in knowledge can make a member feel overwhelmed at times, but it can also provide motivation via the growth of the individual. However, this rate of growth can only be maintained if the environment will support it. As with plants if they grow too fast for their environment they can actually wither and die. This will not cause a team member to die, but it would have a dramatic effect on their motivational outlook.

In the beginning of this book we discussed the leadership equation developed by Kurt Lewin and broke this equation down to its basic sources. From this we were able to ascertain that experience, seen in the equation as Exp, is the primary driver.

$$\mathbf{B = f\,\{(Exp3)\,(A2)\,(DL)\,(T)\}\,\{f\,(P2)\,(GB + GTX)\,(WC)\}}$$

And as we just discussed in the previous paragraph there is a direct relationship between experiences and how, when, where, and why we share knowledge. We can also take this application a step further to motivation if we look at the effect of positive experiences on the rate and development of knowledge sharing which

---

* Kleiner, A. & Senge, P. M. (1994). *The Fifth Discipline Fieldbook*. London: Nicholas Brearley.
† Kleiner, A. & Senge, P. M. (1994). *The Fifth Discipline Fieldbook*. London: Nicholas Brearley.

again amplifies the positive experience yet again increasing motivation. It would almost seem like a perpetual motion machine for development and motivation. When this type of environment is obtained care must be used because as the rate of anything increases there is less reaction time and the momentum could carry the organization, department, group, or individual further away from the goal before it understood. This is where the development of systems thinking and personal mastery assist all those involved.

Tell a Man What Not to Do, And He'll Most Assuredly Do It, Change His Process, and He'll Never Do It Again!

Chapter 9

War Stories

9.1 Bad!

Below are stories that demonstate when things go wrong. This includes unintended consequences along with actions that can downright erode motivation.

9.1.1 Tuition Reimbursement

The following story was provided by Ellen Raim.

I worked with a company that allowed their employees to pay tuition reimbursement to the employees. Several employees worked with their managers at the company to enroll in full masters or bachelor's programs, rather than just a course or two. This was a wonderful perk until times got tight and budgets were being cut.

Someone suggested that an "easy thing to cut out" was the companywide reimbursement program. Loss of the program was demoralizing enough. But there was also no provision made to grandfather the individuals in the middle of getting degrees. So, the managers either had to cut something else out of their group operating budgets to honor their promises to the employees or tell them they would either have to put their degrees on hold or pay themselves.

9.1.2 Patent

The story starts four years earlier with intellectual property provided to this company. This company has a policy providing those who generate intellectual property for the company a monetary reward based upon the achieving of the patent at the conclusion of the process and the patent number assigned to the intellectual property. The employee signs a document (contract) turning over the intellectual property formally to the company in exchange for a specified remuneration should the intellectual property be deemed patent material.

The patent process is slow. The remuneration policy in place at the time of ceding the intellectual property provided the individuals generating them with a bonus for this work. Four years later, the patent finally found its way through the process and has a number at the US Patent Office. Now comes the employee's much anticipated reward. Is it based upon the compensation package at the signing? No. The compensation is not the agreed upon dollar amount at the ceding of the intellectual property—it is a fraction thereof.

Management made a unilateral decision to reduce this compensation, not only for future work, but for those that had already performed the work and were waiting for resolution at the patent office. When asked the logic behind this treatment, the human resources departmental response was "the company reserves the rights to change any policy at any time. This was a policy change that we are making retroactive."

Even the U.S. Constitution forbids *ex post facto* laws. When the questioning of the policy continued, the human resource representative "take away" was the policy change had not been "communicated properly." Generally, the company will have deeper pockets than the employee, so the courtroom is not an option.

What does this say to the employee? Are only some commitments to be honored? Why is it important for the employee to follow through on commitments and not the organization? What constitutes commitment if a signed document is not a commitment?

9.1.3 Deferred Gratification

A long-term employee approaches the manager of the department to discuss advancement in the company. This employee more has decades of experience as well as an advanced degree. The employee also has a track record of saving the company money, providing revenue generating products as well as cost effective systems design. The team member laments he has been with the company for nearly a decade, and there has been no discussion about how the employee can move from their present position in the organization's hierarchy. The manager responds that this is the problem with your generation. You do not understand deferred (or delayed) gratification. This person had a proven track record of performance for the company, as well as undertaken the time and effort of an advanced degrees and applicable certifications. The team member reported he found this incredulous, and recounts sitting back in the chair, telling the manager that he thought the manager was wrong.

9.1.4 Overtime and Mandatory Meetings

A specific project is understaffed with the team members working many hours of overtime with a project that has a tight deadline. The company had mandatory meetings that were focused on developing the organization. This is an admirable objective to be sure, but when the team is already working many hours of overtime because of an understaffed project, this additional drain on the employees is not sustainable or a moral builder. The meeting either adds hours (hours that are uncompensated in salary or via time off) or taking hours away from the project is not productive for the team or the project. Working overtime, uncompensated, and time away from family and outside life is not motivating. Taking time away from an already challenging project reduces the probability of success, and neither of these are helpful nor motivating.

9.1.5 Employee Attitude Surveys (a Mixed Bag)

A company has a survey to gauge the employees' attitude about the work and the company. The surveys are professionally done, with key questions categorized, for example, process questions as well as motivation category questions. At the end of the survey, the data is aggregated around these specific topic areas (departments, geolocation, and topic questions). The data is then statistically processed comparing last year's. The issue is not in the approach up to this point. Understanding the team's perspective (not just technical, but environmental as well) throughout the organization is helpful for improvement.

The company then uses information from the various teams for continuous improvement, starting by reviewing the results within each group and department. The survey is "mandatory," encouraging everybody to participate, and the departments track this performance. Some of the team members lament participating in the survey, as invariably the trouble areas that are pointed out have two categories for resolution, obfuscation, and misassignment.

Obfuscation happens when we use words to explain away or justify the results without sufficient information to make that conclusion. Essentially, we do not like the results so we interpret the results favorably. Getting this incorrect, in this instance, had an impact on the employees, leading some percentage of the employees to the conclusion that the company is not serious about solving problems – especially those with political implication.

Misassignment of the results happens when the survey items not to the organization's liking are assigned for resolution at an inappropriate level. There was considerable complaints that the larger system level problems were pushed down to the employee or worker level when from the worker perspective, to resolve would require more broad understanding of the business along with political wherewithal to actually be able to resolve. The result being, the next time the employees would take the survey, they would select the most favorable rating (Likert scale). This artificially makes things look better than they were in subsequent surveys, as a response to pointing out the problem only brings you action items to fix that which you, by dint of position in the company, are unable to resolve.

9.2 Good!

Not all stories are bad war stories. There are some metaphorical wars wherein the struggle produces a positive result.

9.2.1 Easy Advanced degree

A company had a university in proximity and the business developed a partnership with the university. The employees of this company could go to this university, tuition deferred each semester. The course and the degree were up to the employee with discussions with the manager. The manager would need to agree to the degree or course work, and the employee would still have to keep their day activities up to par. That is, they must be able to perform while at work. The employee would go to these classes at night, or on the weekend, and if the grade they received for the course was a B or better, then the company would pay for that semester's class. There was no limit to the number of classes the employee could undertake, only that their work would not suffer from this additional use of the time. It was about as easy as it could have been to pay for class; the university's remuneration was deferred until after the class was over, and then the business would pay the university, if the employee received a B.

Of course, there were consequences, often considered golden handcuffs. The money the company provided for this education require an investment in time in the organization or the employee would be required to pay back the money.

Other companies do this, but very few (only one that we have ever experienced) set up a relationship between the company and the university that would defer the payment for the coursework as long as the grade expectations were met. Additionally, some companies have an annual limit, for example $5k per year. This company did not have such a limitation.

9.2.2 Team Gets Certified

An organization goes through restructuring, creating a separate verification and test group, starting with a manager and a few of those that have been performing verification and testing work within the organization from some other department. The testing ranges from hardware and environmental to software. The company has strong experience in the environmental and physical testing but are not so strong in software testing. Over time, the manager hires team members from within and outside the company, ultimately building a group of 13 engineers and technicians. The manager takes all of the team to obtain the American Software Testing Qualifications Board (ASTQB) Certification Foundation Level, in two batches. This training gave a common frame of reference (lexicon and process models) upon which the team could build. The certification built a common lexicon and a top-level flow of what is required to successfully test the product.

9.2.3 Machine Support

This story was provided by Steve Lauck.

A machine was being fabricated out of state. The specification required testing at the fabricator before shipping. It had been discussed that the Mechanical Lead and the Lead Designer of the machine would conduct the testing.

The call came that the machine was ready for testing. The fabricator said we were welcome anytime over the next few days; he would have his people available to support the test.

When I notified the Mechanical Lead, in person, it was time to go, he refused. He walked away from me stating emphatically "I am not going." I followed. After a few tense moments he agreed to sit with me and discuss the trip.

The Mechanical Lead finally calmed down. He explained that he had dogs at home, and they could not be left alone when he travelled. I mentioned boarding the dogs. I have dogs and that is the plan when I travel. He said there was only one boarding kennel that he trusted with his dogs and it was a few hours' drive away. I asked if he had time to take the dogs to the kennel could he be on a plane tomorrow morning. He agreed.

I told him to take the afternoon and get his dogs settled at the kennel. He said our management would never agree to time off. I said, "The project needs you to go test this equipment. You need to feel comfortable that your dogs are safe. Go! It is my decision and I will take any heat. Management has to understand there is no one to go in your place and we need to bend whatever rules to meet the schedule."

He left. His dogs got settled at the kennel. The Mechanical Lead and Lead Designer were on the plane early the next morning.

Late in the afternoon on test day, the Mechanical Lead called on a conference call with the fabricator's representative. The test went well and there were a few minor adjustments required to the machine. The Mechanical Lead said he had already secured agreement with the fabricator that their workers would stay late that day to make the adjustments and retest the machine before calling it a day.

In the morning the Lead Designer called. The machine was complete and tested by late evening. The machine was being crated. They were able to get an early flight and preparing to head to the airport. I told him after landing just go on home and take the rest of the day off. I appreciated the effort and control they took at the fabricator to get this done.

Yes, I took heat from management but reminded them about the progress of the project. Ultimately, the client expressed appreciation for the 'above and beyond' steps the team took to hold the schedule. The client never knew about the dogs or any time off. All they knew was two team members worked a double shift to ensure their machine was tested and shipped on time.

The lesson here is everyone has a personal life away from work – spouses, children, pets, and activities they enjoy. Most people work to live, not live to work. I never meddled in any of my employees' lives but I did ask questions about how

I could help with any personal issues that impacted their performance at work. An employee's behavior has implications for possible poor performance. But, to maintain or improve performance (equaling a happy worker), maybe something as simple as giving time off to take care of their dogs is all that is needed.

9.2.4 Database for Learning

An organization that specializes in developing a range of automotive products and systems built a database that was used during the development and post-manufacturing quality of the product. This database was searchable by subsystem (for example exhaust system) and components (for example turbo charger). During development, the results of experiments were recorded, for example, the turbocharger impeller blades were designed using a specific material, and development testing found that the material would not work for that application. This support did not stop at the manufacturing but was extended post-manufacturing as circumstances present. For example, parts that fail within the warranty period are sent back for technical analysis, to determine the nature of the failure. The results of this exploration, when it was deemed a design issue, would be recorded along with the changes to the product to eliminate or reduce this failure mode. This information is available for subsequent development effort, for review prior to starting this interation of the development work. An engineer would consult this database the next time a new turbo charger design was required. This provides a basic understanding of the historical record of the product, what has been tried in the past, and the result of that long line of development projects over the years and many production iterations of the product. The team then can look up specific parts for example, the turbocharger, bearings, exhaust routing, and many other elements, each of which may have historical information recorded that will aid in the development of future iterations of the product. This prevents the team from learning the same lessons from previous teams and effort.

9.2.5 Process and Organization Development

One of us worked at an automotive product development company. This company was a very larger globally distributed company with sites responsible for developing the product within that specific region. The group is made up of a variety of subgroups that work to develop and verify the new products under development.

- Project Management
- Systems Engineering
- Electronics Engineering (embedded hardware and software)
- CAD and mechanical parts of the design
- Electrical Engineering
- Verification and testing

The management decides that it is important to go through how the work is done, and how the workflows through the department. Given the large amount of work going through the department it is necessary to understand how the work goes through the department and equally to the point, the work product exchanges between each group. What does that look like? What are the attributes or what constitutes a good exchange upon which we can build?

Each department was interviewed how they do their work, and what the respective department needs from the interfacing departments. For example, the systems engineering group, for an existing system, will apportioned the function across the myriad of electronic control units on the vehicle. Then the systems group composes a systems document describing how the feature and functions will work. This includes fall back modes, those situations when some sub-portion of the system suffers a failure, for example a sensor failure. This should not cause a catastrophic failure for the vehicle.

Each path for the work was considered, including every exchange between the groups as well as what constitutes a good exchange. Each process step was thought through. The process documentation included:

- Objective - why is this process performed. Knowing this makes it possible to adapt should some of the typical inputs not be available or not be to the expected quality - as in attributes.
- Inputs - what is needed as a prerequisite for this part of the work, and where this work originates, for example, the inputs from the systems engineering group or project management. Sometimes the inputs were a collection of elements and each would be assigned or documented.
- Responsibility - specific talent and expertise within that department that are required to perform the work.
- Process - the steps to accomplish this work.
- Output - the description of what a successful output looks like.

At the end of the work, each of the departments have discussed their work and how it fits into the overall chain of events for the work. The exchanges between each group has been reviewed and what the receiving entity would need from the input. Not only did the team members learn more about their portion of the work, but they learned about how their work impacts the other departments and how the work flows ideally through the department.

Appendix 1: Learning and Organization Development Checklist

This is a brainstormed check list of the things that get in the way of the development of our organization.

- Reduce required billable hours ratio (80% or even less)
- Make time for learning and spreading what is learned
- Gamify the work and learning opportunities
- Encourage exploration by the individual and the team
- Each team member shares their expertise
- Encourage lateral (silo to silo) communication
- Develop communities of practice as a resource to the organization (not a way of usurping the organization)
- Integrate learning and improvement objectives in the daily work
- Schedule recurring point to share the learning of all the department
- Consider online database with searchable metadata tags
- Job rotations, specifically to interfacing or depending departments
- Special assignments for individuals to develop new skills / knowledge the organization will need in the near-term future
- A career development plan for team members that is used act to as if learning and improvement matter create an environment that does not punish failure – but ensures exploration of what happened and why. Baseline expected analytical / statistical tools for the department and team members
- Act as if learning and improvement matter, do not pay lip service
- Create an environment that does not punish failure – but ensures exploration of what happened and why. Failure is not a good thing, nor a bad thing.
- Baseline expected analytical / statistical tools for the department and team members

- Identify teachers / coaches within the team to develop these skills throughout the team
- Create knowledge sharing networks for dissemination of learning
- Develop a culture of questioning. It is okay to say I don't know
- Those that know should not tell, but coach, ask questions, point to places to look and evoke answers from within the student
- The work is learning. Encourage learning beyond the daily, and present activities of the job
- Set up a library or virtual library for the organization – of books and other material that applies to the organization
- Frequent lunch and learns
- Frequent work reviews / critiques a la retrospectives
- Mental or thought experiments
- Develop an environment that grows a common lexicon and shared mental models
- Prioritize learning, slow down to allow it to happen, include learning in work estimates (time & cost)
- Team members teach team members
- Abolish sloganeering
- Develop corporate culture that values learning and sharing
- Managers are teachers and coaches
- Embrace continuous learning in the culture
- Organization subsidized or reimbursement of education – degrees, no degrees, certifications
- 360-degree feedback for employee evaluation
- Display organization objectives and associated metrics for all to see, monitors or other physical boards
- Encourage learning beyond the daily, and present activities of the job
- Develop and implement a mission, vision, and value statement that is actually supported at all levels of the organization.

Appendix 2: Clues! Signals!

A2.1 Overview

The material below is the result of a collaboration with John Cutler, known as @ JohnCuttefish on Twitter. The document started out as a list posed by him, and he was looking for people to comment on it. Upon seeing his list, a bunch of ideas came into my head, and I started adding to it on the Google Drive location. As fast as I was addiing content he was approving of the updates. To me this is another great example of how people can connect to make interesting and perhaps helpful things.

- Might as well do [some extra thing] while we [do the original thing]
  - Distraction consuming hours putting the original thing at risk (hours available and cost) (see 6 myths of product development)
  - Second thing not being communicated with the rest of the team members may come at cost to the system when entirety is assembled
  - something unexpected by other team members = cost poor quality rework
- We don't want to have to revisit [some decision]
  - Staying with a solution that is not a solution, or will end poorly. Wasting time and effort
  - Unable to make a decision or decision takes inordinate amount of time for fear that the decision is irreversible
- While we're waiting on [some blocker], let's start [something new]
  - When the block is removed we are unprepared or distracted due to task switching
  - Too preoccupied with new something to contribute to the blocked cause
  - No learning from blocked cause by those others that are not participating in resolution (which may be okay)
- It would probably be more efficient if we ...
  - Doubled up when things should be consecutive puts depending tasks at risk of rework and unable to adapt to actual outcome

- Neglect some base product management (cutting schedule time is not necessarily efficient)
- Throw talent at the problem believing that 9 women pregnant for a month can produce a baby (do no know the laws of diminishing returns)
■ It's too early to [some interaction with users/customers]
  - Waiting for feedback means more built and the possibility of being farther away from the desired objective (like a pilot that only checks the compass after hundreds of miles from take off)
  - Mockups, quick product demos, and prototypes that look little like the end product can be effective to get this information from the customer the earlier the better
■ If we bundle these things together we will get [some efficiency]
  - Over 80% capacity we are looking at larger delays for small difficulties - queueing theory
■ We don't all need to be in the room for [some decision]
  - Different perspectives help uncover:
    • Unvetted assumptions
    • Different ideas to explore and pursue
    • Communications needs of different people or team members
  - Ultimately project failure due to limited or conflicting communication and excluding voices that should have been heard
■ We can "get ahead of it" by [a series of handoffs]
  - Every hand off is a communication hurdle and opportunity for missed communications
  - Risk dependency, probability of success 1 X probability of success 2 = Sum of probability of success
  - Think of this as the more exchanges the more opportunities for failure (systems engineering))
■ Well [some person] is the only person who can do [some task]
  - Lost opportunity to get rid of this limitation when we do not double this up seasoned person and new but interested person
  - When this person leaves the company we have no one
■ It doesn't work now, but it will work when [some future task is done]
  - How do you know; if you are incorrect, you find out way too late and are unable to respond
■ If we have a little downtime, we might as well try to fit in [another task]
  - If this is not part of the scope this is a waste of time and money
  - Team synchronization / communication that is working on parts that other team members should be aware.
■ We'll have to wait on [some person] to make that decision
  - Delaying decisions delay the project, this consequence must be accepted
  - No escalation plan - could put you in a holding pattern indefinitely
■ It's the right thing to do but [some excuse masquerading as pragmatism]
  - Not looking at long term consequences - lack of systems thinking

- Lack of courage; our team does not feel comfortable saying things that "rock the boat"
■ We just need to "lock down" [some specification] and then we can...
  - Some portions of the specification, certainly. Not the entirety.
  - We do not know what we do not know, requires specification changes, no need to waste time with reworking the specification
■ Just this one time let's [some cut corner] and then we'll fix it, hopefully
  - This become habit; we will do this for any modicum of pressure
  - Those not technically oriented will challenge when you want to resort to no corner cutting
  - People will forget what correct looks like because we now have many ways to do this
  - The path of least resistance becomes common even if this is not the best approach
■ We need to do this to close [one deal]. But I'm sure it will apply elsewhere...
  - See the prior items
■ Oh, I'll just do this on the side. That way it will not be micromanaged...
  - No communication with other team members.
  - Fit issues.
  - Micromanagement is a problem also - that would be what should be solved, your team does not believe they can make decisions and take the initiative. You paid for talent then let it waste away.
■ Oh, this doesn't need UX [or QA, Ops, etc.]
  - You will likely find out later that the product does not meet the customer needs
  - Poor quality in the field comes with rework and replacement in the field, litigation, service costs, reputation impact
  - Not including operations means we may not have the ability to build this thing and ship to customer or deploy
■ So we have this [side project]...can you attend the meeting to [plan in secret]?
  - Missing key players - unvetted assumptions, few possible ways to approach (ideation)
  - Trust issues - don't want to share for whatever reason
  - Distraction of workforce if this person should be working on another project
■ Oh, we can't risk [trying some valuable goal]...
  - No risk = no reward
  - Exploration need not be risky - could find an easy low risk way to explore
  - Eliminating learning opportunity for team members
  - No desire for innovation which comes from this type of exploration
■ Oh, you can't test [some feature] because [some perceived limitation]
  - Testing incremental iterations provides feedback to the developers
  - It is possible to test some portions that work to learn about that work

- Configuration Management (via release notes) provides the map of features able to be tested
- Waiting for all functions available to start testing means finding bugs up against the launch deadline
- You are destroying the iterative and incremental model of working
■ We need individual owners otherwise [some inability to track/punish]
  - Problem when you punish - trust issues in the organization
  - One perspective often does not provide a true view of the field
  - Well, we're unique because [some non-unique challenge]
  - Unique or not unique, there is likely a solution that will meet the objective if you explore, test, and learn. Otherwise you are stuck in this morass for the rest of your days
  - No way to get better living with the limitations without exploration
■ This is too big for one sprint, so we'll do phase one now and....
■ I'm pretty sure I can represent the customer in this case...
  - Not sure any individual nor a customer is in a position to actually
  - Myopic one perspective
  - Likely discovered when the product goes to the customer things that were missed resulting in rework
  - Gets in the habit of making the call for the customer rather than asking the customer
■ [Some effort] is too big to fail. We need to get this right...
  - Still requires attacking incrementally (how do you eat an elephant)
  - Building all, means we find all of the errors and poor decisions late or at the end
  - Requires rework - and late with no time to adequately address
■ We need some quick wins because [normal wins take too long]
  - Then find a way to improve the normal wins rate
  - Work on your corporate discipline - delayed gratification
  - Eroded the corporate discipline and any repeatability
  - If these are to be sequential there is risk of rework of the depending task when the preceding task does not deliver exactly as expected (see compounding impact of risk)
  - Delays delivery of the iteration
■ And then [some other group] can maintain it, right?
  - There was learning in the development of the product that only the group doing it will have
  - Communications challenges with the transition - what should we tell and to whom
  - Better to keep some members of the maintaining group involved during development if this must be a different group
  - Problems with the ability to maintain, constant interaction with the developers
  - Ultimately poor post-development support

Appendix 3: Fallacies, Biases, and Archetypes

A3.1 Logical Fallacies

From know your logical fallacy are flaws in reasoning. These flaws have implications on objectivity as well as negative connotations on communications and problem resolution and fostering an environment of team work. Logical fallacies are different than cognitive biases which we discussed in the chapter. Logical fallacy is an error in logical arguments while cognitive biases are limitations in thinking and knowledge. These limitations originate in memory, social attribution, and errant calculations. We provide a list of logical fallacies that you may find in the work place.

- Strawman: an over exaggeration of another person's argument makes it possible for another to present their arguments as well reasoned and reasonable.
- False cause: the connecting of one thing to another, real or perceived, in that the prior is the cause of the latter; correlation is not causation. Sometimes these events are coincidental.
- Appeal to emotion: the attempt to move the discussion from the merits of the discussion to evoking an emotional response, rather than a valid or compelling argument
- Gambler's fallacy: the belief that runs occur to statistically independent phenomenon such as the flipping of a coin. Each flip event is an independent instance, 50/50; if you have a run of 10 heads, the next flip probability is still 50/50.
- Band wagon: the appeal to popularity or the fact others do something as an attempted form of validation
- Appeal the authority: because an authority says something, it therefore must be true. This is not an argument, but a way to shut down the argument. There are experts and what is said may be true, but to just assume because somebody viewed as an expert says something does not make it valid.

- Fallacy fallacy: The presumption that because a claim has been poorly stated or argued, or a fallacy has been made, then the entire claim must be wrong
- Slippery slope: if we do x then it will lead to y. In this fallacy the issue at hand is avoided and extrapolated to the extreme hypothetical without strong evidence to support.
- Ad hominem: the attack on a person's character or appearance and personal traits rather than on the merits of the argument to undermine their argument.
- Composition: the assumption that one part of something has to be applied to all, or other parts of that thing; or that the whole must apply to its parts.
- No true Scotsman: The making of appeals to purity as a way to dismiss relevant criticisms or flaws in the argument.
- Genetic: the judgment of something as good or bad on the basis of where or from whom the idea originates.
- Tu quoque: answering criticism with criticism, also known as the appeal to hypocrisy. It is a way of distracting one's focus to eliminate the defense of the other's argument, moving the conversation.
- Personal incredulity: because you do not understand something or find it difficult comprehend, you act as if it is probably not true.
- Special pleading: the clinging to a way of thinking in the face of evidence that debunks your perspective, moving the goal posts to allow the prior argument to remain.
- Black or white: the proposition that only two alternatives are possible when many more exist. Also known as the false dilemma.
- Begging the question: circular argument in which the conclusion was included in the premise, originating from deeply held assumption so much so that the assumption is deemed as valid.
- Appeal to nature: the argument that because something is natural it is therefore valid, justified, and inevitable, good or ideal.
- Loaded question: loaded question fallacies are particularly effective at derailing rational debates because of their inflammatory nature - the recipient of the loaded question is compelled to defend themselves and may appear flustered or on the back foot.
- Burdon of proof: the burden of proof lies not with the person making the claim, but with someone else to disprove. Just because others are unable or unwilling to disprove does not make the assertion valid.
- Ambiguity: use of double meaning or ambiguity of language to mislead or misdirect or misrepresent the truth, obfuscation.
- Anecdotal: the use of personal experience no matter how isolated as an example rather than sound arguments and compelling evidence.
- The Texas sharpshooter: using cherry picked data to fit your argument or to find a pattern to fit a presumption rather than developing a hypothesis based upon the evidence.
- Middle ground: the claim that a compromise or middle point between two extremes must be the truth

Appendix 3 ■ 231

There are many more biases and impediments to clear thinking than the selection we just provided, this is but a brief view. It is more difficult than we think to have clear thinking and many times, we are not even aware. These biases can make it difficult to learn, and distribute any learning.

A3.2 Cognitve Bias

In the previous section we discussed teaching and how teaching is just the facilitation of experiences that produces some form of behavioral modification. This section deals with the processing of those experiences. Cognitive Biases is using past experiences or the remembrance of past experiences (how we remember past experiences may be inaccurate or jaded by our position at the time of the experience) to determine our actions for current situations: experiences. While this helps us process information (new experiences) quickly through relating it to previous experiences it comes with the potential for inaccurate assessments or interpretations of a situation. Another part of cognitive biases is its use of the individuals' own likes or dislikes; this emotional context could and commonly does jade our decisions. We all have our own perspectives on every situation. I like to use the example of the angle of view of a quarter: if we look at a quarter from its side while standing up on its end we could assume it's a line, if we look at it from the side while it's laying down it could appear to be a dash, and yet again if we look at it from the front we see it's a quarter. While the quarter never actually changed, what is the position (perspective) of the individual viewing it could have a drastic effect on what they think they are seeing.

For example, let's consider a few of those biases starting with confirmation bias. Confirmation bias impacts product development and project management in many ways. We seek information that supports what we already believe and when we find it, we stop looking and proceed or make some decision. The problem, as pointed out by the great philosopher Karl Popper, is that finding positive evidence does not confirm what you believe to be true. It just gives you the illusion that it is true. Hypotheses are explored for veracity by finding information that refutes our thinking and the hypothesis (falsification). Evidence we find that confirms does not mean what we believe is in fact true. There are many cases where a product after undergoing testing, all is well, the product is good, has catastrophic problems in the field, recalls, and legal action.

There is a tendency to overestimate small runs of data, without understanding the sampling and what that means. Those reviewing the data can see "patterns" in the data and take action on what we see is a pattern, however, the truth is there is no pattern, or our view of the pattern is incorrect. Bad data, or misinterpreted data, amount to the same thing, failure.

In general, people are optimistic, in my experience. We occasionally find the "Marvin the Robots" from the book The Hitchhikers Guide by the late great Douglas Adams, but by and large those are exceptions to the rule. This optimism can become a negative thing with optimism bias, when we are trying to find out what will likely happen. We delude ourselves of the probability of success and the risks associated with our work and the product. We choose to set our project up without due diligence to the risks associated, that is, there is little thinking about what can go wrong. Similarly, when it comes time to launch the product, in the absence of information telling us there could be a defect (see confirmation bias), we put on our rose-colored glasses, and off we launch believing nothing can go wrong.

Lastly, we will review survivor bias. We become subjected to survivor bias when we decide to review our successes to find a common theme, thinking if we do what those earlier projects did, we should be successful. The problem comes when we only look at those success stories. It is possible those things we attribute to those project's successes were also used in those failing projects, and something else drove the project to success. Without looking at the failures, we never know. My friend Kim Pries used to say, "if we walk into Toyota's bathroom, and it is tiled in blue, does that mean if we tile our bathrooms in blue, would we have a successful project and company"?

The impact of cognitive biases can be helpful or extremely detrimental to any progress or process. This is especially true for teaching and learning where the basic premise is providing an experience to modify a behavior. To get past these biases requires a safe environment, one where thoughts can be explored without retribution. As we will discuss in the next section, Communication, the more inferences applied to a topic or items the more likely there is for some error in its assessment. If a new experience is related to an incorrect experience or the recipient's perspective is not that of the individual delivering the experience, what is learned from the experience could and most probably will be not what was intended. We all know that diversity *can* produce great ideas; the premise behind it would seem to counter the idea that cognitive biases can create the potential for issues. It is not diversity or cognitive biases that create anything, but how they are used that creates the gain or loss. We should view these two situations as tools. The tool does neither make nor break how the work is done; it is how they are employed that determines that. Understanding that there is diversity and cognitive biases and engaging these different perspectives to determine the reality of a situation can provide a better starting point and path to the goal at hand.

A3.3 Heuristics

Heuristics are mental shortcuts that are used to reduce cognitive loading; a rule of thumb is an example of a heuristic. Attributes allow us to arrive at an accurate conclusion without taking the mental load and time to calculate or perfectly decide. These shortcuts are developed through the experiences of the individual and as such it is not likely any two of these shortcuts will be perfectly congruent; different experiences provide different mental shortcuts. Heuristics can sometimes lead to biases.

A3.3.1 Availability Heuristic

Availablity heuristic is born out of what comes to our mind immediately when a decision is required, drawing from experiences and knowledge that are relevant to the decision at hand.

> "Are there more words that begin with "r" or that have "r" as their third letter?" To answer this question, you can't help but bring specific words to mind. Words that begin with "r" are easy to think of; words that have "r" as their third letter are harder to think of, so many people answer this question with "words that begin with 'r'" when in fact, that's the wrong answer.*

A3.3.2 Representativeness Heuristic

> The affect heuristic is when we make choices based on emotions at the time of the decision that needs to be made; the mood impacts the decision results. "Linda the bank teller" is one of the most famous examples. It comes from the work of Kahneman and Tversky. In this problem, you are told a little bit about Linda, and then asked what her profession is likely to be. Linda is described as an avid protester who went to an all girls' college. She is an environmentalist, politically liberal, etc. (I'm making up these details, but the information that subjects got in this study is quite similar.) Basically, she's described in such a way that you can't help but think that she must be a feminist, because the prototype/stereotype that you have in your head is that women who are like Linda are feminists. So when people are asked if Linda is more likely to be a bank teller (working for The Man!) or a feminist bank teller, most people say the latter, even though that doesn't make any sense, in terms of probability. In this case, people use a shortcut that involved a stereotype to answer the question, and they ignored actual likelihoods.†

While availability has more to do with memory of specific instances, representativeness has more to do with memory of a prototype, stereotype, or average.‡

---

* http://blog.cambridgecoaching.com/the-psychology-tutor-what-are-heuristics

† Finucane, M. L., Alhakami, A., Slovic, P., & Johnson, S. M. (2000). The affect heuristic in judgments of risks and benefits. Journal of Behavioral Decision Making, 13(1), 1–17. doi: 10.1002/(sici)1099-0771(200001/03)13:1<1::aid-bdm333>3.0.co;2-s

‡ http://blog.cambridgecoaching.com/the-psychology-tutor-what-are-heuristics

A3.4 Archetypes

An archetype is a model of an observed system or behavior that is readily identifiable by the observer into a specific category or classification.

A3.4.1 Systems Archetype

System archetypes are patterns of behavior of a system. Systems expressed by circles of causality have therefore similar structure. Identifying a system archetype and finding the leverage enables efficient changes in a system. The basic system archetypes and possible solutions of the problems are mentioned in the section Examples of system archetypes are provided below. A fundamental property of nature is that no cause can effect the past. System archetypes do not imply that current causes effect past effects.

A3.4.1.1 Circles of Causality

Circles of causality is the concept that all events, have some precedent for cause. An observable phenomenon is the result of some other system or subsystem event or events. For every action, there is some effect, it may be largely imperceptible, we may not know where to look, but there is some impact. Think of everything we do as a net where everything is connected, perhaps not immediately, appreciably, but are connected.

A3.4.1.2 Reinforcing Feedback

Reinforcing feedback (or amplifying feedback) accelerates the given trend of a process. If the trend is ascending, the reinforcing (positive) feedback will accelerate the growth. If the trend is descending, it will accelerate the decline. An avalanche falling, or a snowball rolling dowon hill is an example of the reinforcing feedback process.

A3.4.1.3 Balancing Feedback

Balancing feedback (or stabilizing feedback) will work if any goal-state exists. Balancing process intends to reduce a gap between a current state and a desired state. The balancing (negative) feedback adjusts a present state to a desirable target regardless of whether the trend is descending or ascending. An example of the balancing feedback process is staying upright on a bicycle (when riding).

A3.4.1.4 Limits to Growth

The unprecedented growth is produced by a reinforcing feedback process until the system reaches its peak. The halt of this growth is caused by limits inside or outside of the system. However, if the limits are not properly recognized, the former methods are continuously applied, but more and more aggressively. This results in the contrary of the desired state – a decrease of the system. The solution lies in the weakening or elimination of the cause of limitation. Example: dieting, learning foreign languages.

A3.4.1.5 Shifting the Burden

The problem is handled by a simple solution with immediate effect, thereby "healing the symptoms." The primary source of the problem is overlooked, because its remedy is demanding and has no immediate outcome. The origin of the problem should be identified and solved in the long-term run during which the addiction to the symptomatic remedy decreases. Example: drug addiction, paying debts by borrowing.

A3.4.1.6 Eroding Goals

A kind of shifting the burden archetype. As current problems need to be handled immediately, the long-term goals continuously decline. It can be avoided by sticking to the vision. Example: balancing the public debt, sliding limits of environmental pollution.

A3.4.1.7 Escalation

This archetype could be seen as a non-cooperative game where both players suppose that just one of them can win. They are responding to actions of the other player to "defend themselves." The aggression grows and can result in self-destructive behavior. The vicious circle can be broken by one agent stopping to react defensively and turn the game into a cooperative one. Example: arms race.

A3.4.1.8 Success to Successful

Two people or activities need the same limited resources. As one of them becomes more successful, more resources are assigned to them. The second one becomes less and less successful due to lacking resources, and thus "proves the right decision" to support the first one. Problems occur if the competition is unhealthy and interferes with the goals of the whole system. The two activities or agents might be decoupled or eliminate the competing elements, or perhaps they should receive balanced amount of resources, some examples: two products at one company, work vs. family.

A3.4.1.9 Tragedy of the Commons

Agents use a common limited resource to profit individually. As the use of the resource is not controlled, the agents would like to continuously raise their benefits.

The resource is therefore used more and more, and the revenues of the agents are decreasing. The agents are intensifying their exploitation until the resource is completely used up or seriously damaged. To protect common resources some form of regulation should be introduced. Example: fish stocks (The Fishing Game).

A3.4.1.10 Fixes that Fail

In the fixes that fail archetype, the problem is solved by some fix (a specific solution) with immediate positive effect. Nonetheless, the "side effects" of this solution turn out in the future. The best remedy seems to apply the same solution. Example: saving costs on maintenance, paying interest by other loans (with other interest).

A3.4.1.11 Growth and Underinvestment

The limit to growth is the current production capacity. It can be removed by enough investment in new capacities. If the investment is not aggressive enough (or it is too low), the capacities are overloaded, the quality of services declines, and the demand decreases. This archetype is especially important in capacity planning, for example: small but growing company.

A3.4.1.12 Unintended Consequences

Unintended consequences are those things that arise out of actions we take that we did not anticipate. Experience suggests these unintended consequences originate from incomplete thinking or singular perspective about the topic under consideration. We do not take the time to explore the consequences beyond our immediate consideration.

To be sure there are things we do not know or will not know until we undertake specific actions. There are ways to minimize the probability and the ensuing damage by using multiple perspectives as well as not making large sweeping changes, but rather perform tests and explore what can happen without putting the entire department or organization at risk.

Including multiple perspectives when considering or evaluating the alternatives at hand and what change we should undertake. This multiple perspective approach can help moderate biases and certainly can generate additional ideas on the topic through conversations that help us discover any underlying assumptions and relevant experiences. In this way we may be able to ascertain some of the consequences for our decision before acting, perhaps saving us some unnecessary time and undue stress. Experience suggests many times these unintended consequences could have been predicted if time and effort was spent first exploring the proposed idea. It is important to not stigmatize failure. Failure is where we discover something new, something perhaps in opposition to what we believed to be true. The fear of unintended consequences should not prohibit the exploration. Somethings cannot be known until effort is expended.

Another appropriate approach that is less risky is to devise small scale experiments to learn about our actions. For example, the Total Quality Management approach devised by Shewhart and Deming advocates this incremental exploration via experiments and a review of the results. These results provide more information about the subject we are exploring, and help us to understand these consequences better, or perhaps open our eyes to things we had not considered previously.

Appendix 4: Names and Theories

A4.1 Maslow Hierarchy of Needs*

A4.1.1 Physiological Needs

These include the most basic needs that are vital to survival, such as the need for water, air, food, and sleep. Maslow believed that these needs are the most basic and instinctive needs in the hierarchy because all needs become secondary until these physiological needs are met.

Most of these lower level needs are probably fairly apparent. We need food and water to survive. We also need to breathe and maintain a stable body temperature. In addition to eating, drinking, and having adequate shelter and clothing, Maslow also suggested that sexual reproduction was a basic physiological need.

A4.1.2 Security Needs

These include the needs for safety and security. Security needs are important for survival, but they are not as demanding as the physiological needs. Examples of security needs include a desire for steady employment, health care, safe neighborhoods, and shelter from the environment.

The needs become a bit more complex at this point in the hierarchy. Now that the more basic survival needs have been fulfilled, people begin to feel that they need more control and order to their lives. A safe place to live, financial security, physical safety, and staying healthy are all concerns that might come into play at this stage.

A4.1.3 Social Needs

These include needs for belonging, love, and affection. Maslow described these needs as less basic than physiological and security needs. Relationships such as friendships,

---

* http://psychology.about.com/od/theoriesofpersonality/a/hierarchyneeds.htm last accessed 9/14/2019

romantic attachments, and families help fulfill this need for companionship and acceptance, as does involvement in social, community, or religious groups.

A4.1.4 Esteem Needs

After the first three needs have been satisfied, esteem needs becomes increasingly important. These include the need for things that reflect on self-esteem, personal worth, social recognition, and accomplishment.

At this point, it becomes increasingly important to gain the respect and appreciation of others. People have a need to accomplish things and then have their efforts recognized. People often engage in activities such as going to school, playing a sport, enjoying a hobby, or participating in professional activities in order to fulfill this need.

Satisfying this need and gaining acceptance and esteem helps people become more confident. Failing to gain recognition for accomplishments, however, can lead to feelings of failure or inferiority.

A4.1.5 Self-Actualizing Needs

This is the highest level of Maslow's hierarchy of needs. Self-actualizing people are self-aware, concerned with personal growth, less concerned with the opinions of others, and interested in fulfilling their potential.

A4.2 Herzberg (Two Factor Theory)

A4.2.1 Theory*

Herzberg was the first to show that satisfaction and dissatisfaction at work nearly always arose from different factors, and were not simply opposing reactions to the same factors, as had always previously been (and still now by the unenlightened) believed.

In 1959 Herzberg wrote the following useful little phrase, which helps explain this fundamental part of his theory, i.e., that the factors which motivate people at work are different to and not simply the opposite of the factors which cause dissatisfaction:[†]

"We can expand ... by stating that the job satisfiers deal with the factors involved in doing the job, whereas the job dissatisfiers deal with the factors which define the job context."

---

* https://www.businessballs.com/herzberg.htm last accessed 9/14/2019
† https://www.businessballs.com/herzbergmotivationdiagram.pdf last accessed 9/14/2019

A4.2.2 Motivation

People are only truly motivated by enabling them to reach for and satisfy the factors that Herzberg identified as real motivators, such as achievement, advancement, development, etc., which represent a far deeper level of meaning and fulfillment.

Herzberg's research identified that true motivators were other completely different factors, notably:

■ achievement
■ recognition
■ work itself
■ responsibility
■ advancement

A4.2.3 Hygiene

Herzberg's research proved that people will strive to achieve 'hygiene' needs because they are unhappy without them, but once satisfied the effect soon wears off – satisfaction is temporary. Then as now, poorly managed organizations fail to understand that people are not 'motivated' by addressing 'hygiene' needs. Examples of Herzberg's 'hygiene' needs (or maintenance factors) in the workplace are:*

■ policy
■ relationship with supervisor
■ work conditions
■ salary
■ company car
■ status
■ security
■ relationship with subordinates
■ personal life

A4.3 Victor Vroom (Expectancy Theory)

A4.3.1 Theory

The Expectancy theory states that employee's motivation is an outcome of how much an individual wants a reward (Valence), the assessment that the likelihood that the effort will lead to expected performance (Expectancy), and the belief that the performance will lead to reward (Instrumentality). In short, Valence is

---

* https://www.businessballs.com/herzbergdiagram.pdf last accessed 9/14/2019

the significance associated by an individual about the expected outcome. It is an expected and not the actual satisfaction that an employee expects to receive after achieving the goals. Expectancy is the faith that better efforts will result in better performance. Expectancy is influenced by factors such as possession of appropriate skills for performing the job, availability of right resources, availability of crucial information, and getting the required support for completing the job.

$$MF = \text{Expectancy} \times \text{Instrumentality} \times \Sigma\,(\text{Valence(s)})^*$$

A4.3.2 Expectancy

Expectancy refers to the "effort-performance" relation. Thus, the perception of the individual is that the effort that he or she will put forward will actually result in the attainment of the "performance." This cognitive evaluation is heavily weighted by an individual's past experiences, personality, self-confidence, and emotional state.

A4.3.3 Instrumentality

Instrumentality refers to the "performance-reward" relation. The individual evaluates the likelihood or probability that achieving the performance level will actually result in the attainment of the reward.[†]

A4.3.4 Valence

Valence is the value that the individual associates with the outcome (reward). A positive valence indicates that the individual has a preference for getting the reward as opposed to, vice versa, a negative valence that is indicative that the individual, based on his perception, evaluated that the reward doesn't fill a need or personal goal, thus he or she doesn't place any value towards its attainment.[‡]

A4.3.5 Motivational Force

As the Motivational Force (MF) is the multiplication of the expectancy by the instrumentality it is then by the valence that any of the perception having a value of zero or the individual's feeling that "it's not going to happen" will result in a motivational force of zero.

---

[*] http://managementstudyguide.com/expectancy-theory-motivation.htm last accessed 9/14/2019

[†] http://www.leadership-central.com/expectancy-theory-of-motivation.html#axzz3rHeNHDM3

[‡] http://www.leadership-central.com/expectancy-theory-of-motivation.html#ixzz3rHeuVYlk

A4.4 Douglas McGregor (Theory X and Theory Y)

A4.4.1 Theory

McGregor developed a philosophical view of humankind with his Theory X and Theory Y in 1960. His work is based upon Maslow's Hierarchy of Needs, in that he grouped the hierarchy into lower-order needs (Theory X) and higher-order needs (Theory Y). He suggested that management could use either set of needs to motivate employees, but better results would be gained by the use of Theory Y, rather than Theory X. These two opposing perceptions theorized how people view human behavior at work and organizational life, Theory X and Theory Y.*

A4.4.2 Theory X

With Theory X assumptions, management's role is to coerce and control employees.†

- People have an inherent dislike for work and will avoid it whenever possible.
- People must be coerced, controlled, directed, or threatened with punishment in order to get them to achieve the organizational objectives.
- People prefer to be directed, do not want responsibility, and have little or no ambition.
- People seek security above all else.

A4.4.3 Theory Y

With Theory Y assumptions, management's role is to develop the potential in employees and help them to release that potential towards common goals.‡

- Work is as natural as play and rest.
- People will exercise self-direction if they are committed to the objectives (they are NOT lazy).
- Commitment to objectives is a function of the rewards associated with their achievement.
- People learn to accept and seek responsibility.
- Creativity, ingenuity, and imagination are widely distributed among the population. People are capable of using these abilities to solve an organizational problem.
- People have potential.

---

* http://www.nwlink.com/~donclark/hrd/history/xy.html
† https://www.businessballs.com/mcgregor.htm
‡ https://www.businessballs.com/personalitystylesmodels.htm

A4.5 Argyris

A4.5.1 *Immaturity-Maturity Theory*

Chris Argyris in Personality and Organization (1957) and Interpersonal Competence and Organizational Effectiveness (1962) suggested that directive management styles foster immaturity and dependency and that more participative management styles foster mature and active employees. Indeed, he went beyond the individual level to suggest that an organization might be viewed "as an organism worthy of self-actualization" itself (P & O, p. 58).*

A4.5.2 *Bureaucratic/Pyramidal Value System*

According to Argyris, following bureaucratic or pyramidal values leads to poor, shallow, and mistrustful relationships. Because these relationships do not permit the natural and free expression of feelings, they are phony or non-authentic and result in decreased interpersonal competence. "Without interpersonal competence or a 'psychological safe' environment, the organization is a breeding ground for mistrust, intergroup conflict, rigidity, and so on, which in turn lead to a decrease in organizational success in problem solving."

A4.5.3 *Humanistic/Democratic Value System*

If, on the other hand, humanistic or democratic values are adhered to in an organization, Argyris claims that trusting, authentic relationships will develop among people and will result in increased interpersonnal competence, intergroup cooperation, flexibility, and the like and should result in increases in organizational effectiveness.†

A4.5.4 *Model I-Inhibiting Double Loop Learning*

Argyris tells us that when human beings deal with issues that are embarrassing or threatening, their reasoning and actions conform to a model called Model I.‡ Trying to make change in a Model I organization is difficult because you are dealing with their Espoused Theory. It is neither rewarding nor safe for them to explore or actually change their mental models and decision rules – so there is a wide gap between their Espoused Theory and their Theory in Use. The defensive behavior in Model I organizations create a vicious make this divide even greater. Model I organizations have the following values and supporting behaviors.

---

* http://www.learning-org.com/98.02/0020.html
† http://www.accel-team.com/human_relations/hrels_06i_argyris.html
‡ http://www.dennisstevens.com/2010/07/14/kanban-mental-models-and-double-loop-learning/

1. Define goals and try to achieve them. Participants rarely develop mutual definition of purposes – nor are they open to altering their perception of the task. Participants plan actions secretly and manipulate others to agree with their definition of the situation.
2. Maximize winning and minimize losing. Participants feel that once they have decided on their individual goals it is sign of weakness to change them.
3. Minimize generating or expressing negative feelings. Expressing or permitting others to express feelings is a bad strategy. Participants unilaterally protect themselves.
4. Be rational. Interactions are objective discussions of the issues. Participants withhold the truth, suppress feelings, and offer false sympathy to others.

Model I behavior results in organizational defensive behaviors that block exploring underlying mental models and the resulting maturity that arises. Most organizations exhibit Model I values and behavior most of the time.

A4.5.5 Model II–Encouraging Double Loop Learning

Argyris describes a much more productive type of organization that he calls Model II.* In a Model II organization, it is safe and rewarding to the participants to explore underlying mental models and decision rules. Model II organizations have the following values and supporting behaviors.

1. Valid information. Participants design environments where accurate information is shared and underlying assumptions can be openly explored.
2. Free and informed choice. The participants jointly control tasks and focus on collaborative problem solving.
3. Internal commitment. The participants jointly protect each other in learning and risk taking. Mental models and decision rules are jointly explored.

Model II behavior results in organizational behavior that enhances underlying learning. High maturity organizations exhibit Model II values and behavior.

A4.5.6 Espoused Theory

Espoused theories are those that an individual claims to follow.

This refers to the formalized part of the organization. Every firm will tend to have various instructions regarding the way employees should conduct themselves in order to carry out their jobs (e.g., problem solving). These instructions are often specific and narrow in focus, confining the individual to a set path. An example of

---

* http://www.dennisstevens.com/2010/07/14/kanban-mental-models-and-double-loop-learning/

espoused theory might be "if the computer does not work, try rebooting it and then contact the IT department."*

A4.5.7 Theories-in-Use

Theories-in-use are those that can be inferred from action. This is the actual way things are done. Individuals will rarely follow espoused theory and will rely on interaction and brainstorming to solve a problem. Theory in use refers to the loose, flowing, and social way that employees solve problems and learn. An example of this might be the way someone actually solves a problem with their computer by troubleshooting solutions, researching on forums, asking co-workers for opinions, etc.[†]

A4.6 Argyris and Schön

A4.6.1 Single and Double-Loop Learning

For Argyris and Schön learning involves the detection and correction of error. Where something goes wrong, it is suggested, an initial port of call for many people is to look for another strategy that will address and work within the governing variables. In other words, given or chosen goals, values, plans, and rules are operationalized rather than questioned. According to Argyris and Schön, this is single-loop learning. An alternative response is to question governing variables themselves, to subject them to critical scrutiny. This they describe as double-loop learning. Such learning may then lead to an alteration in the governing variables and, thus, a shift in the way in which strategies and consequences are framed. Thus, when they came to explore the nature of organizational learning. This is how Argyris and Schön described the process in the context of organizational learning:[‡]

Here we come to the focus of organizational effort – the formulation and implementation of an intervention strategy. This, according to Argyris and Schön, involves the 'interventionist' in moving through six phases of work:

- ■ **Phase 1** Mapping the problem as clients see it. This includes the factors and relationships that define the problem, and the relationship with the living systems of the organization.
- ■ **Phase 2** The internalization of the map by clients. Through inquiry and confrontation the interventionists work with clients to develop a map for which clients can accept responsibility. However, it also needs to be comprehensive.

* http://www.actiondesign.com/assets/pdf/AScha3.pdf
† http://www.knowledge-management-tools.net/organizational-learning-theory.html
‡ http://infed.org/mobi/chris-argyris-theories-of-action-double-loop-learning-and-organizational-learning/

- **Phase 3** Test the model. This involves looking at what 'testable predictions' can be derived from the map – and looking to practice and history to see if the predictions stand up. If they do not, the map has to be modified.
- **Phase 4** Invent solutions to the problem and simulate them to explore their possible impact.
- **Phase 5** Produce the intervention.
- **Phase 6** Study the impact. This allows for the correction of errors as well as generating knowledge for future designs. If things work well under the conditions specified by the model, then the map is not disconfirmed.

A4.7 Rensis Likert (Management Theory)

A4.7.1 Theory

The management theory of Rensis Likert brought a new dimension to organizational development theory. The Likert system made it possible to quantify the results of all the work various theorists had been doing with group dynamics. Likert theory also facilitated the measurement of the "soft" areas of management, such as trust and communication.*

Additionally, Likert delineated the characteristics of high- and low-producing organizations and identified the problems with traditional organizational structures. Rensis Likert recognized four management styles, or systems.

A4.7.2 Exploitative-Authoritative

The first system of Rensis Likert theory is characterized by decision making in the upper echelons of the organization, with no teamwork and little communication other than threats.†

A4.7.3 Benevolent-Authoritative

This Likert system is based on a master-servant relationship between management and employees, where rewards are the sole motivators and both teamwork and communication are minimal.

A4.7.4 Consultative

In this style, managers partly trust subordinates, use both rewards and involvement to inspire motivation, foster a higher level of responsibility for meeting goals, and inspire a moderate amount of teamwork and some communication.

---

* http://www.business.com/management/management-theory-of-rensis-likert/
† http://organisationdevelopment.org/the-theorists-rensis-likert/

A4.7.5 Participative-Group

This system is based on managerial trust and confidence in employees; collectively determined, goal-based rewards; a collective sense of responsibility for meeting company objectives; collaborative teamwork and open communication.*

A4.8 Alderfer
A4.8.1 ERG Theory

In an attempt to line up Maslow's Theory of Needs with empirical studies, Alderfer's ERG Theory elicits three core requirements: Existence, Relatedness, and Growth. This categorization reduction is the result of earlier research on Maslow Hierarchy of Needs that indicates some overlap within the middle levels. According to Alderfer, the needs aren't in any order and any desire to fulfill a need can be activated at any point in time.† This results in the the lower level needs not requiring to be satisfied in order to satisfy a higher level need. Alderfer's ERG Theory can actually be utilized as a frustration-regression principle where an already satisfied lower level need can be "re-activated" when confronted with the impossibility of satisfying a higher level one.‡

A4.8.2 Existence

Relates to a person's physical needs such as food, clothing, and shelter.

A4.8.3 Relatedness

Relates to a person's interpersonal needs within his personal as well as professional settings.

A4.8.4 Growth

Relates to a person's needs of personal development.

A4.9 William McDougall
A4.9.1 Instinct Theory of Motivation

One of the pioneers of instinct theories of motivation is the English-born social psychologist, William McDougall, who formed the Hormic Psychology, with

---

* http://www.slideshare.net/vishnuchandradas1/new-microsoft-office-power-point-presentation-23793104
† http://www.leadership-central.com/erg-theory.html#axzz3rHeNHDM3
‡ http://www.envisionsoftware.com/articles/erg_theory.html

'hormic' meaning animal impulse or urge. Hormic Psychology is based on determined and goal-oriented behaviors that are supposed to be motivated by instincts, which are spontaneous, persistent, variable, and repetitive. McDougall highlighted the instinctive nature of purposeful behaviors, but also recognized that learning is possible.[*]

In his theory, instincts are composed of three parts: perception, behavior, and emotion. Human beings have a perceptual predisposition to focus on stimuli that are important to their goals. For example, people pay attention to food odors when hunger instincts are involved. Individuals are also predisposed to move to the goal, like going to the kitchen and checking the refrigerator if there is food, or checking out the source of smell of the food that was identified. And lastly, humans have the drive and energy which is called "emotional core" between perception of the goal and the movement towards it.[†]

A4.10 B. F. Skinner

A4.10.1 Incentive Theory of Motivation

An incentive is either a promise or an act that is provided for the sake of greater action. In business, an incentive may be an additional benefit or remuneration or job promotion given to an employee either to recognize his achievements or encourage him to perform better. Additional remuneration or benefits motivate an employee to accomplish greater things. On the other hand, non-monetary incentives such as job promotion, job security, pride of accomplishment, and job satisfaction are also employee motivators, according to this theory.[‡]

Unlike the drive-reduction theory, the incentive theory states that a stimulus (in this case, an incentive) attracts a person towards it. An individual will more likely behave in order to get himself closer to the incentive. The theory is grounded on the principle of conditioning an incentive to make a person happier. For example, a student who studied hard during his college years is happy to receive a medal on his graduation day.

A4.10.2 Positive Incentives

Incentives that give a positive guarantee for satisfying an individual's needs and wants are called positive incentives. These incentives involve the principle of optimism and are provided to fulfill the employee's psychological requirements. For instance, a

---

[*] http://www.psychologynoteshq.com/instincttheoryofmotivation/

[†] http://psychology.about.com/od/motivation/a/instinct-theory-of-motivation.htm

[‡] https://explorable.com/incentive-theory-of-motivation

supervisor praises a new employee for a job well done. Other positive incentives include recognition, job promotion, additional allowances, trophies, and medals.

A4.10.3 Negative Incentives

As opposed to positive incentives, negative incentives are provided in order to rectify an individual's mistakes and errors for the sake of achieving satisfying results. More often than not, negative incentives are given if the positive incentives do not work, conditioning a person to act to avoid such negative incentives. These include job demotion, penalties, and fines.

A4.10.4 Operant Conditioning

B.F. Skinner coined the term operant conditioning; it means roughly changing of behavior by the use of reinforcement which is given after the desired response. Skinner identified three types of responses or operants that can follow behavior.*

- Neutral operants: Responses from the environment that neither increase nor decrease the probability of a behavior being repeated.
- Reinforcers: Responses from the environment that increase the probability of a behavior being repeated. Reinforcers can be either positive or negative.
- Punishers: Responses from the environment that decrease the likelihood of a behavior being repeated. Punishment weakens behavior.

A4.11 Clark L. Hull

A4.11.1 Drive-Reduction Theory

A "drive" is a state of arousal or tension triggered by a person's physiological or biological needs. These needs include hunger, thirst, need for warmth, etc. In this theory, Hull stated that drives give rise to an individual's motivation. Furthermore, Hull explained that an individual is in a state of need when his survival is threatened. When a person's drive emerges, he will be in an unpleasant state of tension and the person will behave in such a way that this tension is reduced. To reduce the tension, he will begin seeking out ways to satisfy his biological needs. For instance, you will look for water to drink if you are thirsty. You will seek for food if you are hungry.†

According to the theory, any behavior that reduces the drives will be repeated by humans and animals. This is because the reduction of the drive serves as a positive reinforcement (i.e., a reward) for the behavior that caused such drive reduction.

---

* http://www.simplypsychology.org/operant-conditioning.html
† https://explorable.com/drive-reduction-theory

A4.12 Frederick Taylor
A4.12.1 Theory of Scientific Management

Scientific management theory seeks to improve an organization's efficiency by systematically improving the efficiency of task completion by utilizing scientific, engineering, and mathematical analysis. The goal is to reduce waste, increase the process and methods of production, and create a just distribution of goods. This goal serves the common interests of employers, employees, and society.*

Scientific management theory can be summarized by Taylor's Four Principles:†

1. Managers should gather information, analyze it, and reduce it to rules, laws, or mathematical formulas.
2. Managers should scientifically select and train workers.
3. Managers should ensure that the techniques developed by science are used by the workers.
4. Managers should apply the work equally between workers and themselves, where managers apply scientific management theories to planning and the workers perform the tasks pursuant to the plans.

A4.13 Elton Mayo
A4.13.1 Theory of Human Relations

Elton Mayo's theory of motivation examined the social needs of the worker.‡ He believed that pay alone was not sufficient to motivate employees to put forth their best effort. He believed that the social needs of the workers should be taken into consideration. He recommended employers treat their workers in a caring and humane fashion that demonstrates an interest in the individual in order to have them produce their best work.§

A4.14 Senge
A4.14.1 Personal Mastery

Personal mastery is a set of specific principles and practices that enables a person to learn, create a personal vision, and view the world objectively. The concept of personal mastery is one of five disciplines Senge argues is necessary for a learning

---

* http://yourbusiness.azcentral.com/three-major-theories-motivation-1260.html
† http://study.com/academy/lesson/scientific-management-theories-principles-definition.html
‡ http://yourbusiness.azcentral.com/three-major-theories-motivation-1260.html
§ http://www.slideshare.net/ChessenClook/motivation-theory-elton-mayo

252 ■ *Appendix 4*

organization. A learning organization encourages and facilitates learning at all levels so that it may transform and adapt in an ever-changing and dynamic world.*

A4.14.2 Mental Models

"Mental models are deeply held internal images of how the world works, images that limit us to familiar ways of thinking and acting. Very often, we are not consciously aware of our mental models or the effects they have on our behavior."[†]

Mental models are an important component of Senge's conception of a learning organization. You must have a command of mental models in order to effectively build a learning organization. Learning organizations are important because they facilitate and encourage learning within all levels of an organization, permitting the organization to adapt and transform in a complex environment.

A4.14.3 Shared Vision

The practice of shared vision involves the skills of unearthing shared 'pictures of the future' that foster genuine commitment and enrollment rather than compliance. In mastering this discipline, leaders learn the counter-productiveness of trying to dictate a vision, no matter how heartfelt.[‡]

Visions spread because of a reinforcing process. Increased clarity, enthusiasm, and commitment rub off on others in the organization. 'As people talk, the vision grows clearer. As it gets clearer, enthusiasm for its benefits grow.'[§] There are 'limits to growth' in this respect, but developing the sorts of mental models outlined above can significantly improve matters. Where organizations can transcend linear and grasp system thinking, there is the possibility of bringing vision to fruition.[¶]

A4.14.4 Team Learning

Such learning is viewed as 'the process of aligning and developing the capacities of a team to create the results its members truly desire.'[**] It builds on personal mastery and shared vision – but these are not enough. People need to be able to act together. When teams learn together, Peter Senge suggests, not only can there be good results for the organization, members will grow more rapidly than could have occurred otherwise.

---

* http://study.com/academy/lesson/personal-mastery-and-peter-senge-definition-examples-quiz.html
† http://changingminds.org/explanations/models/senge_models.htm
‡ http://infed.org/mobi/peter-senge-and-the-learning-organization/
§ Kleiner, A., & Senge, P. M. (1994). The Fifth discipline fieldbook. London: Nicholas Brearley, p.227
¶ http://www.techrepublic.com/article/shared-vision-a-key-to-project-success/
** Kleiner, A., & Senge, P. M. (1994). The Fifth discipline fieldbook. London: Nicholas Brearley, p.236

The discipline of team learning starts with 'dialog,' the capacity of members of a team to suspend assumptions and enter into a genuine 'thinking together.' To the Greeks dia-logos meant a free-flowing of meaning through a group, allowing the group to discover insights not attainable individually…. [It] also involves learning how to recognize the patterns of interaction in teams that undermine learning.*

A4.14.5 Systems Thinking

Systems thinking – the cornerstone of the learning organization. A great virtue of Peter Senge's work is the way in which he puts systems theory to work. The Fifth Discipline provides a good introduction to the basics and uses of such theory – and the way in which it can be brought together with other theoretical devices in order to make sense of organizational questions and issues. Systemic thinking is the conceptual cornerstone ('The Fifth Discipline') of his approach. It is the discipline that integrates the others, fusing them into a coherent body of theory and practice (ibid.: 12). Systems theory's ability to comprehend and address the whole, and to examine the interrelationship between the parts, provides, for Peter Senge, both the incentive and the means to integrate the disciplines.

Here is not the place to go into a detailed exploration of Senge's presentation of systems theory (I have included some links to primers below). However, it is necessary to highlight one or two elements of his argument. First, while the basic tools of systems theory are fairly straightforward they can build into sophisticated models.

Peter Senge argues that one of the key problems with much that is written about, and done, in the name of management is that rather simplistic frameworks are applied to what are complex systems. We tend to focus on the parts rather than seeing the whole, and to fail to see an organization as a dynamic process. Thus, the argument runs, a better appreciation of systems will lead to more appropriate action.

A4.15 Buckminster Fuller

A4.15.1 Systems Theory

Systems theory is the interdisciplinary study of systems in general, with the goal of discovering patterns and elucidating principles that can be discerned from, and applied to, all types of systems at all nesting levels in all fields of research. Systems theory can reasonably be considered a specialization of systems thinking or as the goal output of systems science and systems engineering, with an emphasis on generality useful across a broad range of systems (versus the particular models of individual fields).

---

* Kleiner, A., & Senge, P. M. (1994). *The Fifth discipline fieldbook*. London: Nicholas Brearley, p.10

A4.16 Fisher

A4.16.1 Theory of Decision Emergence

Fisher's theory of decision emergence includes four phases which a group goes through in the decision making process. According to Fisher the distribution of different tasks and decision making changes a team and, when managed successfully, it makes the team stronger.

The first phase is the orientation phase, where team members establish relationships but also tensions. Effective communication is very important in this phase but it is also quite difficult because team members may not know each other well enough for complete trust to exist.

Next comes the conflict phase. New ideas will be discussed and there may well be significant tension as the proposers and champions of alternative approaches interact. If a natural order within the team emerges then a strong team can result. However, in some teams the conflict continues and competing factions can form.

The next phase is emergence, where the outcome of the conflict phase takes form. During this phase some people may need to soften their positions so as not to seem dominating. Individuals may need to put the interests of the team above their own personal needs and decisions.

The final phase is the reinforcement phase. Here all members of the team need to commit to the objectives and plans, whether they agree with them personally or not.

A4.17 David Bohm

A4.17.1 Theory of Dialog

Bohm has introduced the concept of a dialog stating that* dialog can be considered as a free flow of meaning between people in communication, in the sense of a stream that flows between banks. These "banks" are understood as representing the various points of view of the participants.

> ...it may turn out that such a form of free exchange of ideas and information is of fundamental relevance for transforming culture and freeing it of destructive misinformation, so that creativity can be liberated.
>
> **David Bohm**

A dialog has no predefined purpose, no agenda, other than that of inquiring into the movement of thought, and exploring the process of "thinking together"

---

* https://en.wikipedia.org/wiki/Bohm_Dialog#The_Theory_of_Dialog

collectively. This activity can allow group participants to examine their preconceptions and prejudices, as well as to explore the more general movement of thought. Bohm's intention regarding the suggested minimum number of participants was to replicate a social/cultural dynamic (rather than a family dynamic). This form of dialog seeks to enable an awareness of why communicating in the verbal sphere is so much more difficult and conflict-ridden than in all other areas of human activity and endeavor.

Dialog should not be confused with discussion or debate, both of which, says Bohm, suggest working towards a goal or reaching a decision, rather than simply exploring and learning. Meeting without an agenda or fixed objective is done to create a "free space" for something new to happen.

Dialog is really aimed at going into the whole thought process and changing the way the thought process occurs collectively. We haven't really paid much attention to thought as a process. We have ENGAGED in thoughts, but we have only paid attention to the content, not to the process. Why does thought require attention? Everything requires attention, really. If we ran machines without paying attention to them, they would break down. Our thought, too, is a process, and it requires attention; otherwise it's going to go wrong.

A4.18 Kurt Lewin

A4.18.1 Change Management

This three stage theory of change is commonly referred to as Unfreeze, Change, Freeze (or Refreeze). It is possible to take these stages to quite complicated levels but I don't believe this is necessary to be able to work with the theory. But be aware that the theory has been criticized for being too simplistic.

A lot has changed since the theory was originally presented in 1947, but the Kurt Lewin model is still extremely relevant. Many other more modern change models are actually based on the Kurt Lewin model.

A4.19 Deming*

A4.19.1 14 Points

A4.19.1.1 Constancy of Purpose

Build an environment where there is a constancy of improvement, of the product, process, and individual. Do not take a short term approach to this improvement, but one that expands over the life of the company with the goal of staying in business and providing jobs.

---

* Deming, W. E. (2018). Out of the crisis. Cambridge: The MIT Press.

A4.19.1.2 Adopt New Philosophy

A new era and social changes require change to match these opportunites and requirements. The historical western approach to management exacerbates the 7 deadly diseases. Management needs to adapt, to meet the ever increasing demands such as regulatory and antitrust constraints while improving employees the employees well-being.

A4.19.1.3 Cease Dependence on Inspections

Inspection happens for more than production, but also for those things in product development that eventually culminate in the product. Design reviews, for example, are forms of inspection. Build quality into the product all along the way. Inspections happen after time, money, and materials have been invested in the product, not to mention the inspections also take time and add cost.

A4.19.1.4 End Awarding Business on Cost

Businesses tend to focus on costs, otherwise it would be difficult, even impossible to remain in business. However, rather than award business on the material price tag only, consider the entire cost of the product. For example, how does the product variation impact on quality of ownership. Are incoming material inspections required? Will we need new or specialized equipment or processes to account for this variation? Are there special product or material handling requirements?

In addition to focusing on the entire cost, it is important to develop a partnership with suppliers. The same open mental models and open communication employed internal to the company that drives improvement, is also required to extend improvement areas throughout the supply chain. This is no doubt more difficult than it sounds and requires a relationship beyond just purchasing the material. For standardized parts or commodity parts, perhaps a more stand-off approach can be taken. Even so, organizations should develop a long-term relationship with the suppliers of choice. Purchasing managers need to move from a hard contract negotiation to a symbiotic relationship with the suppliers, and this will require the organization at large to set processes, procedures, and more importantly, culture to support. When suppliers to the business go out of business, can your business be far behind?

A4.19.1.5 Improve Constantly – Forever

Continuously improve the product development, manufacturing, and service processes. The result of this improvement is to improve cost by improving the quality and cost. The product quality originates from the design effort. The constant improvement effort is designed to optimize the product, see the new product as a unique entity optimizing the design around the specific demands of the product. Continue to improve team work as well as product development and testing methods.

A4.19.1.6 Institute Training

Training on the job should occur, not just at the level of employee but also that of the management. Managers and project managers should understand how the work moves through the company. This training includes widespread understanding of variation, which includes expertise with a minimum set of evaluation tools, not just employed on material, or manufacturing processes but processes for the product development work. Management must work to eliminate those things that gets in the way carrying out the work with satisfaction.

A4.19.1.7 Adopt and Institute Leadership

Management and project management are there to help people, processes, and tools to do a better job. Management and project management are not about supervision, or dictating. Management focuses on improvement, and work with those that do the work to find ways to reach those objectives.

When problems arise, management must be able to discern common cause from special cause and understand the limits on the system that would allow this discernment, starting from the clear definition of the objective and what constitutes acceptable quality output.

A4.19.1.8 Drive Out Fear

It is difficult to do your best when you are afraid of making a mistake, or of having a job long term. Encourage learning and a workplace where this learning is shared. We have been seen projects where the people doing the work report favorably, and we knew for a fact that the circumstances were anything but acceptable. Where fear is, there too is false or optimistic reporting. This is not in the least helpful for the project or the organization. Covering up problems just delays the resolution at best and may contribute to the collapse of the company.

A4.19.1.9 Breakdown Barriers Between Staff

An organization's structure can get in the way of being able to effectively work; this can be especially true in organizations that are functionally oriented. This orientation helps refine the competence of each functional area as it focuses on that topic, but often comes at the detriment of communications. These functional areas, research, design and development, manufacturing, aftermarket, sales and marketing, for example, are all part of the same team and free communication between these entities is required for success.

A4.19.1.10 Eliminate Slogans

Slogans amount to unproductive hand waving, and do nothing to help improve the organization.

A4.19.1.11 Eliminate Work Standards

"A quota is a fortress against improvement of quality and productivity. I have yet to see a quota system that includes any trace of a system by which to help anyone to do a better job. A quota is totally incompatible with never-ending improvement."*

This elimination, and for much the same reasons, applies to management. Rather than dwell on numbers, use leadership.

A4.19.1.12 Remove Barriers that Rob People of Pride of Work

It is impossible to have pride in workmanship, of any kind, when there is no measure, identification, or distinguishing characteristis for good work. It is therefore important to establish parameters and specific magnitude for those performing the work. Many project managers and managers too have been bitten by insufficient articulation of what constitutes done, complete or good. In conventional projects this would be described in the WBS dictionary, or in Scrum, the definition of done.

A4.19.1.13 Encourage Education and Self-Improvement for Everyone

People arrive at the organization with some set of skills, not very likely a perfect fit every time, nor over time. As the organization grows, there are opportunities for learning. The company adapts to regulation or external competitive forces; this too requires learning. Some of this happens on the job, some happens at home, and some happens in formal settings.

A4.19.1.14 Take Action

Get every person in the company focused on the transformation. Experiments, learning, and application should be happening every where and from everyone in the company.

---

* Deming, W. E. (2018). Out of the crisis. Cambridge: The MIT Press. p.61

A4.19.2 Seven Deadly Diseases

A4.19.2.1 Lack of Constancy of Purpose

The company has no continuous connection with the market through product or service development to keep the company employing people well into the future. There is a hyperfocus on the immediate, and that includes the products and services presently provided without this long term and continuous exploration into future revenue streams for the company.

A4.19.2.2 Focus on Short Term Profits

A hyper-focus on the short term, often driven by fear, erodes the constancy of purpose. A great many changes are not the sort of thing that can be decided, executed, and funded in a very short term. Therefore there must be focus not only on the short term but the long as well.

A4.19.2.3 Annual Merit Rating

The annual merit rating, besides fostering often unhealthy competition between the team members, inhibits information sharing, and introduces politics, but also comes with a helping of fear from the employees. Individual merits rating drives individual behavior and is not a collaborative and sharing behavior that the organization truly needs to improve.

A4.19.2.4 Mobility of Management

Short tenured management and management rotation of a few years are not congruent with establishing certainty. Working toward quality and productivity requires consistency of leadership, and the plan to rotate managers around runs contrary. However, it is not just management that impacts this constancy, but also the team members. A revolving door of new team members is a very good indicator there is a problem in the organization.

A4.19.2.5 Running Company on Visible Figures Alone

Visible or easily determinable attributes and metrics, for example, sales income, material costs, and taxes, are important, but not the only thing that is important. There are many other things we should consider when we are working our changes, that are no less tangible but much more difficult to measure, for example, poor morale of the employees and team members will have an adverse impact on the company, but measuring what "poor" means and "impact" will be very difficult indeed.

It would be nice if all of the data which sociologists require could be enumerated because then we could run them through IBM machines and draw charts as the economists do. However, not everything that can be counted counts, and not everything that counts can be counted.

William Bruce Cameron
*The Elements of Statistical Confusion Or:
What Does the Mean Mean?*

Index

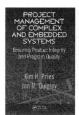

VALUE TRANSFORMATION LLC

Value Transformation LLC provides consulting and training that will heal the wounds of processess gone wild.

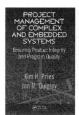
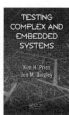

Value Transformation LLC is founded by Kim H. Pries and Jon M. Quigley. We have extensive knowledge and experience in product development (more than 50 years). This experience is largely focused upon software, specifically embedded products, and the subsequent manufacturing of those products and organizational learning and development. Value Transformation has access to additional and similar talent to meet your needs.

- Training online or direct
- Consulting
- Coaching
- Speaking
- Mentoring
- Quick Problem Solving

Visit us on the web at http://www.valuetransform.com or http://valuetransform. com/testimonial. Or you can email us at Jon.Quigley@valuetransform.com

The sooner you call, the sooner you will start to see the change you need.